Poetry of Our Times

Selected and Edited

by

SHARON BROWN
BROWN UNIVERSITY

SCOTT, FORESMAN AND COMPANY
CHICAGO   ATLANTA   NEW YORK

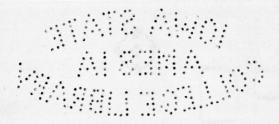

PREFACE

The first aim of this book is to show the readability of contemporary poetry. It may not be possible to forecast the lastingness of a poem, but one can ascertain its present effectiveness by "trying it out" upon all kinds of audiences. Most of the poems in this book have been subjected to such public reading, and they appear here partly because audiences have liked them.

A second aim is, by presenting a sufficient variety of subjects, to give some idea of what poets think of contemporary civilization. In other words, here is, in composite, a poets' picture of the world today.

A third aim is to afford a comprehensive survey of the more important names and influences in recent American and British poetry. Such a survey can hardly be exhaustive, but it can stimulate in the reader such a taste for his subject that he will not rest until he has gained a fuller knowledge of those poets who have most appealed to him. An anthology should be regarded as a handy starting point, a beginning. The books themselves from which these samples have been selected offer the only *complete* survey possible.

Lastly, it is hoped that these poems will be considered good poems—good because they are lovely or strong or tender or delightful or otherwise memorable. There are so many ways in which a poem can be a good poem that every reader must apply his own personal tests; and that, in some degree, is what every anthologist does. This book, however, is not the product of a single reader's preference; each poem has had to survive the judgments of more than one reader, sometimes of many readers. Hence the expectation that people of many tastes

1

will find herein poems which satisfy their several conceptions of "good" poetry.

The alphabetical arrangement of authors has been adopted as the most convenient for reference. American and British authors are separately grouped.

Footnotes have been provided in explanation of unusual words and allusions. In the approach to poetry nothing should be allowed to stand in the way of the reader's comprehension and enjoyment. No doubt there are benefits to be derived from doing one's own research—if one does it—but there is always the temptation to accept a poem with meanings guessed at or half understood. So long as the flesh is weak, the aid of footnotes will be grateful.

Some poems which the ideal anthology might contain are missing from this collection. But the ideal anthology has never been published. Quite likely it never will be so long as the restrictions on copyrighted material make a free choice impossible. For this reason the number or length of selections from an author is not necessarily relative to his importance. But who would measure poetic stature with a yardstick?

The editor gratefully acknowledges his indebtedness to the authors, who have contributed much of the material in the headnotes, have permitted the use of their poems, and have in some instances suggested the choice of selections.

To the publishers and other owners of copyrighted material reprinted here by special arrangement the editor expresses his appreciation and thanks for the patient consideration and ready generosity which he has uniformly experienced.

Indebtedness is also acknowledged to Dr. Benjamin C. Clough, of Brown University, who originally undertook the compilation of this volume and made about a dozen of the selections; to the Widener Library of Harvard University, for access to its excellent collection of modern British and Irish poetry; and to the John Hay Library of Brown University, for the invaluable advantages afforded by its Harris Collection of American Poetry.

Finally, the editor makes grateful recognition of the part played by a collaborator, unnamed here, whose practical assistance and critical judgment have never failed him during the preparation of this book.

S. B.

ACKNOWLEDGMENTS

For permission to reprint copyrighted poems, grateful acknowledgment is made to the following publishers and authors:

Messrs. Allen and Unwin for a selection from *The Temple* by Arthur Waley.

D. Appleton and Company for selections from *Narratives in Verse* by Ruth Comfort Mitchell; *Selected Poems* by Charles Hanson Towne.

E. Benn, Ltd., for a selection from *Poems* (1927) by Camilla Doyle.

Messrs. Basil Blackwell and Mott, Ltd., for selections from *Worms and Epitaphs* by H. W. Garrod; *The Bubble* and *Daedal Wings* by Willoughby Weaving.

Messrs. Boni and Liveright for selections from *Priapus and the Pool* by Conrad Aiken; *is 5* by E. E. Cummings; *Collected Poems of H. D.; The New Spoon River* by Edgar Lee Masters; *Enough Rope* by Dorothy Parker; *Lustra* by Ezra Pound; *Dublin Days* by L. A. G. Strong, published by Boni and Liveright.

Brentano's for selections from *Complete Poems* by Francis Ledwidge.

Messrs. Burns, Oates and Washbourne, Ltd., for selections from *Poems* by G. K. Chesterton; *Verses in Peace and War* by Shane Leslie.

Mr. Joseph Campbell for selections from *The Mountainy Singer*.

Jonathan Cape, Ltd., for selections from *Collected Poems, First Series* and *Second Series*, by William H. Davies.

Constable and Company for a selection from *Selected Poems* by Margaret Sackville.

The Dial for "Marigold Pendulum" by Dudley Poore.

Messrs. Dodd, Mead and Company, Inc., for selections from *The Collected Poems of Rupert Brooke; More Songs from Vagabondia* and *Later Poems* by Bliss Carman; *Poems* by G. K. Chesterton; *Poems New and Old* by Henry Newbolt. Used by permission of Dodd, Mead and Company, Inc.

Messrs. Doubleday, Doran and Company, Inc., for selections from *Tiger Joy* by Stephen Vincent Benét; *Moons of Grandeur* by William Rose Benét; *Poems* and *Ladders through the Blue* by Hermann Hagedorn; *Vigils* by Aline Kilmer; *Trees and Other Poems* by Joyce Kilmer; *Barrack-Room Ballads* by Rudyard Kipling, Copyright, 1899, by Rudyard Kipling; *The Awakening and Other Poems* by Don Marquis; *Chimneysmoke* and *Parsons' Pleasure* by Christopher Morley; *Selected Poems* by Lizette Woodworth Reese; *Out of the Flame* by Osbert Sitwell; *Poems, First Series, Poems, Second Series*, and *Tricks of the Trade* by J. C. Squire; *Leaves of Grass* by Walt Whitman; *Requiem* by Humbert Wolfe.

Gerald Duckworth & Company, Ltd., for selections from *Troy Park* and *The Sleeping Beauty* by Edith Sitwell.

E. P. Dutton and Company, Inc., for a selection from *Cry of Time* by Hazel Hall (copyrighted by E. P. Dutton and Company, Inc., New York, 1928); for "The Spires of Oxford" (by permission from *The Spires of Oxford* by Winifred M. Letts, published by E. P. Dutton and Company, Inc.).

Mr. John Gould Fletcher for selections from *Breakers and Granite*, published by The Macmillan Company.

The Four Seas Company for selections from *Images Old and New* by Richard Aldington; *Willow Pollen* by Jeanette Marks; *Sour Grapes* by William Carlos Williams.

The Freeman for "Examinations" by Howard Mumford Jones.

Messrs. Gelber, Lilienthal, Inc., for selections from *A Tree in Bloom* by Hildegarde Flanner.

Mr. Gerald Gould for a selection from *Lyrics*.

Messrs. Gowans and Gray, Ltd., for a selection from *On Vimy Ridge and Other Poems* by John Ferguson.

Messrs. Harcourt, Brace and Company, Inc., for selections from *The American Rhythm* by Mary Austin; *Poems New and Old* by John Freeman; *Smoke and Steel* and *Slabs of the Sunburnt West* by Carl Sandburg; *The Inner Harbor* by Wilbert Snow; *Roast Leviathan* and *Collected Parodies* by Louis Untermeyer; *The Unknown Goddess* by Humbert Wolfe; *Nets to Catch the Wind* by Elinor Wylie.

Messrs. Harper and Brothers for selections from *Cyclops' Eye* by Joseph Auslander; *Guinea-Fowl and Other Poultry* by Leonard Bacon; *Color* by Countée Cullen; *Astrolabe—Infinitudes and Hypocrisies* by S. Foster Damon; *Poems of the Past and Present* by Thomas Hardy.

Harpers Magazine for "Old Saul" by Lizette Woodworth Reese.

William Heinemann, Ltd., for selections from *Flora* by Walter de la Mare; *War Poems* by Siegfried Sassoon.

Messrs. Hodder and Stoughton, Ltd., for an excerpt from *Collected Parodies* by J. C. Squire.

Henry Holt and Company for selections and extracts from *The Listeners* and *The Veil* by Walter de la Mare; *North of Boston* and *New Hampshire* by Robert Frost; *Chicago Poems* and *Cornhuskers* by Carl Sandburg; *Slow Smoke* by Lew Sarett; *Poems* and *Last Poems* by Edward Thomas; *The Factories with Other Lyrics* by Margaret Widdemer; *Humoresque* by Humbert Wolfe; and "Chicago" from Carl Sandburg's *Chicago Poems*, by permission from Henry Holt and Company, Publishers.

The selections from *The Complete Poems of Thomas Bailey Aldrich*, *Poems 1908-1919* by John Drinkwater, *Clouds and Cobblestones* by Hortense Flexner, *Songs of the Trail* and *Saddle Songs* by Henry Herbert Knibbs, *What's O'Clock* and *Men, Women and Ghosts* by Amy Lowell, and *Harvest Moon* by Josephine Preston Peabody are used by permission of, and by arrangement with, Houghton Mifflin Company, the authorized publishers.

Dr. Douglas Hyde for selections from *The Love Songs of Connacht.*

Mr. Howard Mumford Jones for "Examinations."

Marshall Jones Company for a selection from *New York and Other Verses* by Frederick Mortimer Clapp.

Mr. Mitchell Kennerley for selections from *Sonnets of a Portrait Painter* by Arthur Davison Ficke; *Soldier Songs* and *Songs of the Dead End* by Patrick MacGill; *Manhattan* by Charles Hanson Towne.

Mr. Rudyard Kipling for a quotation from *Barrack-Room Ballads.*

Alfred A. Knopf, Inc., for selections reprinted from *Grenstone Poems* and *A Canticle of Pan and Other Poems* by Witter Bynner; *Colors of Life* by Max Eastman; *Profiles from China* by Eunice Tietjens; *In American* and *To Youth* by John V. A. Weaver; *The Waggoner and Other Poems* by Edmund Blunden, by permission of and special arrangement with Alfred A. Knopf, Inc., authorized publisher.

John Lane, The Bodley Head, Ltd., for a selection from *Orchard and Vineyard* by V. Sackville-West.

The Literary Review of the New York Evening Post for "Marriage" by Mark Van Doren.

The London Mercury for "Cristo Morto" by Francis Brett Young.

John W. Luce and Company for an excerpt from *Riders to the Sea* by John Millington Synge.

The Lyric West for "Montana Wives: Horizons" by Gwendolen Haste.

Robert M. McBride and Company for a selection from *Verses* by Hilaire Belloc.

Erskine MacDonald, Ltd., for a selection by Alexander Robertson from *Soldier Poets.*

The Macmillan Company for selections and extracts not otherwise acknowledged from *Wild Earth and Other Poems* by Padraic Colum; *Collected Poems* by Wilfrid Wilson Gibson; *Poems* by Ralph Hodgson; *Collected Poems* by Vachel Lindsay; and *Early Poems and Stories* and *The Land of Heart's Desire* by William Butler Yeats.

Macmillan and Company, Ltd., for selections from *Collected Poems* by A. E.; *Late Lyrics and Earlier* and *Satires of Circumstance* by Thomas Hardy.

Messrs. Macy-Masius for a selection by David McCord from *The Second Conning Tower Book.*

Miss Mildred E. Marcette for "Query."

Elkin Mathews and Marrot, Ltd., for a selection from *The Halt in the Garden* by Robert Hillyer.

Thomas Bird Mosher for a selection from *A Wayside Lute* by Lizette Woodworth Reese.

Mr. John Murray for selections from *Poetical Works* by Robert Bridges; *Songs of Angus* by Violet Jacob; *Songs from Leinster* by Winifred M. Letts; *Poems New and Old* by Henry Newbolt; *Freedom* by Geoffrey Winthrop Young.

The Nation for "Thoughts at the Year's End" by Babette Deutsch and "Taking away the Banking" by Wilbert Snow.

The New Republic for "Moo!" by Robert Hillyer.

The New York World for "A Critic" by William Foster Elliot and "Battery Park" by David McCord.

The Norman, Remington Company for selections from *Green Days and Blue Days* by Patrick R. Chalmers.

Mr. Seumas O'Sullivan for selections from *Poems* and *The Rosses and Other Poems*.

Messrs. James B. Pinker and Sons, Literary Agents, London, for "Careers" and "Free Verse" from *Fairies and Fusiliers* by Robert Graves.

The Poetry Bookshop (London) for selections from *Spring Morning* by Frances Cornford; *Children of Love* and *Week End Sonnets* by Harold Monro; *Magpies in Picardy* by T. P. Cameron Wilson.

Poetry: A Magazine of Verse for "Who Loves the Rain" by Frances Shaw.

Messrs. G. P. Putnam's Sons for selections from *In Flanders Fields, and Other Poems* by Lieutenant Colonel John McCrae, copyright by G. P. Putnam's Sons, 1919, reprinted by permission of the publishers; *Harvest* by David Morton, by courtesy of G. P. Putnam's Sons, Publishers, New York and London.

Mr. A. M. Robertson for a selection from *Beyond the Breakers* by George Sterling.

The Saturday Review of Literature for "The Ballad of Angel May" by Leonard Bacon and "The Tailor" by Geoffrey Dearmer.

Messrs. Charles Scribner's Sons for selections from *Poems* by William Ernest Henley; *The Poems of Alice Meynell*; *The Town down the River* and *Children of the Night* by Edwin Arlington Robinson; *Poems* by Alan Seeger; *The Black Panther* by John Hall Wheelock.

Scribner's Magazine for "Who Shapes the Carven Word" by David Morton and "Tears" by Lizette Woodworth Reese.

Martin Secker, Ltd., for selections from *The Buzzards and Other Poems* by Martin Armstrong; *Collected Poems* by James Elroy Flecker.

Thomas Seltzer, Inc., for selections from *The Janitor's Boy* by Nathalia Crane; *Poems for the New Age* by Simon Felshin; *7 P. M. and Other Poems* by Mark Van Doren.

Messrs. Selwyn and Blount for selections from *In the Town* and *Streets* by Douglas Goldring.

Mr. R. F. Seymour for selections from *Red Earth* by Alice Corbin.

Messrs. Sidgwick and Jackson, Ltd., for a selection from *The Waggoner and Other Poems* by Edmund Blunden, by permission of the author and of the publishers.

Messrs. Small, Maynard and Company, Inc., for a selection from *The Heart of Peace* by Laurence Housman.

Frederick A. Stokes Company for a selection from *Ardours and Endurances* by Robert Nichols.

The Talbot Press, Ltd., for selections from *Secret Springs of Dublin Song* (Anonymous); *The Three-Rock Road* by H. L. Doak.

Mr. Sherard Vines for "A Song for Grocers."

Miss Marie de L. Welch for "She Never Found Comfort," "Only This Counsel," and "For a Fallen Star."

The Yale Review for "Subjunctive" by Elizabeth J. Coatsworth.

The Yale University Press for selections from *Burning Bush* and *Blue Smoke* by Karle Wilson Baker; *The Falconer of God and Other Poems* by William Rose Benét; *The Middle Miles* by Lee Wilson Dodd.

CONTENTS

	PAGE
PREFACE	1
ACKNOWLEDGMENTS	4
INTRODUCTION	21

AMERICAN POETS

CONRAD AIKEN	58
And in the Hanging Gardens	59
This Is the Shape of the Leaf	62
JOSEPH AUSLANDER	63
The Riveter	64
MARY AUSTIN	66
Neither Spirit nor Bird	67
Lament of a Man for His Son	68
LEONARD BACON	69
The Ballad of Angel May	70
A Concert	74
KARLE WILSON BAKER	75
The Hill Steps	76
Apple and Rose	76
I Shall Be Loved as Quiet Things	77
STEPHEN VINCENT BENÉT	78
The Ballad of William Sycamore	79
WILLIAM ROSE BENÉT	82
The Falconer of God	83
There Lived a Lady in Milan	85
WITTER BYNNER	88
Ghosts of Indians	89
Through a Gateway in Japan	90
A Thrush in the Moonlight	90

PAGE

BLISS CARMAN 91
   A Vagabond Song 92
   Autumn 92

FREDERICK MORTIMER CLAPP 93
   Trade 94

ELIZABETH J. COATSWORTH 96
   Subjunctive 97

ALICE CORBIN 98
   Red Earth 99
   In the Desert 99
   On the Acequia Madre 100

NATHALIA CRANE 101
   The Blind Girl 102

COUNTÉE CULLEN 103
   Heritage 104

E. E. CUMMINGS 108
   here's a little mouse 109
   Sonnet 110

S. FOSTER DAMON 111
   Burning Bush 112
   Greeks 113
   Epilogue 113

BABETTE DEUTSCH 114
   Thoughts at the Year's End 115

LEE WILSON DODD 119
   Lament of a New England Art Student 120

MAX EASTMAN 121
   At the Aquarium 122

WILLIAM FOSTER ELLIOT 123
   A Critic 124

SIMON FELSHIN 125
   My Mother 126

ARTHUR DAVISON FICKE 128
   Sonnets of a Portrait Painter 129

PAGE

HILDEGARDE FLANNER 131
   Philippian 132
   To a Tree in Bloom 132

JOHN GOULD FLETCHER 133
   Arizona Poems: Mexican Quarter 134
   Down the Mississippi: Night Landing 135

HORTENSE FLEXNER 136
   Futility 137
   Masks 137

ROBERT FROST 139
   The Mountain 142
   The Onset 146
   The Fear 147
   Stopping by Woods on a Snowy Evening. 151

H. D. (HILDA DOOLITTLE) 152
   Helen 154
   Sheltered Garden 154

HERMANN HAGEDORN 157
   The Eyes of God 158
   Doors 159

HAZEL HALL 160
   Here Comes the Thief 161

GWENDOLEN HASTE 162
   Montana Wives: Horizons 163

DUBOSE HEYWARD 164
   A Yoke of Steers 165

ROBERT HILLYER 166
   The Halt in the Garden 167
   Moo! 171

ORRICK JOHNS 173
   Failure 174

HOWARD MUMFORD JONES 175
   Examinations 176

PAGE

ALINE KILMER 177
   Things 178

JOYCE KILMER 179
   Trees 180

HENRY HERBERT KNIBBS 181
   Burro 182
   Names 183

WILLIAM ELLERY LEONARD 185
   Indian Summer 186

VACHEL LINDSAY 188
   Kansas 190

AMY LOWELL 192
   Lilacs 194
   Patterns 197

DAVID McCORD 201
   Battery Park 202

MILDRED E. MARCETTE 204
   Query 205

JEANETTE MARKS 207
   White Hair 208

DON MARQUIS 209
   Those That Come Back 210

EDGAR LEE MASTERS 211
   Lucinda Matlock 213
   Rita Matlock Gruenberg 213

EDNA ST. VINCENT MILLAY 215
   God's World 216
   Recuerdo 216
   Journey 217

RUTH COMFORT MITCHELL 219
   The Travel Bureau 220

HARRIET MONROE 221
   The Pine at Timberline 222

PAGE

CHRISTOPHER MORLEY 223
  Nursery Rhymes for the Tender-Hearted 224
  Parsons' Pleasure 226

DAVID MORTON 230
  Winter Twilight 231
  Who Shapes the Carven Word 231

JOHN G. NEIHARDT 233
  O Lyric Master! 234

DOROTHY PARKER 235
  Biographies 236

JOSEPHINE PRESTON PEABODY 238
  Cradle Song 239

EDWIN FORD PIPER 242
  Low Voices 243

DUDLEY POORE 244
  Marigold Pendulum 245

EZRA POUND 249
  Further Instructions 250
  The River-Merchant's Wife: A Letter 250

LIZETTE WOODWORTH REESE 252
  Old Saul 253
  Tears 254

LOLA RIDGE 255
  The Ghetto 256

EDWIN ARLINGTON ROBINSON 260
  For a Dead Lady 262
  Luke Havergal 263
  The Poor Relation 264

JAMES RORTY 267
  Remembering the Mountains 268

PAGE

CARL SANDBURG. 269
    Chicago . . . . —272 —
    Four Preludes on Playthings of the Wind 273
    Prayers of Steel 275
    From *Slabs of the Sunburnt West* 276
    From *The Windy City* 278

LEW SARETT 280
    To a Wild Goose Over Decoys 281
    Four Little Foxes 281

ALAN SEEGER 283
    I Have a Rendezvous With Death 284

FRANCES W. SHAW 285
    Who Loves the Rain 286

WILBERT SNOW 287
    Taking away the Banking 288

GEORGE STERLING 289
    The Last Days 290

SARA TEASDALE 291
    Spring Night 292

EUNICE TIETJENS 293
    The Shop 294

RIDGELY TORRENCE 296
    The Son 297

CHARLES HANSON TOWNE 298
    Manhattan—XI 299

JEAN STARR UNTERMEYER 300
    Clay Hills 301
    Sinfonia Domestica 301

LOUIS UNTERMEYER 303
    Portrait of a Machine. 304
    Rebels 304
    Robert Frost Relates "The Death of the Tired Man" 305

MARK VAN DOREN 308
    Marriage 309

                                             PAGE
JOHN V. A. WEAVER 310
    Legend 311
    To Youth 312

MARIE DE L. WELCH 314
    She Never Found Comfort 315
    Only This Counsel 315
    For a Fallen Star 315

JOHN HALL WHEELOCK 317
    The Black Panther 318
    The Fish-Hawk 318

MARGARET WIDDEMER 320
    Teresina's Face 321

ELINOR WYLIE 322
    The Eagle and the Mole 323

BRITISH POETS

A. E. (GEORGE WILLIAM RUSSELL) 326
    By the Margin of the Great Deep 327
    Reconciliation 327

RICHARD ALDINGTON 329
    The Faun Sees Snow for the First Time 330
    Choricos 331

ANONYMOUS 334
    Ambition in Cuffe Street 335

MARTIN ARMSTRONG 336
    Miss Thompson Goes Shopping 337

HILAIRE BELLOC 345
    The South Country 346

HENRY BRYAN BINNS 348
    Injunction 349

EDMUND BLUNDEN 350
    Almswomen 351

PAGE

ROBERT BRIDGES 353
    A Passer-by 354
    Winter Nightfall 355

RUPERT BROOKE 356
    The Soldier 357
    The Great Lover 357

JOSEPH CAMPBELL 360
    I Am the Mountainy Singer 361
    The Ninepenny Fidil 362

PATRICK R. CHALMERS 364
    A Dream 365

G. K. CHESTERTON 367
    Lepanto 368

PADRAIC COLUM 374
    An Old Woman of the Roads 375

FRANCES CORNFORD 376
    Autumn Morning at Cambridge 377
    In France 377

W. H. DAVIES 378
    A Greeting 380
    The Sleepers 380

GEOFFREY DEARMER 382
    The Tailor 383

WALTER DE LA MARE 385
    Suppose 387
    The Sleeper 388
    Good-bye 389

H. L. DOAK 390
    The Bathers 391

CAMILLA DOYLE 392
    Cuckoos, Larks, and Sparrows 393

JOHN DRINKWATER 394
    Anthony Crundle 395
    Reciprocity 396

                                                        PAGE
JOHN FERGUSON. 397
    The Optimist 398
JAMES ELROY FLECKER 399
    To a Poet a Thousand Years Hence 400
JOHN FREEMAN 401
    The Visit 402
H. W. GARROD 406
    Revolt 407
WILFRID WILSON GIBSON. 408
    Fires 409
DOUGLAS GOLDRING 410
    Dinner-Time (Sloane Street) 411
    The Spanish Sailor 411
    West End Lane 412
GERALD GOULD 414
    Portrait 415
ROBERT GRAVES 417
    Careers 418
    Free Verse 419
THOMAS HARDY 421
    Weathers 423
    Under the Waterfall 423
    In the Servants' Quarters 425
    A Broken Appointment 427
    "Ah, Are You Digging on My Grave?" 427
RALPH HODGSON 429
    Time, You Old Gypsy Man 430
A. E. HOUSMAN 432
    Reveille. 433
    Loveliest of Trees 434
    With Rue My Heart Is Laden 434
    Bredon Hill 435
LAURENCE HOUSMAN. 437
    Gaffer at the Fair 438

PAGE

Douglas Hyde 440
   Ringleted Youth of My Love 441

Violet Jacob 442
   Tam i' the Kirk 443

Francis Ledwidge 444
   Desire in Spring 445
   June 445
   The Shadow People 446

Shane Leslie 448
   Epitaphs for Aviators (Capt. Aidan Liddell, V. C.) 449

Winifred M. Letts 450
   The Spires of Oxford 451
   In Service 452
   Says She 453

John McCrae 455
   In Flanders Fields 456

Patrick MacGill 457
   From Played Out 458

John Masefield 460
   Sea Fever 462
   From Dauber 462

Charlotte Mew 465
   Arracombe Wood 466
   The Farmer's Bride 466

Alice Meynell 469
   The Shepherdess 470
   Renouncement 470

Harold Monro 472
   Milk for the Cat 473
   Overheard on a Salt-Marsh 474

Henry Newbolt 475
   "He Fell among Thieves" 476

Robert Nichols 478
   Last Words 479

PAGE

ALFRED NOYES 481
    The Highwayman 482

SEUMAS O'SULLIVAN (JAMES STARKEY) 487
    Have Thou No Fear 488
    In Mercer Street: A Piper. 488
    The Rosses 489

WILFRED OWEN 490
    The Chances 491

ALEXANDER ROBERTSON 492
    "We Shall Drink to Them That Sleep" 493

MARGARET SACKVILLE 494
    Vale 495

V. SACKVILLE-WEST 496
    Sailing Ships 497

SIEGFRIED SASSOON 500
    The Kiss 502
    Aftermath 502

EDITH SITWELL 504
    Aubade. 505
    The Drum 506

OSBERT SITWELL 509
    Ultimate Judgment 510

J. C. SQUIRE 511
    The Ship 512
    Winter Nightfall 512
    If Mr. Masefield Had Written "Casabianca" 515

JAMES STEPHENS 518
    The Coolun 519
    The Devil's Bag 520

L. A. G. STRONG 521
    The Brewer's Man 522
    The Madwoman of Punnet's Town 522
    Micky-the-Moon 523

PAGE

EDWARD THOMAS 524
   Adlestrop 525
   The New House 525

SHERARD VINES 527
   A Song for Grocers 528

ARTHUR WALEY 530
   Hot Cakes 531

WILLOUGHBY WEAVING 532
   August 533
   Song 533

T. P. CAMERON WILSON 534
   The Mathematical Master to His Dullest Pupil 535

HUMBERT WOLFE 536
   Prelude to the Afternoon of a Faun 537
   Iliad 538
   The Saint 539

WILLIAM BUTLER YEATS 542
   The Wild Swans at Coole 544

FRANCIS BRETT YOUNG 546
   Cristo Morto 547

GEOFFREY WINTHROP YOUNG 550
   Mountain Speed 551

INTRODUCTION

And Milton in the streets no taller
Than sparkling, easy-ambling Waller.
Waller now walks with riming crowds,
While Milton sits above the clouds.

—Walter Savage Landor

WHY STUDY CONTEMPORARY POETS?

The experience of the past shows us that the Wallers are as likely to be exalted by their times as the Miltons, that the Tuppers are frequently preferred to the Brownings. Yet the admission of fallibility in literary judgments should not keep us from the attempt to estimate the worth of living writers. If we approach the task with intelligence, with impartiality, and with humbleness, we shall at least, within our limitations, deal justly with our contemporaries. But if we shun the difficulty for the cheap comfort of long-established judgments, we shall do less than justice to those who ask our friendly appraisement.

Of course a true poet will obey the creative impulse whether or not anyone reads his songs. But he will sing the more freely if he has the encouragement of a critical but sympathetic following. For the stimulus of the understanding reader is essential to the healthy growth of the writer. The poet who, hopeful of an appreciative posterity, writes for no present audience, writes, more often than not, for himself alone and leaves but a poor, ingrown thing as the result of his labor.

Further defense for "the cult of the contemporary" in literature is found in the fact that writers of our own times interpret to us those things which are nearest to our interests, which partake even of our very existence. To the readers, however sympathetic, of some hypothetical future these thoughts and emotions can never come with the same compelling immediacy. Even those infrequent works of genius which bear the stamp of immortality lose, with the passing of the centuries, something of the fresh wonder of the new-born thought. We cannot help the wistful feeling that *The Canterbury Tales* meant more to Chaucer's neighbors of five hundred years ago than to the earnest students of today's seminar. The ideas of "Hertha" which thrilled and shocked Swinburne's readers in 1871 already seem tame and stale.

And if the great works suffer loss, how much more must those lesser works which are important only for their own time! Much of the work of H. G. Wells, for example, has no claim to immortality. Yet Mr. Wells is much more than an intelligent observer of our changing civilization. Repeatedly he has produced a book as the direct result of a moment of crisis and helpful to the solution of that crisis, even though it could not possibly live beyond the moment that provoked it. Such a book, in 1916, was *Mr. Britling Sees It Through*.

But, objects the conservative reader, how can one judge such an intangible thing as the value of a poem unless he has the perspective that time alone can give? Let Robert Frost furnish a reply: "It is absurd to think that the only way to tell if a poem is lasting is to wait and see if it lasts. The right reader of a good poem can tell the moment it strikes him that he has taken an immortal wound—that he will never get over it. That is to say, permanence in poetry, as in love, is perceived instantly. It hasn't to await the test of time. The proof of a poem is not that we have never forgotten it, but that we knew at sight that we never could forget it."

Happily, the study of contemporary literature requires less defense than formerly. In most schools and colleges, although some devotees of the classics may deprecate contemporary literature as "too interesting to be scholarly," those who teach it know that it affords immature students a natural approach to the great, but at first forbidding, body of canonical literature.

DEFINING THE PERIOD

In choosing those poets, American and British, who may fairly be considered contemporaries, the editor of this volume has not restricted himself by arbitrary limits. The aim has been, in general, to include those poets whose work is opposed, in spirit and in substance, to the poetic output characteristic of the preceding literary period. There is little difficulty in discerning a definite contrast between the inertness of *fin de siècle* and pre-war poetry and the vitality of later poetry. Roughly speaking, the year 1914 may be taken as a convenient date to designate the beginning of the "contemporary" period in poetry. The outbreak of the World War in 1914 caused a sudden quickening of poetic fervor in England and coincided, perhaps by accident, with a remarkable manifestation of poetic expression in the United States. No attempt has been made, however, to exclude poems written before 1914 if they are clearly forerunners of the new spirit. Neither has there been any attempt to exclude writers, like Amy Lowell or Thomas Hardy, whose work falls within the period, merely on the ground that they are no longer living. In short, the term "contemporaries" has been used in the broadest sense to embrace any poets of recent years whose work shows differences in manner or in substance from the work of their predecessors. The nature of those differences will be made clear by examining first the poetry of the antecedent period, then the poetry of our own period. Although it might be possible to consider British poetry and American poetry at the same time—for they have many points in common—simplicity and clearness will be served by regarding each subject separately; and since this is a book for American readers, we may pardonably defer the story of modern poetry in England until its progress in America has been traced down to the present.

In order to understand recent American poetry, it is necessary to look briefly at its background.

American Beginnings

The New England poets will at once occur to many readers
as the makers, for all time, of the American poetic tradition.
Such, indeed, has been the conventional opinion, but it is
hardly an accurate one. Longfellow, Bryant, Lowell, Holmes,
Whittier, and Emerson, in spite of their long leadership of
American letters (three of them lived into their seventies,
three into their eighties), have had but a limited influence on
their successors. The reason for this was a willingness, in
most instances, to turn to England and the Continent for substance, style, and inspiration. This statement does not, however, apply to Emerson, whose poetry transcended nationality.
And, so far as substance is concerned, exception must be made
for such fine poems as "Snow-Bound" by Whittier, Longfellow's "My Lost Youth," "Hiawatha," "Evangeline," and
other poems; the Yankee humor of Holmes and Lowell, the
anti-slavery poems, and other such authentic fruits of the native
environment. But in substance largely, in style and inspiration
almost wholly, the New England poets made little effort to
work out an American poetic idiom. They felt no incongruity
in transplanting the literary formulas of Milton, Gray, Wordsworth, and Tennyson from the shaven lawns and burgeoning
hedgerows of old England to the uncouth and rocky pastures
of New England; indeed there was for them no incongruity,
because they transplanted the lawns and hedgerows as well.

The failure of the New England poets to strike out new
paths was understandable enough; it was natural that they
should have considered themselves fellow writers in a common
tongue. Perhaps, too, it was fortunate that they should have
prepared the way for a genuinely native literature by providing,
albeit at second hand, a foundation of culture. Certainly it
had been previously non-existent, as the student of American
manners in the middle of the nineteenth century knows. *Martin
Chuzzlewit* is not all caricature. If the United States was,

apparently, incapable of creating a culture of its own, the next best thing was to borrow one. The New England poets rendered this important service: they established American standards of literary taste and culture in keeping with the best standards of the Old World.

The name of Edgar Allan Poe at once suggests itself in any discussion of our earlier poetry. Yet Poe, originator that he was, had no inheritors. An exotic wonder, he could not be understood by his fellow countrymen; and it was only after he had been appreciated by France that Americans discovered what a great poet had lived and died among them.

The history of genuinely native American poetry begins in 1855 with the appearance of *Leaves of Grass*. Walt Whitman, whatever his place in the final verdict of criticism—and he certainly has been overrated by some admirers—did two important things for American poetry: he turned it to American themes, and he taught it a new manner. With inexhaustible enthusiasm he celebrated "These States" in poem after poem:

I hear America singing, the varied carols I hear . . .

In an early notebook he jots down his determination to "write a book of new things." Deliberately rejecting every inspiration of classical or European origin as inapplicable to his purpose, he wrote, "I will be, also, a master after my own kind, making the poems of emotion, as they pass or stay, the poems of freedom, and the exposé of personality—singing in high tones Democracy and the New World of it through These States." Faithful to this purpose, he glorified not only the "primal sanities" of nature in a continent still largely undisciplined by men, but still more the faces and streets of current American civilization:

Give me faces and streets—give me these phantoms incessant and
    endless along the trottoirs!
Give me interminable eyes—give me women—give me comrades and
    lovers by the thousand!

Let me see new ones every day—let me hold new ones by the hand
    every day!
Give me such shows—give me the streets of Manhattan! . . .
Give me the shores and wharves heavy-fringed with black ships!
Oh, such for me! Oh, an intense life, full to repletion and varied!
The life of the theater, barroom, huge hotel, for me!
The saloon of the steamer! the crowded excursion for me! the torch-
    light procession!
The dense brigade bound for the war, with high-piled military wagons
    following;
People, endless, streaming, with strong voices, passions, pageants, . . .
Manhattan crowds, with their turbulent musical chorus! Manhattan
    faces and eyes forever for me.

As he ranged about the country, traveling South and West
and North, or served as an army nurse in the Civil War, or
mingled in city throngs, he identified himself with all the life
of America. In the period following the Civil War, when the
nation was in the throes of transition, Whitman helped it to
find itself, to become conscious of its spiritual identity. More
than that, he had something which Emerson chiefly of his
contemporaries shared—the capacity to see through the
provincialism of the life about him to the universal aspirations
of humanity. Whitman and Emerson were at once American
and cosmopolitan. The difference between them was that they
reached the same comprehensions by separate routes—Whitman
through the emotions, Emerson through the intellect.

The style of Whitman should have a special significance to
the student of contemporary poetry, because it represents the
first appearance in this country of that metrical freedom which
reappeared in 1914 as "free verse," and which will be more fully
described under a later heading. First encounter with Whitman's manner might suggest that he had written himself completely out of the ranks of orthodox poets, that his sprawling
lines had no relation to the conventions of prosody. But repeated reading of the verses, especially aloud, brings out a

skillfully contrived alternation of many kinds of rhythms. Sometimes these rhythms approach the regularity of meter, as in the following:

THE LAST INVOCATION[1]

At the last, tenderly,
From the walls of the powerful, fortressed house,
From the clasp of the knitted locks—from the keep of the
    well-closed doors,
Let me be wafted.

Let me glide noiselessly forth;
With the key of softness unlock the locks—with a whisper
Set ope the doors, O soul!

Tenderly! be not impatient!
(Strong is your hold, O mortal flesh!
Strong is your hold, O love!)

But always the definite metric pattern is pushed aside, as though the singer's exuberance and exaltation must win free expression. Freedom of thought and freedom of manner are fused with a fine appropriateness that shows that Whitman usually knew what he was about.

In his work as a whole was manifestly the raw stuff of a new and authentically American poetry. If Whitman has fallen short of complete acceptance by posterity, it is because he could not, or would not, exercise sufficient control over his work. But he broke a path which, in the fullness of time, many were to follow.

For the moment, however, Whitman's prodigal originality was without effect. The "black-walnut period" of the eighties and nineties was a period of literary doldrums which calls only for the tribute of a passing shudder. Except for Bret Harte and a few lesser Westerners, no honest American accent broke

---

[1]These lines, "The Last Invocation," may profitably be compared with Tennyson's "Crossing the Bar," an equally great poem on the same theme but in regular meter.

through the sickly-sweet chorus of diluted Byron and senti-
mentalized Tennyson which passed for poetry. How little the
example of Whitman had been heeded is illustrated by such
lines as these by Thomas Bailey Aldrich, descriptive of the
United States:

> Portals that lead to an enchanted land
> Of cities, forests, fields of living gold,
> Vast prairies, lordly summits touched with snow,
> Majestic rivers sweeping proudly past
> The Arab's date-palm and the Norseman's pine—
> A realm wherein are fruits of every zone,
> Airs of all climes, for lo! throughout the year
> The red rose blossoms somewhere—a rich land,
> A later Eden planted in the wilds,
> With not an inch of earth within its bound
> But if a slave's foot press it sets him free.

Here are all the approved ingredients, but the quickening spark
is not in the thing.

One sign that the anemia which afflicted American letters
would not last forever was the appearance, in 1894, of a thin
brown book, *Songs from Vagabondia*, by Richard Hovey and
Bliss Carman. Here was poetry with a tang—not great poetry,
not careful poetry, not particularly American poetry, yet the
product of original inspiration. The poetry-reading public
took the little book and its two successors to its heart. *Songs
from Vagabondia* was, for the nineties, a book of rebellion.
With its love songs, its tavern songs, its songs of the outdoors,
it was a call to the gypsy life. Perhaps because Americans
were just learning to ride the bicycle, they answered with the
greater readiness. Autumn winds, open road, hearty fellowship, "and a good song ringing clear"—today we detect in it
all more than a hint of pose, but in 1894 it was the breath of
life after the stuffy futilities of its predecessors.

Other poets, with a smaller popular appeal, were striking
out lines that followed no familiar modes: Emily Dickinson,

until her death in 1886, was fashioning perversely individual lyrics; Lizette Woodworth Reese, whose first book appeared in 1887, had adopted a style which is still, in her latest book, fresh and modern; Stephen Crane, in *The Black Riders* (1895) and *War Is Kind* (1899), invented a poetic technique which prefigured imagism. But the readers of the nineties failed to recognize the virtue of originality in these poets. Their books kindled no revolt, engendered no consciousness of an American poetic destiny separate from that of Europe. American poetry still hung fire, the sole figure of importance at the turn of the century being William Vaughn Moody, whose premature death cheated him of possible fame. The assertion of America's literary emergence did not come until the voice of America, grown powerful with the expansion of commerce and manufacture, with the headlong settlement of the West, with the impelling urge of high achievements in discovery and invention, insisted on being heard, and when that time came it was not one voice but many voices.

American Poetry Emerges

Of the new American poets, Vachel Lindsay was, appropriately enough, the first who won public attention, for he has always been the most extravagantly American in his effort to translate into the spirit of poetry the blatant energy, the syncopated ragtime rhythms, the multi-racial tumult, which are America. *General William Booth Enters into Heaven* (1913) was the first volume of a literature intensely conscious of its cis-Atlantic origin. Without renouncing conventional meter and rime, Mr. Lindsay put the insistent accents of American life into his verse, sometimes by onomatopoetic devices, sometimes by marginal "stage directions," oftenest by sheer dexterity. In the title poem of his first book, for instance, one is asked to hear bass drums, banjos, flutes, and tambourines, "all in full blast":

Oh, shout Salvation! it was good to see
Kings and princes by the Lamb set free.
The banjos rattled, and the tambourines
Jing-jing-jingled in the hands of queens!

In later poetry Mr. Lindsay gave even freer play to his robust
sense of the dramatic. But in the raucousness of this America
which shrieks and blares and rumbles and explodes, the reader
should not overlook the genuine lyrical sweetness which, ever
and again, rises above the cacophony. In recent poems Mr.
Lindsay shows some falling off from the spontaneity of the early
years, but, judging him by his best, we must concede his importance as an innovator and as a forerunner of the new era.

Shortly before, October, 1912, Harriet Monroe had founded,
in Chicago, *Poetry: A Magazine of Verse*. Although this fact
alone would scarcely account for the awakening interest in
poetry, the hospitality of Miss Monroe's pages went far to
encourage the young writers and give them a hearing.

Close on the heels of Mr. Lindsay's reception came a still
more spectacular success in *Spoon River Anthology* (1915), by
Edgar Lee Masters, a Chicago lawyer. Attracted first to the
book by the sensational repute of its darker passages, readers
discovered in these two hundred and fourteen brief monologues
a crude but powerful realism. These life stories of the men and
women buried in the cemetery of a mid-Western town were
told with compelling candor and devastating irony. Their sum
was offered as the whole history of small-town life in America.
The truthfulness of the sordid picture was hotly questioned,
and a furore of discussion ensued. This was a good thing for
American poetry, for it turned the attention of many readers to
their neglected native poets. They made some astonishing
discoveries.

One of these discoveries was Robert Frost. He was already
known in England for his first two volumes, *A Boy's Will* and
North of Boston, published there in 1913 and 1914, respectively.

Republished in this country in 1915, they brought quick recognition for the finely-tempered artist who could so shrewdly and faithfully interpret the life of the New England countryside. Mr. Frost's popularity was the more surprising because his poems attempted no sensationalism. They were done in quiet tones, apparently with utter simplicity of means. Yet beneath the surface was evidence of a technical mastery which, together with an honest sincerity of purpose, accounted for their unaffectedness. Mr. Frost knows the lanky, loose-jointed rhythms of the New England farmer's speech. He translates it into poetic form without losing its flavor in the process. It has become poetry, but it is still the voice of New England. The purity of Mr. Frost's art and the consistency of his performance encourage the conviction that he is one of the half-dozen preeminent poets of our time in England or America.

Another of the surprises which rewarded the new interest in American poetry was Edwin Arlington Robinson, whose volume *The Man against the Sky* (1916) brought to light his three hitherto all but unrecognized volumes, the first of which had been published as far back as 1897. Through years of obscurity and defeat he had been steadfast to his poetic purpose, patiently fashioning verse of exquisite and polished perfection, packed with intellectual subtleties, which analyzed modern life with searching penetration—and this with no audience worth mentioning until 1916! Although an ingenious experimenter in verse forms, Mr. Robinson is fundamentally conservative in style; it is his use of psychological realism that is new. It is possible that Mr. Robinson's audience may never be large, for his appeal is to the intellect rather than to the emotions; his ideas are sometimes too difficult for transparent rendering; he sometimes places art before passion. Yet, as time passes, and he maintains the same substantial content and the same cool command of his material, he is gaining ever wider acceptance— witness the stir when his *Tristram* appeared in 1927.

FREE VERSE AND IMAGISM

The one feature most strikingly common to the work of these new leaders—Lindsay, Masters, Frost, Robinson—was a desire to challenge the conventional idea that only a narrow range of subjects is proper poetic material. But in style, only Mr. Masters had felt a need to defy restricting formulas. Mr. Lindsay, in spite of his novel effects in rhythm and sound, never departed from the accepted theories of metrics; Mr. Robinson and Mr. Frost were and have remained classicists in meter. Mr. Masters, however, wrote in a form similar to that already employed by Whitman, which came to be known variously as *vers libre*[2], free verse, or, in Amy Lowell's phrase, unrimed cadence. Practitioners of this form, which between 1915 and 1920 attained the proportions of a "movement," repudiated both rime and regular metrical pattern, relying on such cadences or stresses as seemed to them best to reproduce the "organic rhythm" of their subject. They permitted themselves complete freedom in the varying of these cadences, their ideal being to escape the arbitrary restrictions of prosody and to approximate what they considered the more natural rhythms of the speaking voice with its irregular pauses for breath. Such theories, it might be supposed, would result in a form of writing indistinguishable from prose, and that was precisely all that some of the camp-followers of the movement produced —prose chopped into lines of eccentric lengths, and nothing more. Properly written, however, free verse involves a more insistent stress than prose; sometimes it suggests the stately rhythms of the King James Version of the Bible; and always it must strive for a subtle harmony between the movement of the line and its thought or mood. The last quality is particularly well illustrated in the following examples of free verse.

---

[2]The term is adopted from Georges Duhamel and Charles Vildrac, French poets, who tried to evolve a technique based on the example of Walt Whitman. But free verse itself is as old as Hebrew poetry.

"Evening Waterfall," beginning with a regular rhythmic pattern, breaks up, in the eighth and ninth lines, into a melodious cascade of accents, only to return in the end to the serene movement of the first lines; "Evening Song" suggests first the crescendo of the approaching trains, then a meditative interlude, then the swift diminuendo of the outbound trains fading into stillness.

EVENING WATERFALL

What was the name you called me?—
And why did you go so soon?

The crows lift their caw on the wind,
And the wind changed and was lonely.

The warblers cry their sleepy-songs
Across the valley gloaming,
Across the cattle-horns of early stars.

Feathers and people in the crotch of a tree-top
Throw an evening waterfall of sleepy-songs.

What was the name you called me?—
And why did you go so soon?

—Carl Sandburg

EVENING SONG*

Back of Chicago the open fields—were you ever there?
Trains coming toward you out of the West—
Streaks of light on the long, gray plains?   Many a song—
Aching to sing.

I've got a gray and ragged brother in my breast—
That's a fact.

Back of Chicago the open fields—were you ever there?
Trains going from you into the West—
Clouds of dust on the long, gray plains.
Long trains go West, too—in the silence.
Always the song—
Waiting to sing.   *—Sherwood Anderson*

*From *Mid-American Chants* by Sherwood Anderson. New York, The Viking Press, Inc. Copyright 1918.

Imagism, though its vogue coincided with that of free verse, was separate from free verse and should not be confused with it. The Imagists often used free verse, to be sure; but they also used rime and meter. Free verse sought to liberate the form of poetry, imagism to release its spirit. Free verse was never more than a loosely-defined idea which many poets, British as well as American, utilized in varying degrees and with varying success. Imagism, on the other hand, constituted a definite school, the ideas of which were embodied in a definite creed:[3]

1. To use the language of common speech, but to employ always the exact word, not the nearly exact, nor the merely decorative word.

2. To create new rhythms—as the expression of new moods—and not to copy old rhythms, which merely echo old moods. We do not insist upon "free verse" as the only method of writing poetry. We fight for it as for a principle of liberty. We believe that the individuality of a poet may often be better expressed in free verse than in conventional forms. In poetry, a new cadence means a new idea.

3. To allow absolute freedom in the choice of the subject.

4. To present an image (hence the name, "Imagist"). We are not a school of painters, but we believe that poetry should render particulars exactly and not deal in vague generalities, however magnificent and sonorous.

5. To produce poetry that is hard and clear, never blurred nor indefinite.

6. Finally, most of us believe that concentration is of the very essence of poetry.

At first reading it may be hard to see why these apparently innocuous tenets should have caused so much excitement when they first appeared. The inexact or merely decorative word, the narrowly "poetic" subject, the magnificent generality, the blurred, the indefinite, the sprawling—all these things had been open to criticism at least since the time of Wordsworth. The second tenet, "new rhythms," aroused antagonism to be sure, but not separately from the antagonism directed against free

---

[3] *Some Imagist Poets, An Anthology.* Boston, 1915. Houghton Mifflin Company.

verse in general. Typical of the feeling of many critics was the
disgruntled remark of Mr. G. K. Chesterton: "*Vers libre* is
no more a revolution in poetry than sleeping in a ditch is a
revolution in architecture." The real issue between the established order and the Imagists was not so much the qualities
condemned by the Imagists as the extremes which they offered
as substitutes. What these extremes were can best be shown
by an example:

COMPLETE DESTRUCTION

> It was an icy day.
> We buried the cat,
> then took her box
> and set fire to it
> in the back yard.
> Those fleas that escaped
> earth and fire
> died by the cold.

—*William Carlos Williams*

Here, to be sure, are "the language of common speech," freedom
in the choice of subjects, definite particulars, and concentration.
Yet the effect is everything, the matter nothing. The resulting
poem, considered as anything but burlesque, is merely trivial.

Even when the Imagist avoids such extremes, he still runs
the risk of diluting or losing altogether the essential reality by
over-dwelling on the image. He may sacrifice matter to effect.
This trait is defiantly exalted by one member of the group:

> But I have looked down into
> These rain-spear-stung streets
> And found mirrored there
> An unguessed beauty of dingy things:
> Oh, I do not want realities!
> Give me their misshapen lovely images
> And unreached forms.

—*Mark Turbyfill*

Applied with good sense and good taste, however, the imagist theories, within their limitations, produced poetry of worth. Such lines as these are typical:

> Oh, to loose the straining ropes of twisted sunlight
> that tie the white cloud to the hillcrest,
> and rise and sail
> dazzlingly over houses and steeples,
> to see red barns and zigzag fences,
> pastures shouldering green elm parasols,
> rumbling carts that yellow dust clouds lope behind,
> dangling thirsty tongues,
> chugging engines that pant
> sweating up long hills in nodding bonnets
> of curled ostrich or aigrette,
> snaky rivers striped with bridges
> writhing across the haze of level plains
> till the sea sets an icy green heel
> on their envenomed heads,
> while swarming houses run to crowd the wharves
> and dabble their toes in the surf,
> where the sailing ships
> clap shining hands on the horizon,
> and steamers toss dark windy hair.
>
> —*Dudley Poore*

The most significant work of the imagist movement was done by a small group of determined reformers who came together in London in 1914 under the leadership of that eccentric expatriate, Ezra Pound. It included three other Americans, Amy Lowell, H. D. (Hilda Doolittle), and John Gould Fletcher; and three Englishmen, Richard Aldington, D. H. Lawrence, and F. S. Flint. This group it was which formulated the new creed and exemplified its theories by a series of annual anthologies. Miss Lowell soon became head of the cause, throwing herself into it with all the love of a fight which was characteristic of her. If certain poetasters, seeking an easy notoriety, stretched and perverted the imagist doctrines to the point of imbecility, that fact should not detract from our respect for the motives of the sincere Imagists. These latter were explorers in a new idiom, and if their experiments occasionally fell short of success, they were merely suffering the luck of all who engage in research.

Imagism as a movement lasted only five spectacular and controversial years, but it has left its mark all over contemporary British and American poetry. Although, as already suggested, the specific substitutes which they offered were not always satisfactory, the Imagists served poetry well by combating "poetic diction," vague generality, pretentiousness and pompousness, and the sugary romanticism of the nineties. They stimulated the coming of a new order wherein experiment takes the place of unalterable law. Yet out of all the ferment and turmoil, the eternal ingredients of poetry—emotion, idea, physical vision, melody—emerge unchanged; what has occurred is simply an alteration in the mixing proportions of these ingredients. For the time, melody and emotion seem to have been subordinated to image and idea—but only for the time. As the present restless and material age passes on in the sure cycle of change, poetry may reach a point of equilibrium wherein all the poetic ingredients will find their just balance.

With the collapse of imagism as a definite movement there has also been a gradual decline of free verse. In particular, the extravagant and insincere writers of free verse have disappeared—their shoddy stuff has not worn well. The serious advocates of free verse have turned, in many cases, to conventional forms. One reason for this reaction is the extreme difficulty of handling so elusive a medium with the assurance that one has captured just the nuances of cadence, mood, and music which one wishes to achieve. Far from being too easy, free verse is, in reality, infinitely too hard. In the return to regular forms there may be a desire for the satisfaction which comes of working with definite, tangible values. It is something like turning from metaphysics to mathematics.

TWO EXPERIMENTALISTS

One poet who had no need to seek relief from the perplexities of free verse, for she had thoroughly mastered it, was the late Amy Lowell. Yet she did, in her latter years, return to the conventional forms of which she was equally a master. No American poet has equaled Miss Lowell in versatility; her technique was as brilliant as it was inclusive. Although there were few types of poetry which she did not write, she remains best known for her ardent espousal of imagism. Her first characteristic book, *Sword Blades and Poppy Seed* (1914), raised the imagist standard in this country, and introduced her own peculiar contribution of "polyphonic prose." Polyphonic prose is, as the name suggests, a many-voiced form, printed in the semblance of prose but embodying an endless variety of rhythms, both of prose and of verse, as well as occasional deftly-hidden rimes. It had, however, no great vogue. It was one of the experiments that fell by the wayside. Miss Lowell herself questioned the success with which she had adapted the form from French originals.

Miss Lowell's true claim to fame has been a little obscured by her reputation as an indefatigable experimenter. She was that, but she was more—a substantial and thoughtful artist, equally gifted in the lyric and the narrative, and representative of the best intellectual aristocracy. If she fell short of genius, it was in the less palpable values of poetry, the properties of the spirit rather than of the mind. Her work was too deliberately conceived and executed to suggest the presence of the compelling urge under which the greatest poets work. She depended on intelligence rather than inspiration, on brains rather than intuition. In the final reckoning, however, hers was a healthy and a stimulating influence, both as poet and as critic, on the work of her contemporaries.

Last to be considered of the outstanding figures in contemporary American poetry is Carl Sandburg. There is a special fitness in putting him in this climactic position, because his work seems to sum up, perhaps better than that of any other poet, the whole spirit of modern America. Other writers have spoken for their own sections or their own classes of society—Mr. Sandburg comes near to speaking for the United States as a whole, both geographically and socially. It is, then, a mistake to think of him merely as a Chicagoan. True enough, his first volume was entitled *Chicago Poems* (1916), and the first poem in that book was entitled "Chicago":

> Hog Butcher for the World,
> Tool Maker, Stacker of Wheat,
> Player with Railroads, and the Nation's Freight Handler;
> Stormy, husky, brawling,
> City of the Big Shoulders . . .

But though in this and many other poems Mr. Sandburg takes Chicago or other Middle-Western cities for his background, he shows against that background the struggling, laboring, singing, bragging, sweating, loving, dreaming life of a whole nation.

It is, also, a mistake to think of him only as a brawling *enfant terrible* in verse, though "Chicago" is quoted as often by his detractors as by his admirers. There is, admittedly, a want of dignity and melody in such a poem as "Chicago," but it is compensated by the dynamic virility of the utterance. Furthermore, "Chicago" is characteristic of only one side of Mr. Sandburg's work—there is also a constantly recurrent lyricism born of sweetness out of strength, an almost feminine tenderness already illustrated by "Evening Waterfall" on page 33. The truth is that all his faults and eccentricities, banalities and crudities, cannot detract from Mr. Sandburg's stature both as artist and as interpreter of present-day America.

American Poetry in Summary

American poetry is still young and its permanent contribution to the world's literature is still comparatively small. It has not yet entirely found itself. The poetic activity which began about 1914 represented, as we have seen, not one voice but many; and it has produced not one American type but many individual types of poetry, ranging from the polished austerity of Mr. Robinson to the bold innovations of Miss Lowell and Mr. Sandburg. We are still in a period of searching, shifting, experimenting; and the product is uncertain in its total effect, neither classic nor realistic nor romantic.

Yet in the fact of its youth is the greatest hope for the future of American poetry. It is still young enough to learn by trial and error, still young enough to apply its splendid creative vitality to the task of self-development out of which should come, eventually, a national poetic consciousness. That it has not come already is no cause for wonder or despair—such things do not develop overnight, and Whitman, who laid the rough foundation, died as recently as 1892. Furthermore, as Conrad Aiken has remarked, spring freshets are muddy. The flood of poetry that began in 1914 was naturally inchoate, wasteful of its power and careless of its course. A later time will mark the banks and chart the course and perhaps utilize more effectively the energies which have been spent on experimentation. There may be some loss of spontaneity, but there will be a gain of strength and sweetness and a new certainty of purpose.

The British Background

When we turn to the progress of poesy in modern England we find many parallels to recent American literary history. There is the same lassitude in the eighties and nineties, when Victorianism was in the last stages of senescence; there are the same significant forerunners of a new day; there is the same startling impact of revolutionary theories on a complacent conservatism; and there is, to a much greater degree, the powerful stimulus of the World War. But fundamentally there is one striking difference. In America we have seen, about 1914, the definite end of one era and the rise of another—an era whose actual accomplishment is not easily defined because it has been so largely confused with experimentation, but whose main tendencies are at least different from those which preceded it. England, too, has known changes in the poetic mind, but they are no more than superficial eddies and whirlpools in the great onward stream of British poetry. That stream can trace its course for centuries. It represents a body of tradition upon which none of the recent movements or schools has had more than passing effect. In other words, American poetry, young, unrestrained, many-sectional, is still groping its way toward a national standard; British poetry, old and disciplined, feels in the main no need of standards other than those which it has inherited.

The death of Alfred Tennyson in 1892, together with the death of Robert Browning three years earlier, accurately determines the end of the great Victorian period in poetry, for both men continued to write to the ends of their long lives. Although an irreverent younger generation has heaped its criticism upon Victorian smugness, prudery, sentimentality, and materialism, it cannot include in its indictment such men as Browning, Tennyson, Matthew Arnold, Algernon Charles Swinburne, William Morris, Dante Gabriel Rossetti, and George Meredith. In greater part, these poets would not compromise with the meaner standards of their period. In a sense, they were least Victorian of the Victorians.

When they had passed, there was no one immediately fitted to take their places. The eighties and nineties had their poets, men like Austin Dobson, Andrew Lang, Robert Louis Stevenson, Arthur Symons, Ernest Dowson, and others, who strove to keep alive a somewhat languid muse. There was not, in these facile, graceful, and charming writers enough of the consuming

fire of poetic ardor to raise their verse to the high level set by
their predecessors. Their work has survived in varying degrees,
but the total amount to achieve permanence is small. The
rest has passed into the obscurity which overtakes ephemeral
things, for it lacked the qualities which would commend it to
our dynamic age. Less creditable than the work of the poets
just mentioned were the products of the school of decadent
aestheticism which flourished in the nineties under the flashy
leadership of Oscar Wilde, and which took "Art for Art's sake"
as its criterion of wisdom and beauty alike.

The preoccupation of the times with soft themes and merely
decorative fancies had already been challenged by the vigorous
athleticism of William Ernest Henley. Though an invalid
most of his life, he spoke only with a sort of hopeful stoicism.
"In Hospital," written in 1873-1875 while he was confined to
an Edinburgh hospital, anticipated the best in modern realistic
poetry. With a journalist's devotion to fact, Henley stripped
life of sentimental glamour. More than that, he was one of the
first poets to adapt free verse from French and German sources
to the uses of English poetry. Some of his free verse has not
been excelled by any of his successors in this art. Witness his
"Margaritae Sorori," a poem so musical and so expertly
cadenced that a hearer would hardly suspect that it lacks both
rime and regular rhythm:

MARGARITAE SORORI[4]

A late lark twitters from the quiet skies;
And from the west,
Where the sun, his day's work ended,
Lingers as in content,
There falls on the old gray city
An influence luminous and serene,
A shining peace.

---

[4] "To My Sister Margaret."

The smoke ascends
In a rosy-and-golden haze. The spires
Shine and are changed. The lark sings on. The sun,
Closing his benediction,
Sinks, and the darkening air
Thrills with a sense of the triumphing night—
Night with her train of stars
And her great gift of sleep.

So be my passing!
My task accomplished, and the long day done,
My wages taken, and in my heart
Some late lark singing,
Let me be gathered to the quiet west,
The sundown splendid and serene,
Death.

As an editor, Henley was of very practical service to English
literature, for his columns were always open to work of merit,
regardless of its author's fame. It was in Henley's *Scots
Observer* that *Barrack-Room Ballads* (1892) first appeared. Their
author, Rudyard Kipling, was an unknown journalist, whose
work was to achieve the almost instant popularity which
any genuinely fresh and original thing is likely to receive. Not
for forty years had the English-speaking world united in a
popular welcome to a major figure in English poetry. The
expansion of British dominion overseas had brought great
changes to which Mr. Kipling first gave poetic currency. He
was the voice of British imperialism. He realized, too, through
his life in India, the unworked possibilities which lay in Tommy
Atkins and the Indian Civil Service. Finally, in vigorous protest against the enervating aestheticism of his day, he chose
his subjects from practical, active life; with daring realism he
utilized material that never before had been considered the
stuff of poetry. His enthusiasm for machinery, for example,
was a departure from all literary precedent, though it has
become a commonplace of later writers. In style, Mr. Kipling

was also an innovator. His early "ballads" were written in
the vernacular of the British soldier, with insistent, lilting
refrains. His subsequent work has continued this use of vernacular and of catchy, music-hall rhythms. Both traits are
illustrated in the following stanza from "Troopin' ":

> Troopin', troopin', give another cheer—
> 'Ere's to English women an' a quart of English beer.
> The Colonel an' the regiment an' all who've got to stay,
> Gawd's mercy strike 'em gentle—Whoop! we're goin'
> 'ome today.
>> We're goin' 'ome, we're goin' 'ome,
>> Our ship is at the shore,
>> An' you must pack your 'aversack,
>> For we won't come back no more.
> Ho, don't you grieve for me,
> My lovely Mary-Ann,
> For I'll marry you yit on a fourp'ny bit[5]
> As a time-expired man.

Much that is tawdry, much that is hasty, much that is
jingoistic, in Mr. Kipling's poetry has failed of permanence,
and he is judged today, as a poet, on a comparatively small
body of work. His chief importance, which is not to be denied,
arises from the new vitality which he brought into British
poetry by his novel subjects and his racy style. He inspired a
host of imitators who copied his manner without capturing his
spirit. Eventually the rise of new influences diverted the
literary fashion into other channels.

THE CELTIC REVIVAL

One of the first of these influences was the literary revival
which began in Ireland about 1890 and has continued to the
present day. The sources exploited by this revival fall into
two groups: the masterpieces of Gaelic literature, that "reposi-

---

[5] *fourp'ny bit, time-expired*, when this poem was written, the British soldier who had completed his term of service was retired on a pension of fourpence a day.

tory of Irish nationality," which tell, in epic form, the half-mythical history of ancient Ireland; and the folk songs, rich in Celtic tradition, which survive in the countryside. A revived sense of nationality, coupled with a new interest in antiquarian research, furnished the twofold impetus which brought forth translations both of epics and of folk literature. These translations were in turn the inspiration of the new school of Irish poets.

In the eighteenth and nineteenth centuries Irish poetry had merely reflected English poetic style. It was one purpose of the revival to "de-Anglicize" Irish poetry and produce an authentic native idiom. Toward the attainment of this difficult ideal, the services of Douglas Hyde must have special mention. This distinguished Gaelic scholar, seeking a compromise between pure Gaelic and orthodox English, devised for his translations an Anglo-Irish form suggested by the speech of the peasantry, in which English is still dominated by old Gaelic influences. In short, he invented a new literary language. The following specimen of Anglo-Irish prose should be compared with Dr. Hyde's translation of the same poem into conventional English verse on page 440:

O youth of the bound-back hair, with whom I was for a time together, you went by this way last night, and you did not come to see me. I thought no harm would be done you if you were to come and to ask for me, and sure it is your little kiss would give comfort, if I were in the midst of a fever.

If I had wealth and silver in my pocket, I would make a handy boreen[6] to the door of the house of my storeen; hoping to God that I might hear the melodious sound of his shoe, and long since is the day on which I slept, but ever hoping for the taste of his kiss.

And I thought, my storeen, that you were the sun and the moon, and I thought after that, that you were snow on the mountain, and I thought after that, that you were a lamp of God, or that you were the star of knowledge going before me and after me.

---

[6]*boreen*, a lane; *storeen*, darling.

Simultaneous with Dr. Hyde's *Love Songs of Connacht*, first published serially in 1890, were the works of a group of young poets all inspired by the same pride in a heroic tradition, the same consciousness of nationality, the same zeal to revivify the past in poetry that should be free from English influences. Foremost in this group and destined to become its leader was William Butler Yeats, whose *Wanderings of Oisin and Other Poems* had appeared in 1889.

Although Mr. Yeats later became possessed by mysticism and loaded his poetry with so much symbolism that many readers find it obscure, his youthful poems are as fine examples of pure lyricism as any modern poet has composed. The subject-matter, which is, of course, Irish, is idealized and romanticized by the poet's vision. The words and the style are utterly simple. Mr. Yeats first taught modern poetry how to dispense with rhetoric and "poetic diction."

The most brilliant of Mr. Yeats's protégés was John Millington Synge, who did all his work in the six years between 1903 and 1909. Strictly speaking, he was not a poet, for the bulk of his work is dramatic. But such a play as *Riders to the Sea* is so deeply infused with the poetic spirit that it rises above narrow definition and takes its place as poetry in the truest sense. A single passage from this play will show how Mr. Synge, building on Dr. Hyde's foundation, used his first-hand study of the Aran dialect to create an idiom of exquisite beauty and power:

> (*Maurya, an aged islander, is lamenting the death of the last of her six sons, all of whom, as well as their father, have been taken from her by the sea.*)

They're all gone now, and there isn't anything more the sea can do to me. . . . I'll have no call now to be up crying and praying when the wind breaks from the south, and you can hear the surf is in the east, and the surf is in the west, making a great stir with the two noises, and they hitting one on the other. I'll have no call now to be going down and getting Holy Water in the dark nights after Samhain,[7] and I won't

---

[7] *Samhain*, All Saints' Day, November 1.

care what way the sea is when the other women will be keening.[8] . . .
It isn't that I haven't prayed for you, Bartley, to the Almighty God.
It isn't that I haven't said prayers in the dark night till you wouldn't
know what I'd be saying; but it's a great rest I'll have now, and it's
time surely. It's a great rest I'll have now, and great sleeping in the
long nights after Samhain, if it's only a bit of wet flour we do have to
eat, and maybe a fish that would be stinking.

In 1904, A. E. (George William Russell), mystic poet, philosopher, and long a powerful influence in the literary life of
Dublin, sponsored the publication of *New Songs*, a collection
of work by a younger generation of poets. Here Seumas
O'Sullivan and Padraic Colum made their first appearance.
Joseph Campbell and James Stephens, members of the same
group, came only a little later. These men are carrying on the
best traditions of the Celtic Revival. Certain lesser poets, on
the other hand, have affected a pseudo-folklore, called "folk-
smoke" by the earlier men. This tendency does not, of course,
detract from the genuine achievements of the revival. Its positive influence, both in poetry and in drama, has been to encourage directness and simplicity of style together with a fuller
recognition of the beauty, the tragedy, and the humor of
humble lives.

THE WORLD WAR AND LATER

The other chief influence on the formation of modern British
poetry was the World War. In 1914, when the War broke upon
England, a good deal of poetry was just about to take form
under the realistic inspiration of John Masefield, who will be
considered separately in a later section. The devastating experience of the War released a vast amount of poetic energy,
much of it good, some of it painfully bad. On the other hand,
the War was the means of temporarily sharpening and strength-
ening the powers of such young men as Rupert Brooke, Siegfried
Sassoon, Wilfrid Wilson Gibson, Edward Thomas, and Francis
Ledwidge, (to mention the more important), who under normal

---

[8]*keening*, wailing loudly.

circumstances might have developed only a conventional romanticism. Brought up against the terrific facts of modern warfare they tried at first to translate them into the heroic imagery of the age of chivalry. In vain—the facts remained facts, grisly, sardonic, unescapable. And so these poets and many others, such as Wilfred Owen, Robert Nichols, and Robert Graves, described the horror of war from the standpoint of utter disillusionment. Youth of all succeeding time looking back for a true account of the World War will find its features most faithfully recorded in the writings of these Englishmen who fought and, in many cases, died in it.

In the last statement is the clue to much of England's literary history since the War. Death robbed the nation of most of its young poets. The practice of poetry went on in the hands of the older men but without quite the vigor which would have been furnished by the normal influx of young, new blood. The situation has its parallel in the years following the Romantic Period: if there was no poetry of consequence in England for some time after 1832, it was partly because Keats, Shelley, and Byron had all recently died young. Those War poets who survived their military service appear to have suffered a shock from which they cannot fully recover. In no case do they find it possible to regain the point of view which they held before the War. Their genius has been warped by a subject so titanic that all other subjects seem, by comparison, insignificant.

These other subjects, represented in several minor tendencies of contemporary British poetry, are indeed on a different scale from the subjects engendered of the War. There is, in the first place, imagism, which, as already noted, began in England as a definite movement in 1913, a couple of years before it spread to America. Prominent among the British members of the imagist group were Richard Aldington and D. H. Lawrence. Sincere as the work of this group was, the theories of imagism made even less impression on the poetry of England than they were to make on the poetry of America. The force of precedent was too strong. Yet it would be untrue to say that imagism was quite without influence. As in America, it drew attention to outworn conventions of style and called up, albeit with exaggerated emphasis, the function of imagery as an ingredient of poetry.

Since the brief career of imagism, two poetic tendencies have appeared in England, supported largely by the generation of poets that were too young to take part in the World War. These tendencies are so distinct and the conflict between them is so keen that they are entitled to be called schools—the country school and the intellectual school.

The first of these groups, the country school, was, in its beginnings, motivated by a desperate desire to escape from the realities of war. Many of its forerunners, writing in the trenches of Flanders or Gallipoli, turned from present horrors to sing of remembered lovelinesses—the green pastures and still waters of England. Idealized love of country combined with homesickness animated much of such poetry by Rupert Brooke, Francis Ledwidge, and Edward Thomas. When the problems of peace succeeded the rigors of war, it was natural that poets should continue to seek forgetfulness in the "return to nature" which has beguiled poets of every age since that of Theocritus. A further reason why this group turned to the country was to find relief from a civilization rapidly becoming urbanized. The harsh materialism of city life affords them no answer to the "obstinate questionings of sense and outward things" which troubled Wordsworth before them; and, like him, they have found that

> . . . the meanest flower that blows can give
> Thoughts that do often lie too deep for tears.

The country school of contemporary British poetry includes, besides a few surviving War poets, W. H. Davies, Edmund Blunden, Martin Armstrong, Charlotte Mew, Ralph Hodgson, and many others. The weakness of the school is the susceptibility of some of its minor figures to the over-simplification of the obvious. Instead of the Blake-like naïveté for which they strive they accomplish only absurdities. Mr. J. C. Squire has parodied this failing in the following lines, rather unfairly attributed to Mr. Davies:

> I saw some sheep upon some grass,
>   The sheep were fat, the grass was green,
> The sheep were white as clouds that pass,
>   And greener grass was never seen;
> I thought, "Oh, how my bliss is deep,
> With such green grass and such fat sheep!"

The intellectuals or modernists, being primarily city poets, deny any metaphysical property in nature which can interpret a world throbbing to the footbeats of man's progress. Logic, at any rate, seems to be on their side when they assert that the meaning of a city civilization must be sought in the life of the city. If their pitiless analysis discovers very little meaning even there, so much the worse for modern city civilization. The sense of fatuity and futility expressed in the following quotation is typical of their sophisticated attitude:

> The country bumpkins travel to the Fair,
> For night and day and hell and heaven seem
> Only a clown's booth seen in some bad dream,
> Wherefrom we watch the movements of our life,
> Growing and ripening like summer fruits
> And dwindling into dust, a mirage lie.
>
> Hell is no vastness, it has naught to keep
> But little rotting souls and a small sleep.
>
> It has the same bright-colored clarity we knew
> In nursery afternoons so long ago,
> Bright as our childish dreams; but we are old,
> This is a different world; the snow lies cold
> Upon our heart, though midsummer is here. . . .
>   —*Edith Sitwell*

The intellectuals do not stop at a passive world-weariness, however. Like the country poets, they have seen with disgust the sentimentalism and profiteering that accompanied and followed the War; but instead of running away from such things, like the country poets, they have laid them bare with remorseless and acrid mockery.

In style the two schools are even farther apart than in subject-matter. The country poets are accused by their modernist critics of strumming only the familiar strings of bucolic poetry. With biting contempt they are told not to congratulate themselves "on continuing the tradition of English poetry, for the poet who merely derives from his predecessors and presents their thoughts and images worn at second hand does nothing of the sort." The charge is not entirely fair, as the pungency and originality of their best work amply proves: see the poems by Charlotte Mew, page 466. The intellectuals, who get tit for tat from their country critics, have, for the most part, adopted bizarre mannerisms in an effort to represent the bewildering confusion of modern city life. At its best their style crackles with witty and pyrotechnical invention; at its worst, it is either obscure or nonsensical.

The most conspicuous of the British intellectual or modernist group are the three Sitwells, Edith, Osbert, and Sacheverell. A few years ago T. S. Eliot[9] sprang into temporary fame by his long and curious poem *The Waste Land* (1922). The later poetry of Siegfried Sassoon and Robert Graves, War poets, is dominated by the modernist point of view.

Four British Contemporaries

Four men will now be considered from among the outstanding figures in contemporary British poetry: John Masefield, Wilfrid Wilson Gibson, Walter de la Mare, and Thomas Hardy. If they seem a somewhat smaller representation than contemporary American poetry can show, their number must be

---

[9]Though American born, Mr. Eliot has lived in England since 1914.

regarded with a due balancing of their sure distinction, individ-
ually and collectively, against the sometimes fitful groping of
American leadership. Moreover, they have been chosen from
a list too long for comment here, in which occur such names as
John Drinkwater, A. E. Housman, and G. K. Chesterton.

The career of John Masefield, as already hinted, began long
before the World War. As far back as 1902 he had sung the
life of the sea in *Salt-Water Ballads* with a two-fisted romanticism which somehow failed of its due appreciation by a public
attuned to milder music. Yet it was the robust realism of
his four long narrative poems, *The Everlasting Mercy*, *The
Widow in the Bye Street*, *Dauber*, and *The Daffodil Fields*,
which brought him recognition and fame. These poems introduced a poetic manner which could not but profoundly
affect Mr. Masefield's fellow writers. Casting the affectations
and elegances of the current literary custom to the winds, he
transmuted the drab language of common folk into the golden
accents of great imaginative poetry. His means were of the
simplest and the oldest. He adopted a style so casual and so
conversational as to approach banality, even vulgarity. His
rhythms are as ancient as Chaucer and as regular. But it is
by his intimate knowledge of the life he describes and his
passionate understanding of the heroism and the tragedy of
that life that he achieves his power of conviction. And he is
still more than a protagonist of social justice. In everything
he writes, no matter how lowly or how sordid the theme, the
light of beauty shines through. This ability to discover
beauty in unsuspected places is the root secret of his power
and his greatest contribution to the poetry of his time.

The most notable example of Mr. Masefield's effect upon his
contemporaries is found in the record of Wilfrid Wilson Gibson.
His earlier and forgotten books (1902-1910) have nothing in
common with his later; in them is only a placid acceptance of
Tennysonian romanticism. Then he fell under the influence of
Mr. Masefield. He says, himself:

> I caught the stormy summons of the sea.
> And dared the restless deeps that, day and night,
> Surge with the life-song of humanity.

Abruptly he turned realist in order to present the lives of "the poorest, the lowliest, and the lost" with candid revelation of primitive emotions and passionate conviction of social injustice. A third period in Mr. Gibson's work is dominated by the War. Every other interest gives way before the horror which overmasters him. In a series of unforgetable vignettes he flashes the truth in its ugliest aspects. *Battle* is a book eloquent of the author's service as a private in the trenches. Since the War, Mr. Gibson's realism has been considerably softened, as he has turned to the English countryside for new inspiration. Thus, curiously, his career illustrates the whole course of recent British poetry.

Of Walter de la Mare it can only be said that he is one of those timeless and other-worldly beings who refuse to accommodate themselves to any historical scheme or chronology, however artful. His poetry is the poetry of illusion, his world is the world of magic, his time is the eternal childhood of the race. The poems of *The Listeners* and *Peacock Pie* defy any narrower classification. The work of Mr. De la Mare reminds us of the powerful continuity of tradition in English poetry, for it is compact of Keats, Blake, Collins, Donne, and the great sources of English song, Sidney, Spenser, and Shakespeare. Enviably disregardful of the tumult of modern life, and comparatively untouched by the tragedy of the War, Mr. De la Mare allows his romantic fancy to play in the remote regions of the imagination, bringing back to our twentieth century their mysterious and lovely music.

Last to be considered and in many respects greatest is the late Thomas Hardy. Already internationally famous as a novelist, he turned from prose to poetry when he was almost sixty years of age, and most of his poems were written in the last third of his long life. The first impact of Hardy's poems is apt to discourage a faint-hearted reader, for their outward appearance is often uncouth, crabbed, formidable, and their thought is so condensed that it finds no ready understanding. Grace was not unknown to Hardy—notice, especially, his early lyrics. But the ruggedness of his thought sometimes compelled a gnarled and tangled utterance not unlike the language of Browning or Carlyle. In spite of this defect, Hardy has been, by sheer weight of intellect, the most important steadying influence in the poetry of our day. In an age of constant change, he never swerved from his established philosophy. The record of a lifetime was irreproachably consistent. It is useless to measure such monumental constancy to convictions by the scale which one ordinarily uses. Hardy transcends all limitations and schools of style or thought. So far as it is possible to predict, one feels that there is, in his poetry, a solidity of substance and a depth of truth not yet fully realized, which will raise it above the willful perversities of his style and insure its survival among the permanent riches of English literature.

In Summary

British poetry since 1914, or a few years earlier, is not distinguished by the same passion for experiment which has marked American poetry during the same period. The influence of free verse and imagism has been scarcely perceptible in any direct form; the novel conceits of the modernists have attracted only a small following. The greater part of the imposing volume of work produced by contemporary British poets is safely within established literary traditions; Masefield, Gibson, De la Mare, Hardy, the soldier poets, and most of the country poets adhere to the conventions of poetic speech. Thanks chiefly to the example of Mr. Masefield, there is a somewhat greater range of subject-matter than in the past, but, aside from the modernists, there is no considerable tendency toward innovation in matters of style. Yet the general level of contemporary British poetry exhibits a mature and mellow distinction which the general level of contemporary American poetry has not yet attained. This condition results from the inspiration of past achievement in British letters and the consciousness of belonging, in some degree, to a great national tradition. But in this sense of the past there is also the danger of such preoccupation with purely literary values that the substance of poetry is diluted; American poetry may indeed be less meticulous, but it is, perhaps, more vigorous. In the dominating sense of the past is still another possible danger—the danger of complacency. If American poetry lacks the steadying force of a long and honorable tradition, if it has not yet quite found its national consciousness, it has in their stead the spirit of youth which incites to adventure. Though it be still a headlong freshet seeking an outlet, at least it gives no indication of becoming a placid pool.

In the latter part of the period covered by this book there has been, on both sides of the Atlantic, a relaxation from the splendid creative activity of a few years since. In the United States it is significant that a list of the eleven best books of verse published between 1912 and 1926, as determined by the vote of a number of authorities, included only three volumes published since 1920, two of which had been written some time previous to that date. In spite of the sanguine opinions of compilers of the year's best magazine verse, it must be candidly admitted that there is today, both in England and in America, only a relatively small production of verse which rises above the level of technical facility. There seems to be no satisfactory explanation of this lull in poetic energy—perhaps it would not be so conspicuous were it not in contrast to the preceding years of exceptional productivity. Apparently it is simply a breathing-space, a pause rather than an end.

Yet there are some critics who are predicting an end, who say that poetry cannot exist in the modern world of science and invention, commerce and industry, big business and organized labor, a world that is openly and frankly mechanistic and materialistic in its philosophy. To be sure this is a world different from any which poetry has had to deal with in the past. It is an immensely difficult world to translate into poetic terms. No wonder that the singers pause to gird their loins before they attempt the task! But they are only pausing . . . . Poetry is not coming to an end so long as the human spirit struggles to express itself. The poets of the future will grapple with the modern world and on its own conditions. They will discover a synthesis between science and imagination. They will learn to look on the things of their new world as means to an end beyond the material, as symbols of the undying idealism of the race. They will learn, in short, to interpret the contemporary in terms of the timeless.

I

AMERICAN POETS

CONRAD AIKEN

Conrad (Potter) Aiken, born in Savannah, Georgia, in 1889, attended Harvard University, where he was graduated in 1912. There followed several years of travel alternating with graduate study. In 1921 he removed from his home at South Yarmouth, Massachusetts, to the English seaside town of Rye, in Sussex, his present residence, although he spent the academic year of 1927-1928 in the United States.

In spite of his widely-acknowledged mastery over forms of lyric beauty, Mr. Aiken's best audience remains the poets themselves, who cannot but share the delight which he so obviously finds in the discovery of new effects of rhythm and rime. Poetry is for him a laboratory wherein he is forever experimenting to combine the arts of poetry and music; naturally the results of such experimenting are often interesting technically as well as aesthetically. But that is hardly enough to insure a popular appeal. Many readers require a positive and vigorous substance beneath the complex beauties of design, and this, it must be admitted, they do not find in Mr. Aiken's verse. A mood of mild disillusion, a dispassionate introspectiveness, a dream-escape from the life of reality—these he finds sufficient themes upon which to exercise his talent for musical expression.

When Mr. Aiken keeps the length of his poems within reasonable bounds, he proves himself a true lyricist, a singer of exquisite and delicate music. The verses here quoted are examples of pure lyricism; they have been selected from the collection of lyrics called *Priapus and the Pool* (1922), by some considered his finest work. Other books which have come from his fluent pen are: *Earth Triumphant and Other Tales in Verse* (1914), *Turns and Movies* (1916), *The Jig of Forslin* (1916), *Nocturne of Remembered Spring* (1917), *The Charnel Rose* (1918), *The House of Dust* (1920), *Punch: The Immortal Liar* (1921), *The Pilgrimage of Festus* (1923). He is also known as a writer of short stories and, in *Scepticisms* (1919), as a searching critic of his contemporaries. He has also written a novel, *Blue Voyage* (1927) and a book of short stories, *Costumes by Eros* (1928).

AND IN THE HANGING GARDENS

CONRAD AIKEN

And in the hanging gardens there is rain
From midnight until one, striking the leaves
And bells of flowers, and stroking boles of planes,
And drawing slow arpeggios over pools,
And stretching strings of sound from eaves to ferns.
The princess reads. The knave of diamonds sleeps.
The king is drunk, and flings a golden goblet
Down from the turret window (curtained with rain)
Into the lilacs.
                              And at one o'clock
The vulcan under the garden wakes and beats
The gong upon his anvil. Then the rain
Ceases, but gently ceases, dripping still,
And sound of falling water fills the dark
As leaves grow bold and upright, and as eaves
Part with water. The princess turns the page
Beside the candle, and between two braids
Of golden hair. And reads: "From there I went
Northward a journey of four days, and came
To a wild village in the hills, where none
Was living save the vulture and the rat,
And one old man, who laughed, but could not speak.
The roofs were fallen in; the well grown over
With weed; and it was there my father died.
Then eight days further, bearing slightly west,
The cold wind blowing sand against our faces,
The food tasting of sand. And as we stood
By the dry rock that marks the highest point
My brother said: 'Not too late is it yet
To turn, remembering home.' And we were silent
Thinking of home." The princess shuts her eyes

And feels the tears forming beneath her eyelids
And opens them, and tears fall on the page.
The knave of diamonds, in the darkened room,
Throws off his covers, sleeps, and snores again.
The king goes slowly down the turret stairs
To find the goblet.

              And at two o'clock
The vulcan in his smithy underground
Under the hanging gardens, where the drip
Of rain among the clematis and ivy
Still falls from sipping flower to purple flower,
Smites twice his anvil, and the murmur comes
Among the roots and vines. The princess reads:
"As I am sick, and cannot write you more,
Nor have not long to live, I give this letter
To him, my brother, who will bear it south
And tell you how I died. Ask how it was,
There in the northern desert, where the grass
Was withered, and the horses, all but one,
Perished" . . . The princess drops her golden head
Upon the page between her two white arms
And golden braids. The knave of diamonds wakes
And at his window in the darkened room
Watches the lilacs tossing, where the king
Seeks for the goblet.

              And at three o'clock
The moon inflames the lilac heads, and thrice
The vulcan, in his root-bound smithy, clangs
His anvil; and the sounds creep softly up
Among the vines and walls. The moon is round,
Round as a shield above the turret top.
The princess blows her candle out, and weeps
In the pale room, where scent of lilac comes,
Weeping, with hands across her eyelids, thinking
Of withered grass, withered by sandy wind.

The knave of diamonds, in his darkened room,
Holds in his hands a key, and softly steps
Along the corridor, and slides the key
Into the door that guards her.   Meanwhile, slowly,
The king, with raindrops on his beard and hands,
And dripping sleeves, climbs up the turret stairs,
Holding the goblet upright in one hand;
And pauses on the midmost step, to taste
One drop of wine, wherewith wild rain has mixed.

THIS IS THE SHAPE OF THE LEAF

Conrad Aiken

This is the shape of the leaf, and this of the flower,
And this the pale bole of the tree
Which watches its bough in a pool of unwavering water
In a land we never shall see.

The thrush on the bough is silent, the dew falls softly,
In the evening is hardly a sound.
And the three beautiful pilgrims who come here together
Touch lightly the dust of the ground,

Touch it with feet that trouble the dust but as wings do,
Come shyly together, are still,
Like dancers who wait, in a pause of the music, for music
The exquisite silence to fill.

This is the thought of the first, and this of the second,
And this the grave thought of the third:
"Linger we thus for a moment, palely expectant,
And silence will end, and the bird

"Sing the pure phrase, sweet phrase, clear phrase in the twi-
light
To fill the blue bell of the world;
And we, who on music so leaflike have drifted together,
Leaflike apart shall be whirled

"Into what but the beauty of silence, silence forever?" . . .
. . . This is the shape of the tree,
And the flower, and the leaf, and the three pale beautiful
pilgrims;
This is what you are to me.

JOSEPH AUSLANDER

Joseph Auslander was born in Philadelphia, Pennsylvania, in 1897. He attended school in Philadelphia and in Brooklyn, was graduated from Harvard University, and studied at the Sorbonne. For awhile he was an instructor at Harvard.

In Mr. Auslander's first book, *Sunrise Trumpets* (1924), the reader is chiefly conscious of the quality of life. Conventional in form, these poems voice sensations and ideas of a new and sudden originality. In some measure the originality of the poems is in their style. Emily Dickinson is sometimes suggested by the queerly effective phrases. But often the style is queer without being effective. It becomes too obviously an escape from the obvious. More important in this book is the spirit which sees life in eager shapes of beauty and joy, a spirit which led Padraic Colum to call *Sunrise Trumpets* "a book of high-hearted verse." In a foreword Mr. Colum says: "Indeed, it goes some way toward restoring a quality that has been left out of a great deal of verse that is being written in the New World in our time—the quality of delight."

Cyclops' Eye (1927) is a more sober rendering of life. The style is as striking as before, but the spirit which vitalizes the book is a tragic compassion. "The Riveter," in its candor and its pity, is typical of the book.

THE RIVETER

The steam shovels had sunk their teeth
   Through earth and rock until a hole
Yawned like a black hell underneath,
   Like a coal-crater with all the coal
Torn out of her; the shovels bit
The stinking stony broth—and spit.

The Wops went up and down; they spilled
   Cement like a groggy soup in chutes;
They mixed the mortar, and they filled
   The gash with it . . . Short swarthy **brutes**
They were, who reeked of rock and wet
Lime and accumulated sweat.

At first the work was tame enough:
   Only another foundation like
Hundreds before and just as tough
   To stand under a ten-ton spike.
But it was different when a whir
Of steel announced the riveter.

One long lad of them took the crowd
   As he straddled the girders and hooked the nuts
Livid-white hot; and we allowed
   He was the lunatic for guts;
The sidewalk bleachers yelled as he
Speared a sizzler dizzily.

They got to call him the "Rivet Ruth"—
   That crisp corn-shock of gusty hair,
That blue hawk-eye, and devil of youth
   Juggling with death on a treacherous stair,
Tipping his heart on a beam of steel
That made his pavement audience reel.

The riveting hammers stuttered and kicked;
  The ten-ton trestles whined in the winch;
And still this golden Icarus picked
  The hissing rivets by half an inch,
Twirled and nailed them on the spin
Out of the air and rocked them in.

And one fine sun-splashed noon he lunged
  Over the stark deadline—and missed!
Swung for an instant and then plunged
  While the long insane rivet hissed
Him all the way down from truss to truss
And dropped beside its Icarus!

The old strap-hanger thumbed his paper;
  Feet shuffled sidewalks; traffic roared. . . .
Icarus had performed his caper—
  Little New York minced by bored:
Leave the lads with the broken backs,
Soiled feathers and some melted wax!

MARY AUSTIN

Mary Austin's writings are peculiarly the products of her environment—first, the Middle West, where she was born; then the desert country of Southern California, where she passed years of meditation and observation; and latterly, Arizona and New Mexico, where she has acquired an intimate knowledge of Indian life.

Miss Austin's restless intellect has ranged over an unusual variety of subjects and literary forms; her writings include books of travel, critical essays, poetry, novels, and plays. However, she found in the American Southwest one subject of inexhaustible fascination, a subject which she has treated from every angle, and which has thus become the unifying factor in her work.

The Land of Little Rain (1903), a traveler's panorama of desert, arroyo, and mesa revealingly and familiarly unrolled; *The Arrowmaker* (1911), a play which dramatizes the universal conflict between genius and motherhood against a setting of Indian life; *The American Rhythm* (1923), an essay on the Indian's contribution to the founding of a national art in America; and her poetry, which, for the most part, is interpretative of Indian originals—everything which Miss Austin has written is animated by her profound love for the American Southwest and her sympathetic understanding of its people. Through all her work shines the passionate search for "a native poetry that shall not content itself with the deft adaptation of this or that imported, sophisticated mode, but shall go down within the nation till it reaches the basic rhythms, the stroke of the paddle or of the ax, the curves of the landscape, the sequence of the weather and the crops."[1] The "American rhythm" which she defines is not limited to the art of poetry nor even literature, but pervades all native art. Hence it must arise by slow degrees of natural development. In giving voice to the "Amerindian" dialect, Miss Austin has indicated one of the possible roads to her goal, a goal which, she holds, can be reached by intimate communion with the aboriginal American environment.

The poems which follow were selected more for their gracious artistry than for any thesis which they may illustrate. "Neither Spirit Nor Bird" is a Shoshone love song. The "Lament of a Man for His Son" has a poignance which Miss Austin faithfully carries over into English verse.

---

[1]Carl Van Doren: *Many Minds.*

NEITHER SPIRIT NOR BIRD

MARY AUSTIN

Neither spirit nor bird;
That was my flute you heard
Last night by the river.
When you came with your wicker jar
Where the river drags the willows,
That was my flute you heard,
Wacoba, Wacoba,
Calling, "Come to the willows!"

Neither the wind nor a bird
Rustled the lupine blooms.
That was my blood you heard
Answer your garment's hem
Whispering through the grasses;
That was my blood you heard
By the wild rose under the willows.

That was no beast that stirred,
That was my heart you heard,
Pacing to and fro
In the ambush of my desire,
To the music my flute let fall.
Wacoba, Wacoba,
That was my heart you heard
Leaping under the willows.

LAMENT OF A MAN FOR HIS SON

Mary Austin

Son, my son!

I will go up to the mountain,
And there I will light a fire
To the feet of my son's spirit,
And there will I lament him;
Saying,
O my son,
What is my life to me, now you are departed!

Son, my son,
In the deep earth
We softly laid thee in a chief's robe,
In a warrior's gear.
Surely there,
In the spirit land
Thy deeds attend thee!
Surely,
The corn comes to the ear again!

But I, here,
I am the stalk that the seed-gatherers
Descrying empty, afar, left standing.
Son, my son!
What is my life to me, now you are departed?

LEONARD BACON

"The Ballad of Angel May" is the result of a curious collaboration. Rivers S. Browne, who furnished the initial inspiration, is an old cowpuncher and horse-breaker whose insatiable love of scribbling is not backed by a practical knowledge of what editors will publish. Although he has now retired to his own ranch at Salmon Arm, British Columbia, he was at one time connected with a ranch owned by the Bacon family, and there grew up the friendship which resulted in a literary partnership.

Leonard Bacon, born in New York State, in 1887, is a product of St. George's School, Newport, and Yale University, whose experiences have taken him through Europe, Central America, and most parts of the United States. He is the great-grandson of a philosopher, Rowland G. Hazard. Sometimes, as he listened with sympathetic tolerance to the long yarns of Rivers Browne, an episode or a passage caught and held his fancy. It was an isolated line, "the *cavallarda* of the Circle-Bar," which furnished the starting point for "The Ballad of Angel May."

The poem is, of course, a *tour de force*, but so cleverly executed that some of Mr. Bacon's colleagues in the English Department of the University of California were induced to pronounce it apparently a genuine contemporary folk-ballad.

Ballads represent but a small part of Mr. Bacon's manifold versatility. A glance at the titles of his books is informing: *The Scrannel Pipe* (1909), *Heroic Ballads of Servia* (with G. R. Noyes) (1913), *The Song of Roland* (1914), *The Lay of the Cid* (1919), *Ulug Beg* (1923), *Ph. D.'s* (1925), *Animula Vagula* (1926), *Guinea-Fowl and Other Poultry* (1927). Of these, *Ph. D.'s* has perhaps enjoyed the widest audience because of its Byronic flippancy toward the pompous pretense of graduate study when conducted for no end but an advanced degree. Throughout these volumes the thrusts of ridicule are sufficiently keen to make Mr. Bacon one of our foremost satirists in verse.

THE BALLAD OF ANGEL MAY

Leonard Bacon

If you will listen, I'll say my say
About a lady. Her name was May.
And she was pretty and she was limber,
But the Marshal run her out of Big Timber,
And from what she said and done that day,
I reckon they called her Angel May.
Her hair was red, and her eyes was blue.
But I wouldn't go with her, if I was you.
And if I did, I wouldn't go far.
You take it from the Boss of the Circle-Bar.

   With a broken arm he hit Blue Flat,
When May blew by in her Stetson hat,
Painted and powdered, and a sight to see,
And "Boss," she says, "take a whirl with me."
And the Boss he says, "No, May, my girl,
My arm is bruk, and I cannot whirl."
Which proves a fellow don't know his luck
Sometimes, even if his arm is bruk.
"Who's running your beef-herd now?" says May.
Says the Boss: "That piker is Frank McCrea.
His legs is putty. His head is bone.
But I got some trailhands from San Antone.
You come from somewhere down that way.
I think I heerd so, Angel May."
But May she answered in high disdain,
"You think so? Take a think again."

   Now the Boss's arm was hurtin' him bad,
Or he'd 'a noticed why May was mad.
For the only boy in the world for May
Was that pie-faced loafer Frank McCrea.
And every one in the whole Northwest
Knew Frank was an ornery cattle-pest.

And I've hern tell that further South
The Greasers call him "Foot and Mouth."[1]
He couldn't rope, and he couldn't ride.
He hadn't the guts of a man inside.
He couldn't brand or cut or shoot,
But he drew an ace right smart from his boot.
Which don't prove nothing at all, becuz
Frank was a devil with women, he wuz.
They fell for him white and Cree and Sioux,
And Angel May she fell for him, too.
And he was a regular song and dance.
And the sun it rose on the seat of his pants.
All her earnings, every cent,
On that low-life buckeroo she spent,
For all the licker that he could hold,
And that dirty loafer quit her cold.
And she hadn't seen him for nigh two years,
And here he was running the Boss's steers,
Eating overtime, riding slow,
Pushing the herd from Mexico.

Now Angel May didn't wait no more.
The lights was burning in the "Matador,"
Montana laying its aces down,
For half of Texas had come to town.
The drinks was flowing in that den of vice.
I ought to know. I got shot there twice.
And there was the trapper, Two-Dot Jones,
Hitting the red-eye, rolling the bones.
She looks at the gang. "Two-Dot," says she,
"Come here, old timer, and talk with me.
Two-Dot, I know I done you dirt,
But you don't want May to come to no hurt.
Get me a horse, and get me away.
I must see that piker, Frank McCrea.

[1]"*Foot and Mouth*," a contagious disease affecting cattle.

I know he's a half-breed. I ain't no star.
We hit the trail for the Circle-Bar."
   Now I never heard no other report.
Two-Dot Jones was a game old sport.
Three days they rode. They hit, the fourth,
The trail of the beef-herd traveling North.
And through the shadow and the night a-falling
They heard the jingle of the bells calling,
Heard 'em jingle near and far,
The cavallarda[2] of the Circle-Bar.
   She fussed a lot, did Angel May,
Over that piker, Frank McCrea.
She gave him the rough side of her tongue,
But you should have seed the whisky she brung.
There was sure enough to drown the house.
And the whole damn' camp was one big souse.
And Frank McCrea got more 'n' his share,
Which he wouldn't have done, if the Boss was there.
But the Boss by that was a damn' sick man
With a broken arm in Bozeman.
   With his head in her lap, Frank's snoring hard.
It came to the change of the cattle-guard.
He never shifted, he never stirred.
In came Kid Angel from riding herd.
He looks at May, an' he says: "Good night!
There'll be some shooting soon as there's light.
Tomorrow it's me for the Rio Grand',
And Frank, I reckon, for the Promised Land.
He's going to drink just one drink more
Before he starts for the Golden Shore."
And he put a bottle careful by,
For he wouldn't be mean and send him dry.
He rolled in his blanket. And Angel May
Held Frank's head in her lap till day.

---

[2]*cavallarda*, (Spanish), a herd of horses.

Just before sunup Coyote Joe
Blew in. Says May, "Has Frank a show?"
"A chance," says Joe, "but I'm no liar,
Same as a snowball in hell-fire.
The Kid can shoot a bug off the limb.
'Bat' Masterson[3] has nothing on him."

And up the sun come, glum and pale,
And the boys is singing "The Chisholm Trail,"[4]
And chewing his lip, and mad to let drive,
Kid Angel's playing with his forty-five.

And the liquor's burning in Frank McCrea.
And I never want to fight his way.
And she says to him: "McCrea, you're tight.
Pull yourself together. You got to fight."
An' he says, "Where?" An' she says: "Right here!
For this Kid Angel is my brother dear.
An' he says he'll get you, too, by damn,
Because you made me what I am."

And Frank McCrea, he gets to his feet,
And his hands are shaking, an' he's white as a sheet.
Kid Angel's looking mighty mean,
And he says, "You swine!   I'll drill you clean."

Coyote Joe is bossing the show.
He's raised his hand and raring to go.
Frank's head is shaking, and the sweat it run
Down the face of that son-of-a-gun.
The Kid he whipped his gun up spry,
But Angel May heaved her hat in his eye.
He flinched an inch, and the shot went wild—
That May was sure a mischievous child.
And Frankie's bullet, straight and true,
Split the Kid's wishbone right in two.
The Kid he dropped.   And "May," says he,

---

[3] *"Bat" Masterson*, a dead-shot frontiersman.
[4] *"The Chisholm Trail,"* a cowboy song; the Chisholm Trail was the route over which the herds of cattle were driven North to market.

"He's drilled me clean.   The joke's on me.
He's the worst shot I ever saw.
But give my love to Paw and Maw.
Skin out before this show gets pinched.
I don't want no sister of mine to get lynched.
You skip away with Frank McCrea,
And damn you anyhow, Angel May."

A CONCERT

LEONARD BACON

There are fifty million dollars in the room.
The splendid bellow of the baritone
Smites on a note to topple down a throne,
Moussorgsky boding forth an empire's doom.
There is lava in that song that can consume
Wild nations, and artillery's rhythmic drone,
Rebellion yelling, and wild trumpets blown,
And a blood-boltered Czar dragged to the tomb.

As all the bare-backed women sigh applause,
Silk rustles, and the diamond collars glint,
And vacant eyes smile wide, as if no hint
Of horror hung upon the resonant air,
Of white throats cut, perhaps not without cause.
It must be fun to be a millionaire.

KARLE WILSON BAKER

Karle Wilson Baker (Mrs. Ellis Baker) was born in Little Rock, Arkansas, in 1878; she was educated in public and private schools there, and at the University of Chicago, Columbia University, and the University of California. Since her marriage in 1907 she has lived in Nacogdoches, a small town in eastern Texas. Her two volumes of verse, *Blue Smoke* (1919) and *Burning Bush* (1922), illustrate her talent for condensation. Most of her poems are short, incisive; some are exquisitely tender. "The Hill Steps" is an example of vivid landscape painting done in a few strokes, finished off with a touch of realism.

THE HILL STEPS

Karle Wilson Baker

There's a flight of steps running down the hill
Toward the town that lies in the valley below,
And down you come in the paling light
While the roofs are pink with the afterglow.

And there—from the top of the steps—it lies
Like the Town of Pearl in the prince's dream,
In every chimney a plume of blue,
In every window a blazing gleam.

Then, down you come.   And, one, two, three,
Twelve steps, and your foot is on solid land—
And in less than a minute you'll catch the smell
Of onions down at the chilli-stand.

APPLE AND ROSE

Karle Wilson Baker

My little daughter is a tea-rose,
Satin to the touch,
Wine to the lips,
And a faint, delirious perfume.

But my little son
Is a June apple,
Firm and cool,
And scornful of too much sweetness,
But full of tang and flavor,
And better than bread to the hungry.

O wild winds and clumsy, pilfering bees,
With the whole world to be wanton in,
Will you not spare my little tea-rose?
And O ruthless blind creatures,
Who lay eggs of evil at the core of life,
Pass by my one red apple,
That is so firm and sound!

I SHALL BE LOVED AS QUIET THINGS

KARLE WILSON BAKER

I shall be loved as quiet things
Are loved—white pigeons in the sun,
Curled yellow leaves that whisper down
One after one;

The silver reticence of smoke
That tells no secret of its birth
Among the fiery agonies
That turn the earth;

Cloud-islands; reaching arms of trees;
The frayed and eager little moon
That strays unheeded through a high
Blue afternoon.

The thunder of my heart must go
Under the muffling of the dust—
As my gray dress has guarded it
The grasses must.

For it has hammered loud enough,
Clamored enough, when all is said;
Only its quiet part shall live
When I am dead.

STEPHEN VINCENT BENÉT

Born in Bethlehem, Pennsylvania, in 1898, twelve years later than William Rose Benét, his brother, Stephen Vincent Benét has not yet fully attained the sureness and maturity of his brother's poetry. In spite of some tendency to overproduction, he may be expected to overtake his brother, for he has the abounding imagination and whimsical ingenuity that distinguish the work of the older man. Like his brother, he favors the writing of narrative poetry.

In 1923 he won the poetry prize of the New York *Nation* with his widely-discussed poem "King David." The reckless originality and Biblical frankness of this piece commended it to its admirers. His first book of poetry, *Five Men and Pompey* (1915), was published the year that he entered Yale University. It was followed by *Young Adventure* (1918), *Heavens and Earth* (1920), *The Beginning of Wisdom* (1921), a novel, and *Tiger Joy* (1925). "The Ballad of William Sycamore," from the last-named volume, epitomizes in the life of one man the whole story of the American pioneers and foreshadows the epical *John Brown's Body* (1928).

THE BALLAD OF WILLIAM SYCAMORE

Stephen Vincent Benét

My father, he was a mountaineer,
His fist was a knotty hammer;
He was quick on his feet as a running deer,
And he spoke with a Yankee stammer.

My mother, she was merry and brave,
And so she came to her labor,
With a tall, green fir for her doctor grave
And a stream for her comforting neighbor.

And some are wrapped in the linen fine,
And some like a godling's scion;
But I was cradled on twigs of pine
In the skin of a mountain lion.

And some remember a white, starched lap
And a ewer with silver handles;
But I remember a coonskin cap
And the smell of bayberry candles.

The cabin logs, with the bark still rough,
And my mother who laughed at trifles,
And the tall, lank visitors, brown as snuff,
With their long, straight squirrel-rifles.

I can hear them dance, like a foggy song,
Through the deepest one of my slumbers,
The fiddle squeaking the boots along,
And my father calling the numbers.

The quick feet shake the puncheon-floor,[1]
And the fiddle squealing and squealing,

---

[1] *puncheon-floor*, a floor laid with broad, flat slabs of timber.

Till the dried herbs rattled above the door,
And the dust went up to the ceiling.

There are children lucky from dawn till dusk,
But never a child so lucky!
For I cut my teeth on "Money Musk"[2]
In the Bloody Ground of Kentucky!

When I grew tall as the Indian corn,
My father had little to lend me,
But he gave me his great old powder-horn
And his woodsman's skill to befriend me.

With a leather shirt to cover my back,
And a redskin nose to unravel
Each forest sign, I carried my pack
As far as a scout could travel.

Till I lost my boyhood and found my wife,
A girl like a Salem clipper!
A woman straight as a hunting-knife
With eyes as bright as the Dipper!

We cleared our camp where the buffalo feed,
Unheard-of streams were our flagons;
And I sowed my sons like the apple-seed
On the trail of the Western wagons.

They were right, tight boys, never sulky or slow,
A fruitful, a goodly muster;
The eldest died at the Alamo.[3]
The youngest fell with Custer.

---

[2]"*Money Musk*," an old reel tune.
[3]*the Alamo*, a Franciscan mission house in San Antonio, Texas, scene of a battle (1836) in the war for Texan independence; 140 men held the inclosure for ten days against a Mexican army of 4000. The defenders fought to a finish. *Custer*, General George A. Custer (1839-1876), hero of "Custer's Last Stand," a frontier battle in which Custer and his 264 men, outnumbered twenty to one, were surrounded by Indians and massacred.

The letter that told it burned my hand.
Yet we smiled and said, "So be it!"
But I could not live when they fenced the land,
For it broke my heart to see it.

I saddled a red, unbroken colt
And rode him into the day there;
And he threw me down like a thunderbolt
And rolled on me as I lay there.

The hunter's whistle hummed in my ear
As the city-men tried to move me,
And I died in my boots like a pioneer
With the whole wide sky above me.

Now I lie in the heart of the fat, black soil,
Like the seed of a prairie-thistle;
It has washed my bones with honey and oil
And picked them clean as a whistle.

And my youth returns, like the rains of spring,
And my sons, like the wild geese flying;
And I lie and hear the meadow lark sing
And have much content in my dying.

Go play with the towns you have built of blocks,
The towns where you would have bound me!
I sleep in my earth like a tired fox,
And my buffalo have found me.

WILLIAM ROSE BENÉT

William Rose Benét, older brother of Stephen Vincent Benét, also a poet, was born in 1886 at Fort Hamilton, New York Harbor, his father being an army officer stationed there. He was graduated from Yale University in 1907 and at once became a free-lance writer, in California and in New York. His writings have been many and versatile, but he is known best for his poetry. His literary career was interrupted by the World War, in which he was attached to the Air Service. In 1920 he became an associate editor of *The Book Review* of the New York *Evening Post*, a position which he resigned in 1924 in order to help launch *The Saturday Review of Literature*.

His principal volumes of poetry are *Merchants from Cathay* (1913), *The Falconer of God* (1914), *The Great White Wall* (1916), *The Burglar of the Zodiac* (1918), and *Moons of Grandeur* (1920). *Man Possessed* (1927) contains selected poems grouped according to their subject-matter. The contents of these books are as fantastic as their titles would suggest, for Mr. Benét's imagination is as uncurbed as the soaring falcon of his allegory. His poems are chiefly narratives, sometimes of far romance, sometimes of elaborate symbolism, sometimes of unlicensed fancy. "The Falconer of God," from the volume of that name, is reprinted here as one of the most notable of modern didactic poems; yet for all its moral objective, it is first a thing of strange beauty.

THE FALCONER OF GOD

William Rose Benét

I flung my soul to the air like a falcon flying.
I said, "Wait on, wait on, while I ride below!
    I shall start a heron soon
    In the marsh beneath the moon—
A strange white heron rising with silver on its wings,
      Rising and crying
    Wordless, wondrous things;
The secret of the stars, of the world's heartstrings
    The answer to their woe.
Then stoop[1] thou upon him, and grip and hold him so!"

My wild soul waited on as falcons hover.
I beat the reedy fens as I trampled past.
    I heard the mournful loon
    In the marsh beneath the moon.
And then—with feathery thunder—the bird of my desire
      Broke from the cover,
    Flashing silver fire.
High up among the stars I saw his pinions spire.
    The pale clouds gazed aghast
As my falcon stooped upon him, and gripped and held him fast.

My soul dropped through the air—with heavenly plunder?—
Gripping the dazzling bird my dreaming knew?
    Nay! but a piteous freight,
    A dark and heavy weight
Despoiled of silver plumage, its voice forever stilled—
    All of the wonder
    Gone that ever filled
Its guise with glory.   O bird that I have killed,

---

[1] *stoop*, to swoop down; used of birds of prey.

How brilliantly you flew
Across my rapturous vision when first I dreamed of you!

Yet I fling my soul on high with new endeavor,
And I ride the world below with a joyful mind.
I shall start a heron soon
In the marsh beneath the moon—
A wondrous silver heron its inner darkness fledges![2]
I beat forever
The fens and the sedges.
The pledge is still the same—for all disastrous pledges,
All hopes resigned!
My soul still flies above me for the quarry it shall find.

---

[2]*fledges*, provides with wings.

THERE LIVED A LADY IN MILAN

WILLIAM ROSE BENÉT

There lived a lady in Milan
Wrought for a madness unto Man,
A fawn Il Moro[1] could not tame;
Her beauty unbedecked with pearls
More than all Beatrice's[2] girls,
Her eyes a secret, subtle flame.

Brocade wherein her body dressed
Was hallowed; flowers her footstep pressed
Suspired incense ere they died.
Her father, mazed with alchemy,
Wrought in his cellar, ceaselessly.
She lived in quiet, gentle pride.

And by her garden in his hour
Passed Leonardo[3], come with power
From Florence.   So he saw her face
Bending above the shriveled stalks
Of autumn on the garden walks.
And Leonardo drank her grace.

She was as if a sunset were
With fresher colors, clearer air,
And a more golden coil of cloud.
She was as if all citherns swooned
With one rich harmony myriad-tuned,
Haunting, enchanting, pure, and proud.

[1]*Il Moro*, Ludovico Sforza (1451-1508), Duke of Milan, patron of Leonardo da Vinci.
[2]*Beatrice*, Beatrice d'Este (1475-1497), wife of Ludovico; the accomplished mistress of a brilliant court and an important influence in the culture of the Renaissance.
[3]*Leonardo*, Leonardo da Vinci (1452-1519), Florentine painter, sculptor, architect, musician, scientist, mechanician, and military and civil engineer; sometimes called the most versatile genius in history.   The greater part of his life was spent in Milan at the court of Ludovico.

And Leonardo said, "Ladye,
I know not what you do to me
Who have and have not, seek nor find.
The sea shell and the falcon's feather,
Greece and the rock and shifting weather
Have taught me many things of mind.

"My heart has taught me many things,
And so have emperors, popes, and kings,
And so have leaves and green May-flies;
Yea, I have learned from bird and beast,
From slouching dwarf and ranting priest.
Yet, in the end, how am I wise?

"Though with dividers and a quill
I weave some miracle of will—
Say, that men fly—though I design
For peace or war a thousand things
Gaining applause from dukes and kings—
Though soft and deft my colors shine,

"Though my quick wit breed thunderbolts
I may not loose on all these dolts,
Things they are babes to comprehend—
Though from the crevice in stone or lime
I trace grave outlines mocking time—
I know when I am beaten, friend!

"Say that there lived of old a saint
Even Leonardo dared not paint,
Even Leonardo dared not draw—
Too perfect in her breathing prime
For colors to transmit to time
Or quill attempt—aye, ev'n in awe!

"Say this, cold histories, and say
I looked not on her from this day,
Lest frenzied I destroy my art.
O golden lily—how she stands
Listening! Beauty—ah, your hands,
Your little hands tear out my heart!

"Do you not know you are so fair,
Brighter than springtime in the air?
What says your mirror to your mind?"
"Phantom," she whispered, "do you plead
With ghostly gestures? . . . Ah, indeed,
Pity a lady deaf and blind

"Since birth!" . . . Then Leonardo turned
Saluting, though the sunset burned
In nimbus round her—went his way
In daze, repeating "God's defect,
Even he!—and masterpiece elect!"
He never saw her from that day.

WITTER BYNNER

Witter Bynner was born in Brooklyn, New York, in 1881. He was graduated from Harvard University in 1902, recording later the memory of his undergraduate experience in his popular "Ode to Harvard." After a few years as a magazine editor and publishers' adviser, he joined the artists' colony at Cornish, New Hampshire, to give his time to poetry. Later he taught English at the University of California, gathering about him a group of young students of poetry who have since become poets in their own right. He is deeply interested in the encouragement of young talent, and his Annual Undergraduate Poetry Prize has been the means of discovering new writers. Since 1923 he has lived at Santa Fe, New Mexico.

Young Harvard (1907), the first of Mr. Bynner's books, contains the "Ode to Harvard" and is mainly reminiscent of his student days. *The New World* (1915) is both a love poem and a discourse on democracy. *Grenstone Poems* (1917) remains the favorite of many readers of Mr. Bynner—here he draws his subjects mostly from nature, writing with a lyrical ease which must arise from the congeniality of the task. *A Canticle of Pan* (1920) and *Caravan* (1925) cover a surprising variety of subjects and forms, for Mr. Bynner has the gift for emulating without imitating. Some critics, while admiring Mr. Bynner's versatility, regret that it has prevented him from identifying himself with any one particular style or even any one type of subject. It is, however, questionable whether a poet must so limit himself; and even granting that he must, Mr. Bynner has cultivated to a rare degree the one ability of doing small things with perfect ease and grace and clarity. His lyrics are "a silver thread of verse"—as the accompanying poems show.

Spectra (1916), the notorious parody of free verse which Mr. Bynner, as "Emanuel Morgan," concocted with Arthur Davison Ficke ("Anne Knish"), was so successful in deceiving its readers that Mr. Bynner betrayed some tendency toward radical forms in his subsequent verse. Perhaps he regretted that he had to disown *Spectra* as legitimate offspring. On the whole, however, he has chosen to write in the more regular modes.

His travels in the Orient are the basis of *The Beloved Stranger* (1919), and his residence in China accounts for *The Jade Mountain*, a forthcoming collection of T'ang Dynasty poems in English versions.

GHOSTS OF INDIANS

Witter Bynner

Indian-footed move the mists
From the corner of the lake,
Silent, sinuous, and bent;
And their trailing feathers shake,
Tremble to forgotten leapings,
While with lingerings and creepings
Down they lean again to slake
The dead thirst of parching mouths,
Lean their pale mouths in the lake.

Indian-footed move the mists
That were hiding in the pine,
Out upon the oval lake
In a bent and ghostly line,
Lean and drink for better sleeping . . .
Then they turn again and—creeping,
Gliding as with fur and fins—
Disappear through woods and water
On a thousand moccasins.

THROUGH A GATEWAY IN JAPAN

Witter Bynner

A torii[1] stood, three miles above the bay,
 A gate of sacred ground,
And when I wandered through a little way,
 I paused and found
No temple-steps, no lanterns, and no shrine;
 Only divinity:
The solitary presence of a pine
 Facing the sea.

A THRUSH IN THE MOONLIGHT

Witter Bynner

In came the moon and covered me with wonder,
 Touched me and was near me and made me very still.
In came a rush of song, like rain after thunder,
 Pouring importunate on my window sill.

I lowered my head, I hid it, I would not see nor hear;
The birdsong had stricken me, had brought the moon too near.
But when I dared to lift my head, night began to fill
With singing in the darkness.   And then the thrush grew still.
And the moon came in, and silence, on my window sill.

[1]*torii*, a gateway, usually before a Shinto temple

BLISS CARMAN

(William) Bliss Carman is a Canadian by birth and by sympathies. Born in Fredericton, New Brunswick, in 1861, he has never lost touch with the Maritime Provinces, though he has lived in the United States since 1889. His education was acquired at the University of New Brunswick, at Edinburgh, and at Harvard University.

His first book, *Low Tide on Grand Pré: A Book of Lyrics* (1893), was enthusiastically received. It offered a refreshing departure from senescent literary traditions. His next three books were written in collaboration with his friend Richard Hovey, and did more than any other American poetry of their day to clear the stage of empty imitations of French verse forms and sentimental confections feebly suggestive of Byron and Tennyson. The three books which brought "jest and youthful jollity" back into the world were *Songs from Vagabondia* (1894), *More Songs from Vagabondia* (1896), and *Last Songs from Vagabondia* (1900), published the year of Hovey's death. They still retain with little diminishment their gay and honest appeal to those who look on life with youthful eyes.

Mr. Carman's later books betray something of the inevitable sobering that comes with age. Always a conservative in matters of style, Mr. Carman has lost much of the rebellious spirit which so endeared him to his earlier followers. But much remains to please the thoughtful reader in his *Ballads of Lost Haven* (1897), *From the Book of Myths* (1902), *Songs of the Sea Children* (1904), *April Airs* (1916), and other volumes. In 1927 he edited the *Oxford Book of American Verse*.

A VAGABOND SONG

Bliss Carman

There is something in the autumn that is native to my blood—
Touch of manner, hint of mood;
And my heart is like a rime,
With the yellow and the purple and the crimson keeping time.
The scarlet of the maples can shake me like a cry
Of bugles going by.
And my lonely spirit thrills
To see the frosty asters like a smoke upon the hills.
There is something in October sets the gypsy blood astir;
We must rise and follow her,
When from every hill of flame
She calls and calls each vagabond by name.

AUTUMN

Bliss Carman

Now when the time of fruit and grain is come,
When apples hang above the orchard wall,
And from a tangle by the roadside stream
A scent of wild grapes fills the racy air,
Comes Autumn with her sunburnt caravan,
Like a long gypsy train with trappings gay
And tattered colors of the Orient,
Moving slow-footed through the dreamy hills.
The woods of Wilton, at her coming, wear
Tints of Bokhara and of Samarkand;
The maples glow with their Pompeian red,
The hickories with burnt Etruscan gold;
And while the crickets fife along her march,
Behind her banners burns the crimson sun.

FREDERICK MORTIMER CLAPP

Frederick Mortimer Clapp, born in New York City in 1879, has paid affectionate tribute to his native city in his most notable volume, *New York and Other Verses* (1918), from which the accompanying poem is chosen. Yet most of his life has been spent in travel far from "the grandiloquent city" of which he writes. After graduation from Yale University, he studied at European universities and received a degree from the Sorbonne. He has lived in France, Italy, and Switzerland, and has traveled on art pilgrimages through China, Japan, and Korea. The fruits of this experience are a number of books on Italian and Oriental art. Early in the World War he joined the Royal Flying Corps and was attached to several British squadrons. Later he became a lieutenant in an American Aero Squadron.

Mr. Clapp has preferred to experiment with free verse, in which medium he achieves striking word-pictures without sacrifice of clarity or sense. That is to say, he is not an extremist. In his search for novelty he does not forget the accepted requirements of literary taste.

TRADE

Frederick Mortimer Clapp

Her derricks thrust their yellow booms through the lilac air,
like the naked sticks of a shuffled fan,
and her wireless sags between slanting masts.
Rusty teeth of winches chatter and grate,
as bale after bale,
jerked up on a tawny rope,
dodders an instant over the river
to flash from a wailing block
into the thudding grumble of the hold.
Like a huge bassoon her loose-lipped whistle flibbers.
I see the puffed flurry of the steam
grip her smokestack like a hand
and drift out into lingering torn undulations.
She is peeling the rooted wharf away from her side,
and her lifeboats seem to slide along its pebbled roof.
Tugs waddle around her, whipping the river to a cream of foam;
they are panting and ringing frantic little bells;
they are heaping around her great drab walls
a snowdrift of heaving steam.
At last she emerges—
she strides toward the sea, a-quiver with the shake of her
    engines,
and the proud lust of the deep water is upon her.
At last the boiling spine and fluffy silver ribbon of her wake,
the wet shoulder of her rudder, and her name, and the quicken-
    ing snap-snap
of her little red flag.
How flapped about she is with the veering squeal of gulls;
how dense and foreboding and gray the mist is that she steams
    into;
how, as I think, like a vast green mass of glass, the sea
that she will scratch her white hair-line across

lies immovable in its deep drowned valleys
and sunken mountains.
A thousand unconquerable thoughts have become
her delicate wires and wheels and rods;
a thousand patient hands have fitted them together
and heaped a fire among them until they have made her creep
on the bright skin of the sea.
She is taking a thousand souls with her,
each with his hands full of treasure,
each with a lifetime of love and hope
flowering like a living tree in the hollow of his heart.
Yet how dim her stern light's wink, now the sun has set.
So dim and far it seems, that, watching her, I wonder
how she can ever reach England,
with her hull no bigger than a water-fly,
and her humming screw a pin point
grazing the filmy face of the unending dark green death.
And yet can it be she will ever sink down,
in a fluttering sheath of bubbles,
to some ledge laid bare like a spectral claw,
among sodden ocean ranges,
to rot into the very stuff
of eternal darkness and silence?

A dray clanks jangling over the cobbles past the pier;
its rumble is slashed into bits
by the sliding clink of the horses' hoofs.
It is life taking up the unshaken prose of existence.
It is the clicking of the rushing and eternal looms
of calculation,
reeling forever out their unchanging pattern
of profit and loss,
that counts her, and all who peer across her trembling rail
and see no land now,
only a shuttled thread.

ELIZABETH J. COATSWORTH

Elizabeth J. Coatsworth was born in Buffalo, New York, in 1893. Her early education was acquired in private schools in Buffalo and in California; she was graduated from Vassar College and received a master's degree the following year from Columbia. The great influence of her life has been travel. Not only has she divided her home life between the Atlantic and Pacific coasts, but since the age of five she has frequently traveled abroad. At fifteen she was taken to Mexico; after completing her college work, she visited the Far East. The latter trip resulted in *Fox Footprints* (1921), a successful venture in the compact subtleties of Oriental style. "At present," she writes, on a January day, "we live in New England in an old house above Hingham harbor—a quiet sort of life, a matter in these days of snowshoes and tea beside the fire."

Atlas and Beyond (1924) covers a wide range of travel and defines both the quality of foreign places and the lives of their people. Her most recent poems, as yet published only in magazines, display a charming lightness of humor and fancy, well illustrated in "Subjunctive"—a quality which cannot but attract many readers.

SUBJUNCTIVE

Elizabeth J. Coatsworth

Suppose Marie Antoinette *had* come to Wiscasset,[1]
Escaped from Paris, escaped from violence, escaped
   from fear,
Would she have lived, soberly and quietly,
Talking to the women in the square white houses there?

Where they saw gray water, she would have seen steel
   flashing,
Where they saw autumn leaves, blood she would have seen.
The shivering white birches would have seemed like
   frightened ladies,
Where the Wiscasset eyes found only moving green.

And when she saw the women go out into the barnyards,
Then she would have felt her tired heart fail,
Remembering the Trianon[2] and a dress of flowered satin,
And herself going milking with a silver milking pail.

---

[1]*Wiscasset.* There is a tradition in Wiscasset, Maine, that a house was bought there as a refuge for Marie Antoinette. (Author's note.)

[2]*Trianon,* the Petit Trianon, a pavilion at Versailles, favorite residence of Marie Antoinette, where she played peasant with the ladies of her court.

ALICE CORBIN

Although Alice Corbin (Mrs. William P. Henderson), a native of St. Louis, Missouri, has produced a smaller number of poems than some other women lyricists of America, she has performed important services to American poetry, first as Harriet Monroe's chief assistant in the editorship of the magazine *Poetry;* second, as her collaborator in the compiling of the anthology, *The New Poetry* (1917, revised 1923), an exhaustive collection of the work of the younger and more experimental writers. That she is a poet herself, however, is amply attested by the rich quality of her *Red Earth* (1920).

Red Earth, from which all the following selections are taken, is the product of her residence in New Mexico since 1916. It is a faithful interpretation of much that must seem alien to the rest of America, a civilization which was already old when the Pilgrims landed at Plymouth. Miss Corbin captures successfully the barbaric colorings of desert and mesa, the primitive life of Indian pueblo and Mexican village. She has worked her field lovingly and well. Her only other volume, which is less typical of her work, is *The Spinning Woman of the Sky* (1912). Her most recent verse, which includes skillful adaptations of Southern folk-poetry, has appeared only in magazines.

RED EARTH

ALICE CORBIN

After the roar, after the fierce modern music
Of rivets and hammers and trams,
After the shout of the giant
Youthful and brawling and strong
Building the cities of men,
Here is the desert of silence,
Blinking and blind in the sun—
An old, old woman who mumbles her beads
And crumbles to stone.

IN THE DESERT

ALICE CORBIN

The hill cedars and piñons
Point upward like flames,
Like smoke they are drawn upward
From the face of the mountains.
Over the sunbaked slopes,
Patches of sundried adobes straggle;
Willows along the acequias[1] in the valley
Give cool streams of green;
Beyond, on the bare hillsides,
Yellow and red gashes and bleached white paths
Give foothold to the burros,
To the black-shawled Mexican girls
Who go for water.

---

[1]*acequias*, irrigation ditches.

ON THE ACEQUIA MADRE[1]

ALICE CORBIN

Death has come to visit us today.
He is such a distinguished visitor
Everyone is overcome by his presence—
"Will you not sit down—take a chair?"
But Death stands in the doorway, waiting to depart;
He lingers like a breath in the curtains.
The whole neighborhood comes to do him honor—
Women in black shawls and men in black sombreros
Sitting motionless against whitewashed walls;
And the old man with the gray, stubby beard,
To whom death came,
Is stunned into silence.
Death is such a distinguished visitor,
Making even old flesh important.

But who now, I wonder, will take the old horse to pasture?

[1] *acequia madre*, the main irrigation ditch, from which branch ditches proceed.

NATHALIA CRANE

The child prodigy is easily the most uncertain quantity in literature; rare indeed is the one who fulfills the promise of a precocious beginning. Therefore it would be rash to predict the future of Nathalia Crane, who, before she was ten years old, was contributing verses to *The Sun*, New York, the editors of which were unaware that she was a child. Yet there is no denying that she has a natural poetic gift, expressing itself now in rich music, now in impish humor, now in baffling subtleties of suggestion.

The Janitor's Boy (1924) illustrates both the good and the bad of which she is capable; for in spite of her uncanny semblance of maturity, she cannot resist two childish weaknesses—a fondness for conundrums without an answer and a passion for archaisms which recalls the "marvelous boy," Thomas Chatterton. But in this book, and still more in *Lava Lane* (1925), *The Singing Crow* (1926), and *Venus Invisible and Other Poems* (1928), there are so much of sheer inexplicable brilliance, such wealth of startling imagery, such whimsical invention, that one can simply wait to see what she will do next—whether her abilities will steady into the quality of genius or whether she will flicker into the limbo of child prodigies who sang their snatch of song and then were silent. Her capture, in 1927, of the first prize in a contest for a poem commemorative of Lindbergh's transatlantic flight showed that, at fourteen, she maintained her talent unimpaired.

Nathalia Crane was born in New York City in 1913. If there is any sure indication in heredity, her chances of future fame should be considerably enhanced by the curious mixture of her blood: on one side the Pilgrim simplicity of John Alden, on the other the romantic turbulence of the Spanish Jews. And she is also related to that unappreciated master of American literature, Stephen Crane.

THE BLIND GIRL

Nathalia Crane

In the darkness, who would answer for the color of a rose,
Or the vestments of the May moth and the pilgrimage it goes?

In the darkness who would answer, in the darkness who would
care,
If the odor of the roses and the wingéd things were there?

In the darkness who would cavil o'er the question of a line,
Since the darkness holds all loveliness beyond the mere design?

Oh, night, thy soothing prophecies companion all our ways,
Until releasing hands let fall the catalogue of days.

In the darkness, who would answer for the color of a rose,
Or the vestments of the May moth and the pilgrimage it goes?

In the darkness who would answer, in the darkness who would
care,
If the odor of the roses and the wingéd things were there?

COUNTÉE CULLEN

Countée Cullen was born in New York City in 1903; he attended the New York public schools, was graduated from New York University in 1925, and pursued graduate study at Harvard University. His first volume of poetry, *Color*, appeared in 1925. Its contents command high respect for the sure poetic technique, the pungency of phrasing, and the terrible candor of thought which distinguish *Color* from the common run of soft and pretty little books of verse. As the outspoken revelation of some of the deeper emotions of the American negro, the volume also merits special attention. "Heritage" has been selected as showing best the racial emotion of the author; "Shroud of Color" (not reprinted here) is another but more mystical expression of the same idea. No one who enjoys the art of mordant epigram should fail to read Mr. Cullen's "Epitaphs." *Copper Sun* (1927) and *The Ballad of the Brown Girl* (1928) continue the rich and vivid distinction of the initial volume. Mr. Cullen has also edited *Caroling Dusk, An Anthology of Verse by Negro Poets* (1927). In 1928 he married the daughter of W. E. B. Du Bois, eminent negro editor.

HERITAGE

Countée Cullen

What is Africa to me:
Copper sun or scarlet sea,
Jungle star or jungle track,
Strong bronzed men, or regal black
Women from whose loins I sprang
When the birds of Eden sang?
One three centuries removed
From the scenes his fathers loved,
Spicy grove, cinnamon tree,
What is Africa to me?

So I lie, who all day long
Want no sound except the song
Sung by wild barbaric birds
Goading massive jungle herds,
Juggernauts of flesh that pass,
Trampling all defiant grass
Where young forest lovers lie,
Plighting troth beneath the sky.
So I lie, who always hear,
Though I cram against my ear
Both my thumbs, and keep them there,
Great drums throbbing through the air.
So I lie, whose fount of pride,
Dear distress, and joy allied,
Is my somber flesh and skin,
With the dark blood dammed within
Like great pulsing tides of wine
That, I fear, must burst the fine
Channels of the chafing net
Where they surge and foam and fret.

Africa? A book one thumbs
Listlessly, till slumber comes.
Unremembered are her bats
Circling through the night, her cats
Crouching in the river reeds,
Stalking gentle flesh that feeds
By the river brink; no more
Does the bugle-throated roar
Cry that monarch claws have leapt
From the scabbards where they slept.
Silver snakes that once a year
Doff the lovely coats you wear,
Seek no covert in your fear
Lest a mortal eye should see;
What's your nakedness to me?
Here no leprous flowers rear
Fierce corollas in the air;
Here no bodies sleek and wet,
Dripping mingled rain and sweat,
Tread the savage measures of
Jungle boys and girls in love.
What is last year's snow to me,
Last year's anything? The tree
Budding yearly must forget
How its past arose or set—
Bough and blossom, flower, fruit,
Even what shy bird with mute
Wonder at her travail there,
Meekly labored in its hair.
One three centuries removed
From the scenes his fathers loved,
Spicy grove, cinnamon tree,
What is Africa to me?

So I lie, who find no peace
Night or day, no slight release
From the unremittent beat
Made by cruel padded feet
Walking through my body's street.
Up and down they go, and back,
Treading out a jungle track.
So I lie, who never quite
Safely sleep from rain at night—
I can never rest at all
When the rain begins to fall;
Like a soul gone mad with pain
I must match its weird refrain;
Ever must I twist and squirm,
Writhing like a baited worm,
While its primal measures drip
Through my body, crying, "Strip!
Doff this new exuberance.
Come and dance the Lover's Dance!"
In an old remembered way
Rain works on me night and day.

Quaint, outlandish heathen gods
Black men fashion out of rods,
Clay, and brittle bits of stone,
In a likeness like their own,
My conversion came high-priced;
I belong to Jesus Christ,
Preacher of humility;
Heathen gods are naught to me.

Father, Son, and Holy Ghost;
So I make an idle boast;
Jesus of the twice-turned cheek,
Lamb of God, although I speak

With my mouth thus, in my heart
Do I play a double part.
Ever at Thy glowing altar
Must my heart grow sick and falter,
Wishing He I served were black,
Thinking then it would not lack
Precedent of pain to guide it,
Let who would or might deride it;
Surely then this flesh would know
Yours had borne a kindred woe.
Lord, I fashion dark gods, too,
Daring even to give You
Dark, despairing features, where,
Crowned with dark, rebellious hair,
Patience wavers just so much as
Mortal grief compels, while touches
Quick and hot, of anger, rise
To smitten cheek and weary eyes.
Lord, forgive me if my need
Sometimes shapes a human creed.

All day long and all night through,
One thing only must I do:
Quench my pride and cool my blood,
Lest I perish in the flood;
Lest a hidden ember set
Timber that I thought was wet,
Burning like the dryest flax,
Melting like the merest wax,
Lest the grave restore its dead.
Not yet has my heart or head
In the least way realized
They and I are civilized.

E. E. CUMMINGS

Born in Cambridge, Massachusetts, in 1894, Edward Estlin Cummings is, at first glance, far removed from the fashion of those poets who made his native city a center of sweetness and light. For Mr. Cummings distorts punctuation's artful aid and even largely rejects the use of capitals on the theory that punctuation and capitalization give an artificial, mechanical emphasis to poetry instead of leaving the word, phrase, or rhythm to convey its own natural emphasis. The individual reader can test this theory for himself by writing out a Cummings poem with conventional punctuation and capitalization, and comparing its effect with that of the original. Such an experiment is likely to show that there is nothing intrinsically misleading in commas and capitals, and that the form which is nearer to accepted custom is actually the one that seems the less artificial. Such an experiment will also show that Mr. Cummings is not always the radical that he seems: that his couplets do rime, that his rhythms are regular, that his sonnets usually consist of fourteen lines. Once the irritation of his idiosyncrasies is tolerated, the reader will perceive a refreshing inventiveness of phrase and an occasional evocation of magic which entitle Mr. Cummings to rank as a poet of promise. His poetry is dealt with at considerable length in *A Survey of Modernist Poetry* (1927) by Laura Riding and Robert Graves.

If he follows the course of other youthful revolutionists, it is not impossible that he may shed his eccentricities and so gain a wider reception. His books are *The Enormous Room* (1922), a description in prose of his experiences in a French prison camp, *Tulips and Chimneys* (1923), *XLI Poems* (1925), *&* (1925), privately printed, *is 5* (1926), and *him* (1927), a play in prose.

HERE'S A LITTLE MOUSE

E. E. Cummings

here's a little mouse) and
what does he think about, i
wonder as over this
floor (quietly with

bright eyes) drifts (nobody
can tell because
Nobody knows, or why
jerks Here &, here,
gr(oo)ving the room's Silence) this like
a littlest
poem a
(with wee ears and see?

tail frisks)
                    (gonE)
"mouse,"
          We are not the same you and

i, since here's a little he
or is
it It
? (or was something we saw in the mirror)?

therefore we'll kiss; for maybe
what was Disappeared
into ourselves
who   (look).   ,startled

SONNET

E. E. Cummings

if i have made, my lady, intricate
imperfect various things chiefly which wrong
your eyes (frailer than most deep dreams are frail)
songs less firm than your body's whitest song
upon my mind—if i have failed to snare
the glance too shy—if through my singing slips
the very skillful strangeness of your smile
the keen primeval silence of your hair

—let the world say "his most wise music stole
nothing from death"—
                                you only will create
(who are so perfectly alive) my shame:
lady through whose profound and fragile lips
the sweet small clumsy feet of April came

into the ragged meadow of my soul.

S. FOSTER DAMON

Samuel Foster Damon was born at Newton, Massachusetts, in 1893. He is a member of a family which settled in Massachusetts in 1635, and has lived there ever since. He was graduated from Harvard University in 1914; in 1920-1921 he held a traveling fellowship of the American-Scandinavian Foundation, as a result of which he collaborated with Robert Hillyer in *A Book of Danish Verse* (1922), translations of Danish poetry in the original meters. For several years he held an instructorship at Harvard, resigning in 1927 to become assistant professor of English at Brown University.

Astrolabe: Infinitudes and Hypocrisies (1927), the volume into which he has collected the best of his philosophical poems, strongly reflects his interest in the mystical and visionary, an interest already employed in the writing of his *William Blake—His Philosophy and Symbols* (1924). "Burning Bush," in its attempt at mystic identification of self and nature, is typical of much of Mr. Damon's poetry. "Greeks" illustrates the touch of epigram which serves as a foil to his metaphysics. Another side of Mr. Damon's work will be shown in *Tilted Moons*, a forthcoming book of love poems.

BURNING BUSH

S. FOSTER DAMON

One morning in eternity,
I thought myself into a tree.
I felt my breast push with the sheen
Of leaves expanding into green;
I felt my arms like living wood
Thrill with resilience as I stood;
I felt the sap within my spine
Rise like the heart-blood of the pine.

Put off thy shoes (there was no sound)
And root thy feet in holy ground.

I stripped my body to the breeze,
The naked fellow of all trees,
And stood again with arms outspread,
My self almost untenanted.

Then, with a roar, there rose in me
The flames of a strange ecstasy.
My leaves, my branches, unconsumed,
With blossoms terrible I bloomed;
So tense, the whole world was obscured,
While, for a moment, I endured.

Then the fierce heat, the brilliance, died.
I shuddered, cold. On either side
The sun and moon stared like dead thieves.
My arms seemed naked of their leaves.

GREEKS

S. FOSTER DAMON

Hamlet once met William Blake.
They chatted for politeness' sake.
Said Hamlet: "Do you see that cloud?"
Said William: "Yes! It is a crowd
Of seraphim shouting 'Glory! Hail!' "
Said Hamlet: "No. It's like a whale."
And so they parted, each one glad
That the other, and not he, was mad.

EPILOGUE

S. FOSTER DAMON

Sometimes I think that I shall live again;
And chancing on these records of my times,
I'll wonder dimly at the hidden pain
Faded to quaintness in my early rimes.

And then, maybe, I shall be vaguely pleased
To feel again the torture of myself;
And by the ancient anguish gently eased,
I shall return my own book to its shelf.

BABETTE DEUTSCH

Born in New York in 1895, Babette Deutsch (Mrs. Avrahm Yarmolinsky) was graduated from Barnard College and afterwards attended the School for Social Research. The masculine sobriety and thoughtfulness of her poetry are relieved by a feminine lyricism. One has the feeling that her poetry is more to her than a creation of beauty, that it freely reflects her inmost experience, rich, dark, bitter, rebellious, or whatever the mood may be. Her books are *Banners* (1919) and *Honey out of the Rock* (1925). The poem reprinted here received *The Nation's* poetry prize for 1925.

In collaboration with her husband, Miss Deutsch has edited valuable anthologies, *Modern Russian Poetry* (1921) and *Contemporary German Poetry* (1923), both in translation.

THOUGHTS AT THE YEAR'S END

Babette Deutsch

Draw a clean breath of crisp and moonless air;
Fix eyes upon the dark;
set ears to catch
the knocking of the wind along the ground,
whereto no grass replies, being numb as wire.
The traveling clock you carry everywhere
about with you, the jewel of your bones,
ticks with too little sound,
keeping the time no other soul may share,
making you know
here's night, here's winter, here's year's end
to bear
once more,
and without a god's help, now,
without a devil, and without desire.

O happy Egypt!   O most eloquent stones,
heaped like a hill of thunder, frescoed in gold
and black and rusted vermilion,
to comfort a god, the son of the Sun, with riches.
O wise embalmers'
bandages tightly wound, to keep the dignity of the Pharaoh's
        bones
unbitten by any tooth, save, it may be,
the envy of a slave.
O black marble nostrils, spread like wings,
squat dark doorways
open to eternal life.
We come upon you, fifty centuries having passed,
we, the sorrowful heirs and assigns
of your grave-treasure, your bread, your heart, your rings,

buried with you—
we remember, O son of the Sun,
that even the first Father, shining
on the Moskva as on the Rhein, the Seine as on the
    Thames, the Hudson
as on old Nile—
even the Sun is doomed,
and dooms us in a little while.
In His eyes
two thousand years are as a moment.
Now at the winter solstice, when the light is squeezed
like a drop of watery chrome on the faded earth,
to be lapped up by a brumous blotter of darkness,
does He remember
the long December night through which the chosen
virgin labored to bring
peace to the people?

(Sing:
holy, holy, holy,
Lord God Almighty!)
He endured much—
the kiss of betrayal,
the heavy way up the hard hill,
the ropes, the nails, the spear,
the death agony, the slow, long rending, most the mockery
He cast upon Himself when He cried out,
"*Elohai, Elohai, lama sabachthani?*"[1]
That moment is over
And we, who have seen His peace
shredded by Huns and Romans, priests and kings, rich men
    and rabble,
we whom He could not save
(Himself He could not save)

---

[1]"*Elohai, Elohai . . .*" See *Mark xv,* 34.

now watch the wintry dark as a sick seaman watches
his coldly tossing grave.

But who are we
that we should envy the Pharaoh,
the Keeper of the House, who built his house forever,
or that we
should rate the God of the Hebrews, One and Eternal,
because He turned into a Trinity, and, soon thereafter,
    ceased?
We are so small
that the fleas that crawled over behemoth bulked
larger to that huge pasture than we to the stars,
and to the night the blinking stars are less
than fireflies to the whole wilderness.
O vanity
of man! that would spin Cosmos out of a small gray clot
locked in a fragile shell.
Say: God is not.
Say: man dies,
every man, alone
(Bite on this iron at midnight, when you lie
sleepless, in bed, with half a life gone by, eaten away—
the day
will be undone,
love and ambition be ashy on your tongue,
and oblivion
will roll its weight over upon you, ton and giant ton).
Say: God is not, death's instant, history's
a fever the moon died of—
what way now?
There's no help in the hills, for they will crumble,
nor in the skies, for earth is a dropped stitch
in their pattern.
(But even to fumble, there must be Fingers,

and for a pattern—Mind) . . .
Reach out, reach out, you will touch nothing,
you will find
nothing,
but yet reach,
with the balked pressure of the blind on emptiness,
reach, grope, seize, shape.
Or, let the ice-blue winding-sheet
that waits for earth
swaddle your infant wisdom at the birth,
or, from the cracked bones of despair
suck marrow,
and bend Now
backward and forward in your spirit's heat.
And bear . . . and bear . . .

LEE WILSON DODD

Lee Wilson Dodd was born in Franklin, Pennsylvania, in 1879; his childhood was spent in New York City. He went to Yale University and to the New York Law School, afterwards practicing law for five or six years. Writing is his vocation, however, and for this, his extensive travels in England, France, and Italy have given him a cosmopolitan background. He says: "I have tried my hand at almost everything— verse, essays, short stories, plays, novels, criticism," and he mentions various theatrical experiences *en tour* as a working playwright.

The poem "Lament of a New England Art Student," besides being amusing verse, suggests that Mr. Dodd is none too grateful to his long line of Presbyterian ancestors for bequeathing him a large measure of Puritanism. One feels here that he might have readily agreed with Amy Lowell when she spoke of Puritanism as "that virulent poison which saps vitality and brings on the convulsions of despair."

His volumes of verse are *A Modern Alchemist* (1906) and *The Middle Miles and Other Poems* (1915). Among his plays are *The Changelings* (1924) and *Pals First* (1925). He has also written a non-sense tale, *The Sly Giraffe* (1925).

LAMENT OF A NEW ENGLAND ART STUDENT

Lee Wilson Dodd

(Adagio, ma non troppo . . .)[1]

In the Luxembourg Gardens below the Queens of France
Brown-legged urchins scamper with hair and eyes a-dance;
And down the shadier alleys beneath the browning trees
Frail lovers of the Quarter[2] stroll delectably at ease
In Zion; and I mark them with a wistful, envious smile,
And I would that I were twenty in the happy pagan style
Of being French and twenty, and I would that I could taste
The naïve joy of Gaston when his arm is around her waist.
But woe is me, my forebears chose to agonize and pray
To a God who lived on vengeance in a most appalling way,
Who kept a strong fire burning for souls that couldn't kill
The joy of life within them—and I am suffering still
Because in lonely Salem-town they agonized and prayed
To be delivered from the wiles of Satan and a maid.
So I sit alone and watch them with a wistful wondering sigh,
Frail lovers of the Quarter who are happier than I;
And I would that I were twenty in the unassuming style
Of being French and twenty, and I half-contrive a smile
Of superior disenchantment . . . but my timid pulses dance
Like the brown-legged urchins singing there below the Queens
    of France,
In the Luxembourg Gardens—below the Queens of France.

[1] *adagio, ma non troppo,* slowly but not too much so.
[2] *the Quarter,* the Latin Quarter, a district in Paris where art students live.

MAX EASTMAN

Max Eastman was born in Canandaigua, New York, in 1883. He was graduated from Williams College in 1905. For four years thereafter he taught philosophy at Columbia, then succumbed to the greater attraction of social reform. As editor of the radical magazine, *The Masses*, he attained some fame and much notoriety. His poetic production has been somewhat limited by his unwillingness to concentrate his attention upon this branch of writing. *Child of the Amazons* (1913) and *Colors of Life* (1918) contain so much good verse that one must regret that the wide range of Mr. Eastman's activities has prevented a more substantial poetic accomplishment.

The Enjoyment of Poetry (1913) is a treatise of the first importance upon the aesthetic philosophy indicated by the title. Written in non-technical terms, with a sprightliness that suggests the style of William James, Mr. Eastman's book has something to offer every reader of poetry and much to offer the young reader.

AT THE AQUARIUM

Max Eastman

Serene the silver fishes glide,
Stern-lipped, and pale, and wonder-eyed!
As through the aged deeps of ocean,
They glide with wan and wavy motion!
They have no pathway where they go,
They flow like water to and fro.
They watch with never-winking eyes,
They watch with staring, cold surprise,
The level people in the air,
The people peering, peering there:
Who wander also to and fro,
And know not why or where they go,
Yet have a wonder in their eyes,
Sometimes a pale and cold surprise.

WILLIAM FOSTER ELLIOT

William Foster Elliot, born of American parentage in Halifax, Nova Scotia, in 1893, grew up on a California ranch. As a child he had the run of a good library and, according to his own testimony, "could and did read Shakespeare and such like" when he was five years old. Since finishing high school "under protest," he has done "nearly everything from punching cattle to newspaper work," and prefers the former. He appears, however, to be committed to a writing career, since his poems and short stories are frequently printed in magazines, and he is working on a novel. During the World War he served in France as an aërial photographer and observer. For several years he has been an editorial writer on *The Fresno Bee*, at Fresno, California.

"A Critic," originally contributed to The Conning Tower of the *New York World*, amusingly analyzes the conflict between the dreaming artist-poet and the well-disciplined writer of newspaper jargon.

A CRITIC

WILLIAM FOSTER ELLIOT

Seeing her dance, he thought the fleet
White marvel of her limbs more sweet
   Than love told in a secret place,
   Or silences that interspace
Their needless words when lovers meet.

He scribbled on his program's edge:
"O grace like that of windblown sedge;
   O beauty by slow time untouched,
   Borne back to one whom time has smutched
Since first behind some Attic hedge

"He kissed your knees." . . . The lights flared up;
Out of her veils as from a cup
   She rose and poised. . . . "Dark wine of hearts,"
   He wrote, "young breath of older arts,
Your bounty bids a world to sup

"On healing when its soul grows parched."
The spotlights died; she overarched
   The foots to bow; and so he fell
   To scrawling: "Angels over hell
Might bend so while the damned souls marched."

He typed at midnight: "Grace La Verne
Presents a barefoot dancing turn
   Which is distinguished by a rare
   Technique and that exotic air
Which, so it seems, few dancers learn

"This side the pond." . . . From overhead
A yellow incandescent shed
   Strange fantasies across his page—
   A rose-crowned Pierrot bent with age,
A wreathéd faun whose wreath was dead.

SIMON FELSHIN

Simon Felshin, whose American verses are reminiscent of Old Testament poetry, was born in Galilee, Palestine, in 1896, and grew up in a frontier colony of Zionists at the foot of Mount Hermon, near the source of the River Jordan. Surrounded by reminders of a glorious past, witnessing the struggle to reëstablish the Jewish homeland in the face of constant attacks by hostile Arab tribesmen, he could not but acquire a faith in the new birth of his people. His poetry is ardent with a proud race-consciousness, somber with the dignity of the ancient Hebrew poets. A strong sympathy with ultra-modernist movements in art and literature is also reflected in his two books, *Free Forms* (1921) and *Poems for the New Age* (1924), a result, perhaps, of his travels in France, Germany, Italy, and Soviet Russia. His more formal education was acquired in the public schools of New York City, at Columbia University, and in the Universities of Paris and Berlin. He is at present a teacher in a New York high school.

The experience of this poet shows how powerful an inspiration the reading of contemporary literature may be. He writes in a letter, "It is the same type of people who dote on the masters of the past who at the time when those masters were alive disregarded them and made the struggle hard for them just as it is hard for the living writers today. I myself was introduced to writing poetry, not by reading Longfellow or even Shakespeare, but by reading the living American poets. They lit a spark in me, they brought a response in me which the Tennysons and the Wordsworths could not do. And I only began appreciating the poets of the past when the living poets awoke in me a love for poetry."

MY MOTHER

Simon Felshin

My mother was born in Jerusalem.
As a little girl she played on the Mount of Olives,
And she went with her mother to say prayers
By the ruins of the Temple—
By the Wailing Wall.[1]

With her understanding
My mother has spanned the old world
And she stands in the new abreast with her children.
At fifteen she was a wife.
She has borne eight sons and daughters,
And she fed them all at the breast.
Tall and strong are her children,
And they will utter her praises all their days.
I want to lift her name high.
I will bring to her my achievements,
And lay them at her feet.
She will accept them,
And they will be jewels bedecking her.

When I was a child I loved my father and feared him;
My mother I simply loved.
My mother is so human and so intimate,
And for this I love her.
She has given me her strength and her weakness,
And for this I love her.
She divides her love equally among her children.
For her there is no good child or bad,
Because they all lay under her heart,
And they were borne with pain and with tears.

[1] *Wailing Wall*, a portion of the western wall of the Temple, where devout Jews gather to pray and to bewail the past glory of their race.

Sad is the lot of a mother.
When her children are with her
They are young and have not enough understanding
To know her sacrifice.
And when they are old enough to understand
They leave her to go their ways.
She suffers the tyranny of her children.
She toils to give them comfort,
And they receive her favors with avarice.
They rob her of sleep, and they cause her tears,
And what is the thanks she receives?
Some letters sent from across an ocean.
With my fist I strike on my breast
For any harsh words that I spoke to her.
Oh, I will go back to her,
And she will put her hands on my aching head,
And the pain will disappear.
I will bring to her my achievements,
And they will be jewels bedecking her.

ARTHUR DAVISON FICKE

Arthur Davison Ficke was born in Davenport, Iowa, in 1883; he was graduated from Harvard University in 1904. He is a lawyer but has not practiced his profession since the World War; perhaps, like many others who served in France, he found his old interests unsettled by his war experience. His poetic production has been small but fine. *Sonnets of a Portrait Painter* (1914), from which the following selections were made with the author's advice, represents Mr. Ficke's best work. Carefully conventional in form, these sonnets are far from formal in feeling. They represent an important contribution to the small but increasing yield of American writers in this difficult medium.

As the "Anne Knish" to Witter Bynner's "Emanuel Morgan," he helped to perpetrate *Spectra* (1916), the parody which hoaxed a public rendered gullible by the prevailing epidemic of experimentation. In 1917 Mr. Ficke published *An April Elegy*.

SONNETS OF A PORTRAIT PAINTER

Arthur Davison Ficke

VIII

Come forth! for Spring is singing in the boughs
Of every white and tremulous apple tree.
This is the season of eternal vows;
Yet what are vows that they should solace me?
For on the winds, wild loveliness is crying;
And in all flowers, wild joy its present worth
Proclaims, as from the dying to the dying—
"Seize, clasp your hour of sun upon the earth!"
Then never dream that fire or beauty stays
More than one April moment in its flight
Toward regions where the sea drift of all days
Sinks in a vast, desireless, lonely night.
O wind from flushing orchards!—give me breath
Of one white hour here on the marge of death!

X

I am in love with high, far-seeing places
That look on plains half-sunlight and half-storm—
In love with hours when from the circling faces
Veils pass, and laughing fellowship glows warm.
You who look on me with grave eyes where rapture
And April love of living burn confessed—
The gods are good! The world lies free to capture!
Life has no walls.   Oh, take me to your breast!
Take me—be with me for a moment's span!—
I am in love with all unveiléd faces;
I seek the wonder at the heart of man;
I would go up to the far-seeing places.
While youth is ours, turn to me for a space
The marvel of your rapture-lighted face!

XV

It was the night, the night of all my dreams.
Across the lofty spaces of that room
You stole; and where the moonlight's silver streams
Cloudily slanted in upon the gloom,
More silver radiance met them where you moved;
And all the beauty of the hazéd west,
Wherein the moon was sinking, lay approved
Because thus lay your pale, slow-curving breast.
I shall remember—aye, when death must cover
My soul and body with its rayless tide—
The madness and the peace of that wild lover
Drunken with life's whole wonder at your side.
I shall remember in life's stormiest deep—
Even as that night I knew you there in sleep.

HILDEGARDE FLANNER

Hildegarde Flanner was born in Indianapolis, Indiana, in 1899; she has lived for some years in California. She was graduated from Sweet Briar College, Virginia, and the University of California. Her first book, *Young Girl* (1920), was published when she was only twenty-one and gave her a place in the group of American women— Genevieve Taggard, Leonora Speyer, Hazel Hall, Lola Ridge, and Elinor Wylie—who were coming of poetic age about that time. Her first book and *This Morning* (1921) represented a stage in her growth which she was to leave definitely behind her. In these first works is evident the influence of Edna St. Vincent Millay's early and flippant moods.

In *A Tree in Bloom* (1924), from which the following poems were selected, there emerged a mature personality in which the serious purpose to explore the more baffling passages of life is tinged with a wistful mysticism. Withal, the pretty grace of her earlier style has not forsaken her. The lover of the exquisite and the subtle will find satisfaction in *A Tree in Bloom* and *That Endeth Never* (1926).

PHILIPPIAN
HILDEGARDE FLANNER

"Whatsoever things are lovely"—ah, Saint Paul,
I dare not think on loveliness at all,
For fear I see a face I must not see,
And long for hands that are not stretched to me;
For fear I break a flower and wish a thing
That is not mine for garnering.

"Whatsoever things are lovely . . . think on these."
Oh, bring the eyes to beauty, bend the knees!
Was it a silent or a singing way
That Paul of Ephesus knelt down to pray?
No matter, for all lovely things are pain
To me become Philippian in vain.[1]
Ah, Paul, I practice in perverted guise
The word you sent from Rome to make men wise.

TO A TREE IN BLOOM
HILDEGARDE FLANNER

There is no silence lovelier than the one
That flowers upon a flowering tree at night.
There is no silence known beneath the sun
That is so strange to bear, nor half so white.
If I had all that silence in my heart,
What yet unfinished heavens I could sing!
My words lift up and tremble to depart,
Then die in air, from too much uttering.
It must have been beneath a tree like this
An angel sought a girl in Galilee,
While she looked up and pondered how the kiss
Of God had come with wings and mystery.
It may be that a single petal fell,
Heavy with sorrow that it could not tell.

---

[1]*Philippian in vain.* The poet longs for the loveliness of this world, although she recalls the exhortation of Paul (see the *Epistle to the Philippians*, iv, 8) to think on the beauty of spiritual things.

JOHN GOULD FLETCHER

Although John Gould Fletcher was born in Little Rock, Arkansas, in 1886, was educated at Phillips Academy, Andover, and Harvard University, has traveled extensively in this country, and has written much poetry about America, he has chosen to live in England for many years. He was resident in England when the imagist movement began, and was one of the six poets who issued the manifesto of 1914. He had already been dabbling in experimental verse forms. These experiments then appeared in Ezra Pound's *Des Imagistes* (1914) and in the annuals entitled *Some Imagist Poets* (1915-1917).

His own first book of importance was *Irradiations—Sand and Spray* (1915), in which the reader will find extravagantly vivid color used to nearly futile purpose. *Goblins and Pagodas* (1916) is again splashed with all the hues of a much-daubed palette, but the volume is chiefly notable for its statement of Mr. Fletcher's theory of rhythms. *The Tree of Life* (1918) was followed by *Breakers and Granite* (1921) wherein he arrives at the fullness of his power. *Breakers and Granite* is a most satisfying presentation of the far-flung American pageant, from the clipper ships of Down-East Yankees to moonlight on the Mississippi or the Mexican villages and red-buttressed mesas of the Southwest. A whole continent is comprehended in his sweeping lines. *Branches of Adam* (1926) is the first part of an epic poem.

In the matter of rhythms Mr. Fletcher is a revolutionary, yet he does not disregard the essential of cadence. Even his polyphonic prose has suggestions of cadence, though it is poetry only in a somewhat loose definition of that abused term. When Mr. Fletcher falls short of lyrical heights it is because he is more interested in appearances than in realities. He sits down before his subject to study it in a mood of artistic detachment rather than to identify himself with it. As Harriet Monroe has said of him, "His ecstasy is invoked, not inspired."

ARIZONA POEMS*
MEXICAN QUARTER
John Gould Fletcher

By an alley lined with tumble-down shacks,
And street-lamps askew, half-sputtering,
Feebly glimmering on gutters choked with filth, and dogs
Scratching their mangy backs;
Half-naked children are running about,
Women puff cigarettes in black doorways,
Crickets are crying;
Men slouch sullenly
Into the shadows.
Behind a hedge of cactus,
The smell of a dead horse
Mingles with the smell of tamales frying.

And a girl in a black lace shawl
Sits in a rickety chair by the square of unglazed window,
And sees the explosion of the stars
Fiercely poised on the velvet sky.
And she seems humming to herself:
"Stars, if I could reach you
(You are so very clear that it seems as if I could reach you),
I would give you all to the Madonna's image
On the gray plastered altar behind the paper flowers,
So that Juan would come back to me,
And we could live again those lazy, burning hours,
Forgetting the tap of my fan and my sharp words.
And I would only keep four of you—
Those two blue-white ones overhead
To put in my ears,
And those two orange ones yonder
To fasten on my shoe-buckles."

*From *Breakers and Granite* by John Gould Fletcher. Copyright 1921 by the Macmillan Company. Reprinted by permission.

A little further along the street
A man squats, stringing a brown guitar.
The smoke of his cigarette curls round his hair,
And he too is humming, but other words:
"Think not that at your window I wait.
New love is better, the old is turned to hate.
Fate! Fate! All things pass away;
Life is forever, youth is but for a day.
Love again if you may,
Before the golden moons are blown out of the sky,
And the crickets die.
Babylon and Samarkand
Are mud walls in a waste of sand."

DOWN THE MISSISSIPPI*
NIGHT LANDING

JOHN GOULD FLETCHER

After the whistle's roar has bellowed and shuddered,
Shaking the sleeping town and the somnolent river,
The deep-toned floating of the pilot's bell
Suddenly warns the engines.

They pause like heartbeats that abruptly stop;
The shore glides to us, in a wide low curve.

And then—supreme revelation of the river—
The tackle is loosed, the long gangplank swings outward;
And poised at the end of it, half naked beneath the searchlight,
A blue-black negro with gleaming teeth waits for his chance to
    leap.

*From *Breakers and Granite* by John Gould Fletcher. Copyright 1921 by the Macmillan Company. Reprinted by permission.

HORTENSE FLEXNER

Hortense Flexner (Mrs. Wyncie King) is a native of Louisville, Kentucky, where for a number of years she pursued the profession of journalism. She attended the University of Michigan, both as undergraduate and as graduate student. She married into a family widely known for its work in education and other fields of public service.

Although her work is frequently published in magazines, the only collection of her poetry is *Clouds and Cobblestones* (1921). This modest book will prove a surprise to the reader not already acquainted with Mrs. Flexner's ability—every page is crisp, the observation of life racy and penetrating. "Futility" is more typical of her compact style than "Masks," but the latter poem is included here as a particularly able reproduction of one phase of contemporary life in America. It should be noted that Mrs. Flexner's technical range is wide, but that her personal preference favors the more conventional verse forms.

FUTILITY

Hortense Flexner

Across the iron wheel
Of the powerful engine
A tiny spider has spun in the night
His fragile web.
Now, at magnificent ease,
He sits in the center
Awaiting his prey.
It does not occur to him
That the eight-forty-five will start on time,
In spite of his preparations for quarry
And a long day
Of hunting.

MASKS

Hortense Flexner

A pleasant scent is on the steamy air
Of oils and herbs and soap.   Women half sleep
Before the lighted mirrors while their hair
Is brushed, or while deft fingers ply and creep
Over face-muscles or a sagging throat
That shows a little yellowish when bare. ——
The room is still, a sunny blind is drawn,
A chair shifts, or one voice remote
Drones gossip through a smothered yawn;
A young girl smiles, tilts up a lovely head
In a rare way, that makes the attendant note
How she would lie in bed.

Matrons are here, erect, well-cared-for, dressed
To flash, for all who look, the best

That may be had in living—
Furs, motors, servants, warmth, and ease,
All taking, little giving;
Women cast in a mold half perfume, paste,
Passionate, idle, kind, in varying degrees,
Their souls in stays, upright and firmly laced.
And there are old maids, frail and overbred,
With long-boned hands that twist a silver chain,
While puffy blondes decide to have, "Instead
Of gold this time, a bit of henna stain."
And brave old ladies who have lost the fight,
Yet quite ignore the point,
Rustle and preen themselves, though dim of sight,
And very stiff of joint.

So they come in, gracious, aloof, serene,
And sit before the glass in a bright stall,
And face themselves, as if they had not seen,
As if it mattered not at all
How in the glass,
A certain thing, avoided and put by,
Comes more and more to pass.
They sit and turn their heads and vaguely try,
With an old gesture, an unyielding trace
Of pride—to cut, ignore, deny
The gently crumbling face,
Like a worn mask—that gently drowses here
Above a fear—a great crude fear,
A half-seen thing,
Such as rude peasants know, who front the black,
Strange night, with club and sling,
Hearing draw near, by leaves and twigs that crack,
Some prowling thing!

ROBERT FROST

Robert (Lee) Frost, who makes his poetry out of New England, was born in 1875 in San Francisco, California, where he lived until the age of ten. His father's family had lived in New England for nine generations, however, and it was to New England that the boy eventually went. Lawrence, Massachusetts, a cosmopolitan manufacturing city whose textile mills line the Merrimac River for miles, was an unpromising environment and the job of bobbin boy an uninspiring occupation for a future poet, especially one who was to interpret the life of the older Yankee stock in rural New England.

Until he was twenty-two, Mr. Frost's education was limited to the high-school course in Lawrence and a brief stay at Dartmouth. Then, having married in the meantime, he consented, at his wife's suggestion, to try what Harvard might do for him. It was not much, evidently, for he stayed in Cambridge only two years, disinclination for formal education partly accounting for his leaving.

In the meantime he was writing poetry, but not selling it. He followed a variety of occupations: school-teaching, cobbling, editing a weekly paper, and finally, in 1900, farming at Derry, New Hampshire. Although he persisted in the last calling for the next eleven years, he barely earned a living at it.

The easy negligence of his manner, the deliberate drawl of his voice, the comfortable leisureliness of his every movement, suggest a man of easy-going purpose; but the record is quite otherwise. Only a conscious and stubborn determination could have kept him writing poetry through twenty years devoid of recognition or encouragement!

Then came the lucky move of his life. In 1912 he determined to visit England. In London he happened to fall in with a group of eager young poets who had the critical perception to accept him as a fellow artist. They gave him the sympathy he had long needed, and through their help he found his first publisher. For them there could be little doubt, after the appearance of *A Boy's Will* (1913) in England, that a new major poet had arisen. Yet *A Boy's Will* represents only a small and scarcely typical part of Mr. Frost's literary personality. These lyrics, delicately subjective, introspective, sometimes enigmatic, are very different from the homespun narratives which comprise the bulk of *North of Boston* (1914), *Mountain Interval*

(1916), *New Hampshire* (1923), and *West-Running Brook* (1928). Mr. Frost created a new poetic style, peculiarly his own—blank verse of apparently conversational casualness until one examines its "light meter" more closely and observes that the fabric is woven firmly and with skill. It was *North of Boston*, republished in America in 1915, that brought Mr. Frost wide and enthusiastic recognition.

In the meantime, he had returned to this country and to his New Hampshire farm. He has continued to live on the soil to the present time, alternating agriculture with excursions into teaching and lecturing. At the University of Michigan, Amherst, and other colleges he has conducted classes in the writing and appreciation of poetry. An excellent volume of *Selected Poems* appeared in 1923.

Much of Mr. Frost's poetry is as stern and stony as the New England hill pastures themselves, but Amy Lowell was mistaken in saying that it showed New England in a state of degeneration. The picture is not always so grim as in "Home Burial," for instance. More often, as in "The Death of the Hired Man," the harshness is softened by a sensitive tenderness. Warren, a farmer, is debating with his wife whether they shall once more take in the old and useless farmhand who has returned to them:

> "Warren," she said, "he has come home to die:
> You needn't be afraid he'll leave you this time."
>
> "Home," he mocked gently.
>
>   "Yes, what else but home?
> It all depends on what you mean by home . . . ."
>
> "Home is the place where, when you have to go there,
> They have to take you in."
>
>   "I should have called it
> Something you somehow haven't to deserve."

The same quiet understanding of humble lives appears in poem after poem. In "The Mountain" ("my best, as I see it"), the inert, incurious life of a whole community is condensed into a chance conversation by the roadside.

A philosophy of wider implications, but simple always, appears in "Birches," "Mending Wall," and especially the poems in *A Boy's*

Will and *New Hampshire*. For it is a mistake to think of Mr. Frost as exclusively a narrative poet. Often, indeed, the narrative is only the vehicle for a lyrical commentary on life.

Finally there are in Mr. Frost's poems glints of shrewd Yankee humor (for example, in "The Code" and "Paul's Wife") and pictures of nature no less faithful than the human portraits. The supreme example of Mr. Frost's ability to enter into the life of nature, as it is also the most memorable of his lyrical achievements, is "Stopping by Woods on a Snowy Evening."

The following **group** of poems has been selected with the friendly help of Mr. Frost.

THE MOUNTAIN

Robert Frost

The mountain held the town as in a shadow.
I saw so much before I slept there once;
I noticed that I missed stars in the west,
Where its black body cut into the sky.
Near me it seemed; I felt it like a wall
Behind which I was sheltered from a wind.
And yet between the town and it I found,
When I walked forth at dawn to see new things,
Were fields, a river, and beyond, more fields.
The river at the time was fallen away,
And made a widespread brawl on cobblestones;
But the signs showed what it had done in spring;
Good grassland gullied out, and in the grass
Ridges of sand, and driftwood stripped of bark.
I crossed the river and swung round the mountain.
And there I met a man who moved so slow
With white-faced oxen in a heavy cart,
It seemed no harm to stop him altogether.

"What town is this?"   I asked.

                    "This?   Lunenburg."
Then I was wrong: the town of my sojourn,
Beyond the bridge, was not that of the mountain,
But only felt at night its shadowy presence.
"Where is your village?   Very far from here?"

"There is no village—only scattered farms.
We were but sixty voters last election.
We can't in nature grow to many more:
That thing takes all the room!"   He moved his goad.
The mountain stood there to be pointed at.
Pasture ran up the side a little way,

And then there was a wall of trees with trunks:
After that only tops of trees, and cliffs
Imperfectly concealed among the leaves.
A dry ravine emerged from under boughs
Into the pasture.

     "That looks like a path.
Is that the way to reach the top from here?—
Not for this morning, but some other time;
I must be getting back to breakfast now."

"I don't advise your trying from this side.
There is no proper path, but those that *have*
Been up, I understand, have climbed from Ladd's.
That's five miles back.   You can't mistake the place:
They logged it there last winter some way up.
I'd take you, but I'm bound the other way."

"You've never climbed it?"

     "I've been on the sides
Deer-hunting and trout-fishing.   There's a brook
That starts up on it somewhere—I've heard say
Right on the top, tiptop—a curious thing.
But what would interest you about the brook,
It's always cold in summer, warm in winter.
One of the great sights going is to see
It steam in winter like an ox's breath,
Until the bushes all along its banks
Are inch-deep with the frosty spines and bristles—
You know the kind.   Then let the sun shine on it!"

"There ought to be a view around the world
From such a mountain—if it isn't wooded
Clear to the top."   I saw through leafy screens
Great granite terraces in sun and shadow,
Shelves one could rest a knee on getting up—

With depths behind him sheer a hundred feet;
Or turn and sit on and look out and down,
With little ferns in crevices at his elbow.

"As to that I can't say.   But there's the spring,
Right on the summit, almost like a fountain.
That ought to be worth seeing."

                              "If it's there.
You never saw it?"

                              "I guess there's no doubt
About its being there.   I never saw it.
It may not be right on the very top;
It wouldn't have to be a long way down
To have some head of water from above,
And a *good distance* down might not be noticed
By anyone who'd come a long way up.
One time I asked a fellow climbing it
To look and tell me later how it was."

"What did he say?"
                              "He said there was a lake
Somewhere in Ireland on a mountain top."

"But a lake's different.   What about the spring?"

"He never got up high enough to see.
That's why I don't advise your trying this side.
He tried this side.   I've always meant to go
And look myself, but you know how it is:
It doesn't seem so much to climb a mountain
You've worked around the foot of all your life.
What would I do?   Go in my overalls,
With a big stick, the same as when the cows

Haven't come down to the bars at milking time?
Or with a shotgun for a stray black bear?
'Twouldn't seem real to climb for climbing it."

"I shouldn't climb it if I didn't want to—
Not for the sake of climbing.   What's its name?"

"We call it Hor: I don't know if that's right."

"Can one walk round it?   Would it be too far?"

"You can drive round and keep in Lunenburg,
But it's as much as ever you can do,
The boundary lines keep in so close to it.
Hor is the township, and the township's Hor—
And a few houses sprinkled round the foot,
Like boulders broken off the upper cliff,
Rolled out a little farther than the rest."

"Warm in December, cold in June, you say?"

"I don't suppose the water's changed at all.
You and I know enough to know it's warm
Compared with cold, and cold compared with warm.
But all the fun's in how you say a thing."

"You've lived here all your life?"

                    "Ever since Hor
Was no bigger than a —"   What, I did not hear.
He drew the oxen toward him with light touches
Of his slim goad on nose and off-side flank,
Gave them their marching orders, and was moving.

THE ONSET

Robert Frost

Always the same, when on a fated night
At last the gathered snow lets down as white
As may be in dark woods, and with a song
It shall not make again all winter long
Of hissing on the yet uncovered ground,
I almost stumble looking up and round,
As one who, overtaken by the end,
Gives up his errand, and lets death descend
Upon him where he is, with nothing done
To evil, no important triumph won,
More than if life had never been begun.

Yet all the precedent is on my side:
I know that winter death has never tried
The earth but it has failed; the snow may heap
In long storms an undrifted four feet deep
As measured against maple, birch, and oak,
It cannot check the peeper's silver croak;
And I shall see the snow all go downhill
In water of a slender April rill
That flashes tail through last year's withered brake
And dead weeds, like a disappearing snake.
Nothing will be left white but here a birch,
And there a clump of houses with a church.

THE FEAR

Robert Frost

A lantern light from deeper in the barn
Shone on a man and woman in the door
And threw their lurching shadows on a house
Near by, all dark in every glossy window.
A horse's hoof pawed once the hollow floor,
And the back of the gig they stood beside
Moved in a little.   The man grasped a wheel,
The woman spoke out sharply, "Whoa, stand still!"
"I saw it just as plain as a white plate,"
She said, "as the light on the dashboard ran
Along the bushes at the roadside—a man's face.
You *must* have seen it too."

> "I didn't see it.

Are you sure—"

> "Yes, I'm sure!"

> "—it was a face?"

"Joel, I'll have to look.   I can't go in,
I can't, and leave a thing like that unsettled.
Doors locked and curtains drawn will make no difference.
I always have felt strange when we came home
To the dark house after so long an absence,
And the key rattled loudly into place
Seemed to warn someone to be getting out
At one door as we entered at another.
What if I'm right, and someone all the time—
Don't hold my arm!"

> "I say it's someone passing."

"You speak as if this were a traveled road.
You forget where we are.   What is beyond

That he'd be going to or coming from
At such an hour of night, and on foot too?
What was he standing still for in the bushes?"

"It's not so very late—it's only dark.
There's more in it than you're inclined to say.

Did he look like—?"

"He looked like anyone.
I'll never rest tonight unless I know.
Give me the lantern."

"You don't want the lantern."

She pushed past him and got it for herself.

"You're not to come," she said. "This is my business.
If the time's come to face it, I'm the one
To put it the right way. He'd never dare—
Listen! He kicked a stone. Hear that, hear that!
He's coming toward us. Joel, *go* in—please.
Hark!—I don't hear him now. But please go in."

"In the first place you can't make me believe it's—"

"It is—or someone else he's sent to watch.
And now's the time to have it out with him
While we know definitely where he is.
Let him get off, and he'll be everywhere
Around us, looking out of trees and bushes
Till I shan't dare to set a foot outdoors.
And I can't stand it. Joel, let me go!"

"But it's nonsense to think he'd care enough."

"You mean you couldn't understand his caring.
Oh, but you see he hadn't had enough—

Joel, I won't—I won't—I promise you.
We mustn't say hard things. You mustn't either."

"I'll be the one, if anybody goes!
But you give him the advantage with this light.
What couldn't he do to us standing here!
And if to see was what he wanted, why
He has seen all there was to see and gone."

He appeared to forget to keep his hold,
But advanced with her as she crossed the grass.

"What do you want?" she cried to all the dark.
She stretched up tall to overlook the light
That hung in both hands hot against her skirt.

"There's no one; so you're wrong," he said.

                    "There is. ——
What do you want?" she cried, and then herself
Was startled when an answer really came.

"Nothing." It came from well along the road.

She reached a hand to Joel for support:
The smell of scorching woolen made her faint.

"What are you doing around this house at night?"

"Nothing." A pause: there seemed no more to say.

And then the voice again: "You seem afraid.
I saw by the way you whipped up the horse.
I'll just come forward in the lantern light
And let you see."
                    "Yes, do. —Joel, go back!"

She stood her ground against the noisy steps
That came on, but her body rocked a little.

"You see," the voice said.

                    "Oh."   She looked and looked.

"You don't see—I've a child here by the hand."

"What's a child doing at this time of night—?"

"Out walking.   Every child should have the memory
Of at least one long-after-bedtime walk.
What, son?"

                    "Then I should think you'd try to find
Somewhere to walk—"

                    "The highway as it happens—
We're stopping for the fortnight down at Dean's."

"But if that's all—Joel—you realize—
You won't think anything.   You understand?
You understand that we have to be careful.
This is a very, very lonely place.
Joel!"   She spoke as if she couldn't turn.
The swinging lantern lengthened to the ground,
It touched, it struck it, clattered and went out.

STOPPING BY WOODS ON A SNOWY EVENING

Robert Frost

Whose woods these are I think I know.
His house is in the village though;
He will not see me stopping here
To watch his woods fill up with snow.

My little horse must think it queer
To stop without a farmhouse near
Between the woods and frozen lake
The darkest evening of the year.

He gives his harness bells a shake
To ask if there is some mistake.
The only other sound's the sweep
Of easy wind and downy flake.

The woods are lovely, dark and deep,
But I have promises to keep,
And miles to go before I sleep,
And miles to go before I sleep.

H. D. (HILDA DOOLITTLE)

The reticence of Hilda Doolittle (Mrs. Richard Aldington) is suggested by the near-anonymity of her pen name, H. D., by which she is always known. It is not profitable to explore beyond those simple initials, for the poet's shy dignity is impenetrable. She has admitted her readers to the world of beauty in which she lives; her personality she has not disclosed.

H. D. was born in Bethlehem, Pennsylvania, in 1886, and lived as a child in the neighborhood of Philadelphia; she attended Bryn Mawr College. A few years later she went to Europe, where she traveled and lived in various countries, finally settling in England at the moment when imagism was making its appearance. With Amy Lowell and others she was associated in the first group of imagist poets, and remains today the most notable exponent of their theories. Only second to her in this respect is her husband, Richard Aldington, the English Imagist. With the exception of a single year in this country, she has continued to live abroad, and in recent years has chosen Switzerland as her place of residence.

The poetry of H. D. will not appeal to all readers, nor will it appeal to any who regard it carelessly or hastily. It maintains a splendid aloofness from contemporaneous concerns, and speaks in a language of rarefied emotion which is not at once easy of apprehension. Sometimes, too, the extreme concentration on the specific image helps to obscure her real intention. More frequently, however, her pictures have a blinding clarity, a lean economy of line which recalls the triumphant simplicity of Greek art. She has a passion for driving straight to the heart of her subject and, without a single adventitious word, achieving the full revelation of its intrinsic meaning.

Through all the changing winds of poetic doctrine, she has remained faithful to her own idea of free verse, which, it must be agreed, she writes with admirable feeling for essential rhythm. This fact may be put to the test by reading any of her poems aloud, slowly, and noting the ease with which the lines flow, seemingly of themselves. A little analysis of her meters will show that they are not so irregular as they appear. In subject-matter, H. D. shares the pagan's intimate acceptance of nature. The determination to see the thing as it really is leads her to examine natural beauty with eyes unsophisticated by civilized preconceptions.

Her poems first appeared in the several imagist anthologies and were gathered in *Sea Garden* (1916). This book was followed by *Hymen* (1921), *Heliodora and Other Poems* (1924), and *Collected Poems* (1925).

HELEN

H. D. (Hilda Doolittle)

All Greece hates
the still eyes in the white face,
the luster as of olives
where she stands,
and the white hands.

All Greece reviles
the wan face when she smiles,
hating it deeper still
when it grows wan and white,
remembering past enchantments
and past ills.

Greece sees unmoved,
God's daughter, born of love,
the beauty of cool feet
and slenderest knees,
could love indeed the maid,
only if she were laid,
white ash amid funereal cypresses.

SHELTERED GARDEN

H. D. (Hilda Doolittle)

I have had enough.
I gasp for breath.

Every way ends, every road,
every footpath leads at last
to the hill-crest—

then you retrace your steps,
or find the same slope on the other side,
precipitate.

I have had enough—
border-pinks, clove-pinks, wax-lilies,
herbs, sweet-cress.

Oh, for some sharp swish of a branch—
there is no scent of resin
in this place,
no taste of bark, of coarse weeds,
aromatic, astringent—
only border on border of scented pinks.

Have you seen fruit under cover
that wanted light—
pears wadded in cloth,
protected from the frost,
melons, almost ripe,
smothered in straw?

Why not let the pears cling
to the empty branch?
All your coaxing will only make
a bitter fruit —
let them cling, ripen of themselves,
test their own worth,
nipped, shriveled by the frost,
to fall at last but fair
with a russet coat.

Or the melon —
let it bleach yellow
in the winter light,

even tart to the taste —
it is better to taste of frost —
the exquisite frost —
than of wadding and of dead grass.

For this beauty,
beauty without strength,
chokes out life.
I want wind to break,
scatter these pink-stalks,
snap off their spiced heads,
fling them about with dead leaves —
spread the paths with twigs,
limbs broken off,
trail great pine branches,
hurled from some far wood
right across the melon-patch,
break pear and quince —
leave half-trees, torn, twisted,
but showing the fight was valiant.

Oh, to blot out this garden,
to forget, to find a new beauty
in some terrible
wind-tortured place.

HERMANN HAGEDORN

Hermann Hagedorn was born in New York City in 1882. He attended Harvard University, Columbia University, and the University of Berlin, and was at one time an instructor in English at Harvard. In 1919 he became secretary of the Roosevelt Memorial Association; in connection with this position he has written a number of biographical studies of Theodore Roosevelt.

Of his several volumes of verse the most notable are *Troop of the Guard* (1909), *Poems and Ballads* (1912), and *Ladders through the Blue* (1925). In technique he is faithful to the conventions and has been especially successful in his sonnets. His poetic voice is a light one; in the short lyric his lines often rise to a spirited beauty.

THE EYES OF GOD

Hermann Hagedorn

I see them nightly in my sleep.
The eyes of God are very deep.
There is no cave, no sea that knows
So much of unplumbed depth as those,
Or guards with walls or specters dumb
Such treasures for the venturesome.

I feel them burning on my back.
The eyes of God are very black.
There is no substance and no shade
So black as God His own eyes made;
In earth or heaven no night, no day,
At once so black, so bright as they.

I see them wheresoe'er I turn.
The eyes of God are very stern.
The eyes of God are golden fires
That kindle beacons, kindle pyres;
And where like slow moon-rays they pass
They burn up dead things as dry grass.

They wait, and are not hard to find.
The eyes of God are very kind.
They have great pity for weak things
And joy in everything with wings;
And glow, beyond all telling bright,
Each time a brave soul dares a flight.

DOORS

Hermann Hagedorn

Like a young child who to his mother's door
   Runs eager for the welcoming embrace,
   And finds the door shut, and with troubled face
Calls and through sobbing calls and, o'er and o'er
Calling, storms at the panel—so before
   A door that will not open, sick and numb,
   I listen for a word that will not come,
And know, at last, I may not enter more.
Silence! And through the silence and the dark
   By that closed door, the distant sob of tears
   Beats on my spirit, as on fairy shores
The spectral sea; and through the sobbing, hark!
   Down the fair-chambered corridor of years,
     The quiet shutting, one by one, of doors.

HAZEL HALL

Hazel Hall was born in St. Paul, Minnesota, in 1886, but most of her life was spent in Portland, Oregon. From the age of twelve until her death in 1924 she was confined to a wheel chair, a helpless but by no means hopeless invalid. Her poetry expresses the outlook of one who sees the world only through her window, who hears only the sound of footsteps passing in the street. Her verses have an exquisite quiet, and a delicacy of finish which recalls the fact that she partly supported herself by fine needlework. But there is something more than neat verbal embroidery in her pages; she is an eager and clear-eyed observer and interpreter of the life in which she could have no active part. Miss Hall's art is summed up in the titles of her two books: *Curtains* (1921) and *Walkers* (1923). A third book, *Cry of Time*, will appear in 1928.

HERE COMES THE THIEF*

HAZEL HALL

Here comes the thief
Men nickname Time,
Oh, hide you, leaf,
And hide you, rime.
Leaf, he would take you
And leave you rust.
Rime, he would flake you
With spotted dust.
Scurry to cover,
Delicate maid
And serious lover.
Girl, bind the braid
Of your burning hair;
He has an eye
For the lusciously fair
Who passes by.
O lover, hide—
Who comes to plunder
Has the crafty stride
Of unheard thunder.
Quick—lest he snatch,
In his grave need,
And sift and match,
Then sow like seed
Your love's sweet grief
On the backward air,
With the rime and the leaf
And the maiden's hair.

*From *Cry of Time* by Hazel Hall. Copyrighted by E. P. Dutton and Company, Inc., New York, 1928.

GWENDOLEN HASTE

Although a native of Illinois and a graduate of the University of Chicago in the class of 1912, Gwendolen Haste went to Montana shortly after leaving college and lived there for a number of years. This experience, added to the stories of her father's childhood on a pioneer farm in Wisconsin, intensified a natural love of history and folk-ways and fixed her attention on the great migration across the plains and the subsequent history of western homesteading. Thus, the subject of much of her work is the American West, a field still comparatively fresh for the hand of the artist. Her work has not been issued in book form as yet, though she has contributed to *The Century*, *Scribner's*, *Poetry*, *The Lyric West*, and other magazines and has received *The Nation's* 1922 poetry prize for her "The Ranch in the Coulee."

MONTANA WIVES

HORIZONS

Gwendolen Haste

I had to laugh,
For when she said it we were sitting by the door,
And straight down was the Fork
Twisting and turning and gleaming in the sun.
And then your eyes carried across to the purple bench[1] beyond
   the river
With the Beartooth Mountains fairly screaming with light and
   blue and snow
And fold and turn of rimrock and prairie as far as your eye
   could go.
And she says: "Dear Laura, sometimes I feel so sorry for you,
Shut away from everything—eating out your heart with lone-
   liness.
When I think of my own full life I wish that I could share it.
Just pray for happier days to come, and bear it."

She goes back to Billings to her white stucco house,
And looks through net curtains at another white stucco house,
And a brick house,
And a yellow frame house,
And six trimmed poplar trees,
And little squares of shaved grass.

Oh, dear, she stared at me like I was daft.
I couldn't help it!   I just laughed and laughed.

---

[1]*bench*, a long, level strip of ground, rising above the adjacent region.

DUBOSE HEYWARD

The poetry of DuBose Heyward has every right to be considered representative of the South, for not only was the author born in Charleston, South Carolina (1885), but he is a direct lineal descendant of Thomas Savage Heyward, who signed the Declaration of Independence for South Carolina. Furthermore he received his education in the public schools of Charleston and has spent all his life either in the low country of South Carolina or in the mountains of North Carolina, both of which have furnished settings for his finest poetry. To express the spirit of the South in prose as well as in verse is the chief aim of his life. He has been especially active in the encouragement of societies and magazines for the promotion of this cause.

With Hervey Allen, the gifted biographer of Edgar Allan Poe, Mr. Heyward first produced *Carolina Chansons* (1922), followed by his independent volume of verse, *Skylines and Horizons* (1924), from which the following selection has been chosen. His two novels, *Porgy* (1925) and *Angel* (1926), have enjoyed a deserved popularity. The dramatic version of the former captured Broadway by its terribly candid exposition of a negro's frustration.

DuBose Heyward has already gained distinction for the strength and beauty of his poetry. See, as an interesting example of syncopated "jazz" rhythms, his "Jasbo Brown" in *The American Mercury* for September, 1925.

A YOKE OF STEERS*

DuBose Heyward

A heave of mighty shoulders to the yoke,
Square, patient heads, and flaring sweep of horn;
The darkness swirling down beneath their feet
Where sleeping valleys stir, and feel the dawn;
Uncouth and primal, on and up they sway,
Taking the summit in a drench of day.
The night winds volley to a rainbow spray
Under the slow-moving, cloven feet.

There is a power here that grips the mind;
A force repressed and inarticulate,
Slow as the swing of centuries, as blind
As destiny, and as deliberate.

They will arrive at their appointed hour
Unhurried by the goad of lesser wills,
Bearing vast burdens on.
                         *They are the great
Unconquerable spirit of these hills.*

*From *Skylines and Horizons* by DuBose Heyward. Copyright 1924 by The Macmillan Company. Reprinted by permission.

ROBERT HILLYER

Robert (Silliman) Hillyer was born in East Orange, New Jersey, in 1895, of a family which settled in Connecticut in 1630. His youth was passed at Kent, Connecticut, in the Housatonic River Valley, an environment so pleasantly suited to his taste that he has written, "The Housatonic Valley has made me reluctant ever to enter a city or to leave Connecticut." He was graduated from Harvard University in 1917 and spent a year in Copenhagen as a fellow of the American-Scandinavian Foundation, the fruit of the latter experience being *A Book of Danish Verse* (1922), translations in the original meters done in collaboration with S. Foster Damon. Although he has traveled and lived abroad, he calls himself "a born provincial." He is at present in the Department of English at Harvard.

Mr. Hillyer's reputation rests only partly on his poems, for he has had published in magazines a number of thoughtful and substantial critical essays. His chief volumes of verse are *Sonnets and Other Lyrics* (1917), *The Five Books of Youth* (1920), *Alchemy* (1920), *The Hills Give Promise* (1923), *The Halt in the Garden* (1925), and *The Seventh Hill* (1928).

As for "Moo!"—the author writes from Pomfret, Connecticut— "The cow herself, whom I see every day for a brief conversation, is always vastly flattered at each reprint of the poem, and, I assure you, has actually waxed sleek and portly as her vanity is gratified."

THE HALT IN THE GARDEN

Robert Hillyer

Hesperides? Right here! the faithful keeper,
Sir, at your service. Won't you step this way?
The shadows round the elm are growing deeper,
You cannot go much farther on today.
Sit here, this rock will hold the heat awhile,
And later, if you're so inclined, we'll sup
Over at my house in the hollow there.
It must be you I saw that clambered up
The rock ledge and came through the broken stile?
The other road is shorter by a mile,
But you are young—I don't suppose you care.

Yes, help yourself, but don't take three or four;
Take one and eat it to the very core.
Hell! that young Pan's a scoundrel! Nibbles one,
Throws it away, nibbles another, shakes
The bough—and nine times out of ten it breaks—
Spilling my finest beauties by the score
To rot away and stink under the sun.
These be no common apples;—no, not gold,
If people said so then it's lies they told—
They're all the seasons bottled in one fruit,
Autumn a-top and April at the root.
And what a savor to the nose and tongue!
No, sir, I never touch them, I am here
To guard, not eat . . . but once, oh, years ago,
Long before you were thought of . . well, I know
Their taste and smell, and I should still be young
If I had gone on eating year to year.

The gods, now, 'tis their right, but even they
Come seldom. Not that I'm complaining, only

As I grow old I seem to grow more lonely.
Life isn't as it was for them or me;
There's more time to remember, less to play,
And somehow one pretends at being gay.
When they have picnics by the linden tree
Across the valley, one or two come over
And lie here at my feet among the clover,
Picking the petals off the daisies, while
I tell them fairy tales to make them smile.
For, between us, sir, they are children still,
Ready to burst with laughter as with tears,
In spite of all that time has done—and will.

I've loved them now over three thousand years,
And served them as you see, not well or ill,
And I can tell you, sir, my blood runs cold
To think I shall be dead when they are old.
Oh, most of all, Hermes and Artemis
I love—the immortal Girl, the immortal Boy!
To see them is a sort of awful joy,
To touch them, unimaginable bliss.
Many have tried to snare them, and in vain;
For when you spread the usual sort of mesh,
Music and wine, to catch them, then they are
As ghostly and remote as the white train
Of seven moons that swarm about the star
Of Zeus. White flame of spirit and of mind,
Held in twin columns of triumphant flesh!
And yet, they say how each has given his heart
Unto the other, and how they take their joys;
Touching with one aërial kiss, to part—
She with her virgins, he among his boys. . . .
You smile that love so far outdoes my wit,
Words being finite and love infinite.

Compare with these immortals, if you will,
The latter pieties I entertain.
They mope along the summit of the hill
As though the landscape pleased them not, and strain
To find a blemish on my apple trees—
A blemish! here in the Hesperides!
I vow, sir, it's my duty I perform,
And neither more nor less, when that pale swarm
Come buzzing down on me and call me "Brother"
As though it were a virtue so to do!
We take our liberties in all the ranks,
But none takes liberties with any other—
You understand, sir—well, this pious crew,
Instead of dining in the hall outside,
Invite themselves to take their meat with me,
Seeming to think I ought to render thanks
Because they sacrifice my servant's pride
To make a show of their humility!
By Hera! then my blood all turns to gall. . . .
I serve cold porridge in the outer hall.

No tolerant stream can ever irrigate
Those arid minds. No kindly flower or shrub
Wakes on those desert hearts. Early and late
The scorpion and the unwholesome grub
Gnaw round the cactus and the prickly thorns.
Why, sir, that aged Jew who wears the horns[1]—
His name escapes me—played so vile a trick
That even Ares wept to hear the tale.
He found young Arothyx, Campaspe's faun,
Playing all naked in the woods at dawn
Beside the tarn, the way our children do.

---

[1] *that aged Jew who wears the horns*, Moses. See *Exodus xxxiv*, 29, 30; the Hebrew word for "shone" may be translated "sent forth beams" or "sent forth horns." The Vulgate uses the latter translation.

What then? The old man took a briary stick
And laid it on his haunches like a flail
Until the creature was all black and blue,
His infant flesh shot through and through with hurt.
It's blame and scold from dawn to dark, and still
Despising, they remain to vent despite.
We plant the rose, and they unearth the dirt.
There is no peace upon the sacred hill,
No songs at noon or drinking bouts at night,
It's not "Do as you please and so will I,"
But "Do my will; if not, be damned thereby."
Some of my Greeks are lechers and all that,
But everyone's a born aristocrat!

The curious thing is this: that gentle man
They call their Master is a different kind.
He comes to supper with me when he can,
And eats there in my room, but I don't mind.
He doesn't pose and condescend to me,
But just as any friend to friend might be,
Sits down and eats, asks me about the weather,
Are apples ripe? and how is Aphrodite
Since her last lying-in?   No high and mighty
From him; he's just a dreamy sort of friend,
Not hard to talk with or to comprehend.
The only time he ever lost his head
Was once when we were talking here together,
I told about his people.   Then he said . . .
Perhaps I ought not tell you what he said,
But if words kill those holy goats are dead!

Forgive me, sir, an old man, the late year,
We all drift on, and night is close at hand.
The planets now are ripe, harvest is near,
And they will sow new planets where we stand.

See there, the flock of yellow butterflies
That chase September down the western slope
Have flashed their last against the smoky skies.
Your hand, sir, if you please.   Blear eyes must grope
And clear still lead . . . Hark! do you hear them shouting
Over the hill where the red sun has set?
While we sit here conjecturing and doubting
The gods of Greece are gods of laughter yet.
Over the hill, the young with blowing hair
Forget the season of the singing reapers
Who come to bind the yellow planets in.
Forget the season of the silent sleepers,
The ruined barn, the harvest in the bin.

Come in, and drink and eat, and still forgive
That lonely age should be so talkative.
I'll quench the burning itch that jerks my tongue
In drafts of wine that still remembers Greece,
And you shall hear but silence while you sup.
Once in this garden when the world was young,
At cool of evening . . . No, I'll hold my peace!
Yonder's a Chian vintage.   Fill your cup!

MOO!

Robert Hillyer

Summer is over, the old cow said,
And they'll shut me up in the drafty shed
To milk me by lamplight in the cold;
But I won't give much, for I am old.
It's long ago that I came here
Gay and slim as a woodland deer;
It's long ago that I heard the roar
Of Smith's white bull by the sycamore.

And now there are bones where my flesh should be,
My backbone sags like an old rooftree,
And an apple snatched in a moment's frolic
Is just so many days of colic.
I'm neither a Jersey nor Holstein now,
But only a faded sort of cow.
My calves are veal, and I had as lief
That I could lay me down as beef.
Somehow, they always kill by halves;
Why not take me when they take my calves?
Birch turns yellow and sumac red,
I've seen all this before, she said.
I'm tired of the field and tired of the shed.
There's no more grass, there's no more clover,
Summer is over, summer is over.

ORRICK JOHNS

Orrick Johns was born in St. Louis, Missouri, in 1887. He attended the University of Missouri and studied architecture at Washington University. Instead of becoming an architect he chose writing as a profession, coming naturally by the choice, for his father is a St. Louis newspaper editor. His poetry is only a part of his total output, which includes magazine articles, book reviews, a novel, and a comedy.

Asphalt and Other Poems (1917) will come as a shock to readers who have made the poet's acquaintance through the elusive lyrics of his later manner, for in this first book he fumbled what John V. A. Weaver was later to capture successfully—a representation of American life in the language of the streets. The effect is disappointing because the harshness of Mr. Johns's medium gets in the way of his art. Mr. Weaver discovered a means to rise above his medium through the saving grace of sympathy. There were other poems in Mr. Johns's first book not written in slang which, by virtue of their delicate beauty, forecast the lyrical art of *Black Branches* (1920) and *Wild Plum* (1926). In the short, singing line of utter simplicity Mr. Johns has found the form in which he can work with distinction.

FAILURE*

ORRICK JOHNS

Five-score years the birds have flown
   Back from March to May,
And this land has never known
   A man who made his way.

Flocks have passed of faces here,
   Jovial and sour,
And never a single one of them
   Became a man of power.

Year on year these slopes were plowed
   By man and boy, and still
Hardly have they yielded more
   Than the burying bill.

Five-score years they've risen green
   Almost from the snow;
Now they're beautiful and clean. . .
   Failure made them so.

HOWARD MUMFORD JONES

Howard Mumford Jones, like William Ellery Leonard, David Morton, Edwin Ford Piper, S. Foster Damon, and Robert Hillyer, is a college teacher of English who can create as well as criticize. He was born at Saginaw, Michigan, in 1892; his higher education was acquired at the Wisconsin State Normal School, the University of Wisconsin, and the University of Chicago. Since 1916 he has been a member of the English Department of the University of Texas. His only volume of verse is *Gargoyles* (1918), which reveals a pleasant fluency with frequent notes of lyrical feeling. "Examinations," which appeared in the admirable but short-lived *Freeman*, is, like many of his other poems, drawn from his experience as a college teacher. The student reader may accept it as a trustworthy reflection of every English teacher's occasional despair.

EXAMINATIONS

Howard Mumford Jones

"Shelley was born in seventeen ninety-two,
And died at thirty, and he was a poet;
He wrote an elegy called 'Adonais'
And many minor works.   Lord Byron lived
From eighty-eight to eighteen twenty-four;
He led a reckless life.   He was romantic,
'Childe Harold' being his first successful work.
He died, I think, in Italy or Greece.
I don't know Southey's dates or poems.   Also
Keats was a poet, and he was romantic.
He died in eighteen hundred twenty-one."

Thus with laborious pen my struggling scholar,
It being term-time and the meadows green.

Now from the Grasmere[1] meadows larks ascend,
And all the silent hills like pools of water
Are troubled by the singing silver rain;
Also a pyramid in Rome[2] grows warm
Beneath the radiant Italian noon,
And Spezia's bay[3]—ah, that is flecked with sunlight
As once it was a hundred years ago.

Shelley is dead, and Keats.   What would you more?

---

[1]*Grasmere*, a village in the English lake country where Wordsworth made his home.
[2]*a pyramid in Rome*, Keats's grave.
[3]*Spezia's bay.*   The poet Shelley was drowned in the bay of Spezia when a storm capsized his boat.

ALINE KILMER

So radiant is the vitality which shines through the writings of
Aline (Murray) Kilmer that it is no belittlement of their poetic quality
to say that they are first of all valuable for the personality which
they reveal. To read Mrs. Kilmer is to make contact with a spirit
in love with life and finding its deepest satisfactions in the joys of
home and children. The intensity of her emotional life appears
throughout her books of verse: *Candles That Burn* (1919), *Vigils*
(1921), and *The Poor King's Daughter* (1925).

Mrs. Kilmer, whose ancestry can be traced through her father's
family to John Alden, was born in Norfolk, Virginia, in 1888. She
attended Rutgers Preparatory School, New Brunswick, New Jersey,
and the Vail-Deane School, Elizabeth, New Jersey. In the former
place she met Joyce Kilmer, also a writer and in every way a fellow
spirit, whom she married in 1909. In close companionship she shared
his short, crowded, zestful life, terminated by his death in action
during the World War.

THINGS

Aline Kilmer

Sometimes when I am at tea with you,
   I catch my breath
At a thought that is old as the world is old
   And more bitter than death.

It is that the spoon that you just laid down
   And the cup that you hold
May be here shining and insolent,
   When you are still and cold.

Your careless note that I laid away
   May leap to my eyes like flame,
When the world has almost forgotten your voice
   Or the sound of your name.

The golden Virgin da Vinci[1] drew
   May smile on over my head,
And daffodils nod in the silver vase,
   When you are dead.

So let moth and dust corrupt, and thieves
   Break through, and I shall be glad,
Because of the hatred I bear to things
   Instead of the love I had.

For life seems only a shuddering breath,
   A smothered, desperate cry;
And things have a terrible permanence,
   When people die.

---

[1]*da Vinci.* See footnote 3, page 85. Leonardo painted a number of pictures of the Virgin.

JOYCE KILMER

(Alfred) Joyce Kilmer was born in New Brunswick, New Jersey, in 1886. In 1908 he received an A. B. from Rutgers College and an A. B. from Columbia University. In 1909 he married Aline Murray, also a poet, and became a teacher of Latin in the high school at Morristown, New Jersey. At one time and another he was an editorial assistant on the *Standard Dictionary*, editor of *The Churchman*, and a reviewer for the *New York Times Review of Books*. Whatever he did he did ardently and exuberantly; every day began for him a new adventure. The World War promised the greatest adventure of all—the chance of furthering the spiritual issues which he and other idealists saw implicit in the struggle. Within three weeks after America declared war he had enlisted. He served on the French front, was made a sergeant, and was killed in action in July, 1918.

Trees and Other Poems (1914) caught the universal ear with its title poem, the lovely simplicity of which has saved it from becoming hackneyed in spite of endless repetition. *Main Street and Other Poems* (1917) shows the influence of his experience as a newspaper reporter; the title anticipated Sinclair Lewis. Neither book represents the maturity which Kilmer might have reached had he lived to develop his art.

The personality of the man is more satisfactorily revealed in his letters (*Joyce Kilmer: Poems, Essays and Letters; with a Memoir by Robert Cortes Holliday*, 1918). It was a personality which William Rose Benét has described in the words of all Kilmer's friends: "As a man he was lovable, always quick to 'give a leg up' to any writer in need, a remarkably hard worker, a buoyant spirit in spite of it, a man with the strongest sense of responsibility, with a kind heart and a very noble side to his character."

TREES

Joyce Kilmer

I think that I shall never see
A poem lovely as a tree.

A tree whose hungry mouth is prest
Against the earth's sweet flowing breast;

A tree that looks at God all day,
And lifts her leafy arms to pray;

A tree that may in summer wear
A nest of robins in her hair;

Upon whose bosom snow has lain;
Who intimately lives with rain.

Poems are made by fools like me,
But only God can make a tree.

HENRY HERBERT KNIBBS

Henry Herbert Knibbs was born in Niagara Falls, Ontario, in 1874, but is a naturalized citizen of the United States, where he has lived since youth. After a knockabout career in various vocations, he decided at the age of thirty-five that his education was deficient and attended Harvard University for three years. Here the inspiration of Dean Briggs's famous course in advanced composition brought out his talent as a writer, and he wrote his first book, a novel, as part of the class work. He left Harvard to gather experience in the wilds of western Canada. In his several novels and books of verse he has given a picture of the West which is, in general, faithful and sympathetic. Occasionally it is a romanticized West, the West of Robert W. Service, but usually Mr. Knibbs is too forthright, too much in love with life as he finds it, to stop for sentimentality. His whimsical humor appears in "Burro," and his ability as a lyricist is shown in the musical "Names." His verse is contained in *Songs of the Outlands: Ballads of the Hoboes and Other Verse* (1914), *Riders of the Stars* (1916), *Songs of the Trail* (1920), and *Saddle Songs and Other Verse* (1922).

BURRO

Henry Herbert Knibbs

Beloved burro of the ample ear,
   Philosopher, gray hobo of the dunes,
Delight of children, thistle-chewing seer,
   From Lebanon and eld, how many moons?

Muse of Mañana:[1] sturdy foe of haste;
   True to yourself in every attitude;
A statue of dejection, shaggy-faced,
   Or plodding with your pack of cedar-wood;

Stopping to turn about, with motion stiff,
   As though you half imagined something wrong:
Wondering if you were there complete, or if
   The other half forgot to come along.

What melancholy thoughts bestir your heart
   When, like an ancient pump, you lift a tone,
Lose it and lift another—with an art
   Bequeathed to none on earth, save you alone?

Your melody means something deep, unseen;
   Desert contralto you are called: perchance
An ear attuned to mysteries might glean
   More from your song than simple assonance.

You sing the truth, without a touch of guile:
   And truth were sad enough—yet your fond guise
Of bland sincerity provokes a smile,
   And so the world is richer—burro-wise.

---

[1]*Mañana* (Spanish), tomorrow, a term of procrastination.

Thus do you serve twofold, in that you please
  That subtle sense that loves the ludicrous
Nor scorns affection. Oh, Demosthenes
  Of Andalusia,[2] left to preach to us!

Dogging the shadows of some empty street,
  Content with what your indolence may find,
You let the world roll on, and keep your feet,
  Or let it run, and still you stray behind.

NAMES

Henry Herbert Knibbs

It's when you name Cheyenne or Laramie,
  Laredo, Magdalena, San Antone,
You set me thinking of what used to be:
I knew a blue-eyed girl in Laramie—
  But, somehow, I just drifted on, alone.

A man got shot in Laramie one night;
  It wasn't me. I fanned it out of town
And headed South. I reckon I did right—
  The Magdalena girl, her eyes were brown.

I didn't know the Southern country then;
  I tried it for a year, then came away;
Homesick, I hit the trail for old Cheyenne—
  I recollect her eyes were warm and gray.

The sheriff came to town; so I rode South;
  For every man, he likes a change of scene—
Laredo? Well, she had a rose-red mouth,
  And eyes you couldn't read—just cool and green.

---

[2] *Andalusia*, a province in Spain.

Laredo it was heaven, for a spell,
   Then hard times hit the range, and work was slack;
I wouldn't say that San Antone was hell,
   But she was Spanish—and her eyes were black.

Some folks they settle down and make a home,
   And some keep chasing after fame or gold;
And while it seems I always had to roam,
   I'm glad I didn't see their eyes grow old.

So when you name Cheyenne or Laramie,
   Laredo, Magdalena, San Antone,
You're making music that sounds good to me;
I knew a blue-eyed girl in Laramie,
   But, somehow, I just drifted on, alone.

WILLIAM ELLERY LEONARD

William Ellery Leonard, born in Plainfield, New Jersey, in 1876, and holder of degrees from Harvard, Göttingen, and Bonn Universities, is a conspicuous example in present-day American letters of the scholar as poet. Professor of English at the University of Wisconsin since 1906, he has mingled learning with art, never permitting pedantry to stifle the fine fire of his convictions. The learning is there, a solid training in the classics, a love of modern German; but it is almost always in the background. When it obtrudes, as in the curious Greek-English and German-English sonnets in *Two Lives*, it detracts from the directness and simplicity of the author's usual style, without, however, damaging its sincerity. For scholarship is plainly a passion with this poet. As a rule, Mr. Leonard subordinates this passion to the far greater passion of his life, the protest against social injustice. See, for examples, the scathing invective of "The Lynching Bee" and "The Quaker Meeting House."

Two Lives (1925) has been his most discussed, as it is his most pretentious, work. In sonnet form it narrates a tragic personal experience, a story so intimate that the reader identifies himself with its pitiful actors. For years this poem remained in manuscript form, until none of those concerned could take exception to its publication. "Indian Summer," reprinted here, was originally published as a separate poem and afterwards incorporated into "Two Lives" as its final and best stanzas. It sums up, in short space, the idea of the longer poem and gives some suggestion of its plaintiveness.

Mr. Leonard's remaining books are *The Vaunt of Man* (1912), *The Lynching Bee and Other Poems* (1920), *The Quaker Meeting House* (1922), *Tutankhamen and After* (1924), and a number of translations from classic authors; *The Locomotive God* (1927) is autobiography by psycho-analysis.

INDIAN SUMMER*

WILLIAM ELLERY LEONARD

(After completing a book for one now dead.)

(O Earth-and-Autumn of the Setting Sun,
  She is not by, to know my task is done!)
In the brown grasses slanting with the wind,
Lone as a lad whose dog's no longer near,
Lone as a mother whose only child has sinned,
Lone on the loved hill, ... and below me here
The thistle-down in tremulous atmosphere
Along red clusters of the sumac streams;
The shriveled stalks of goldenrod are sere,
And crisp and white their flashing old racemes.[1]
(. . . forever . . . forever . . . forever . . .)
This is the lonely season of the year,
This is the season of our lonely dreams.

(O Earth-and-Autumn of the Setting Sun,
  She is not by, to know my task is done!)

The corn-shocks westward on the stubble plain
Show like an Indian village of dead days;
The long smoke trails behind the crawling train,
And floats a-top the distant woods ablaze
With orange, crimson, purple.   The low haze
Dims the scarped bluffs above the inland sea,
Whose wide and slaty waters in cold glaze
Await yon full-moon of the night-to-be,
(. . . far . . . and far . . . and far . . .)
These are the solemn horizons of man's ways,
These are the horizons of solemn thought to me.

---

*From *Two Lives*, by William Ellery Leonard; The Viking Press, Inc.   Copyright 1925 by B. W. Huebsch, Inc.

[1]*racemes*, flower-clusters arranged at intervals about a central stem.

(O Earth-and-Autumn of the Setting Sun,
She is not by, to know my task is done!)

And this the hill she visited, as friend;
And this the hill she lingered on, as bride—
Down in the yellow valley is the end.
They laid her . . . in no evening autumn tide . . .
Under fresh flowers of that May morn, beside
The queens and cave-women of ancient earth . . .

This is the hill . . . and over my city's towers,
Across the world from sunset, yonder in air,
Shines, through its scaffoldings, a civic dome
Of piled masonry, which shall be ours
To give, completed, to our children there . . .
And yonder far roof of my abandoned home
Shall house new laughter . . . Yet I tried . . . I tried
And, ever wistful of the doom to come,
I built her many a fire for love . . . for mirth . . .
(When snows were falling on our oaks outside,
Dear, many a winter fire upon the hearth) . . .
(. . . farewell . . . farewell . . . farewell . . .)
We dare not think too long on those who died,
While still so many yet must come to birth.

VACHEL LINDSAY

As everyone who has read his poetry knows, (Nicholas) Vachel Lindsay was born (1879) in Springfield, Illinois, the town made famous by its association with Abraham Lincoln. He grew up there, in the heart of the Middle West, attending Hiram College, at Hiram, Ohio, and the Art Institute of Chicago. It is a fact not generally known that Mr. Lindsay considers himself more an artist than a poet. Three years at the Art Institute were followed by a year at the New York School of Art. The product of this training is seen in the fantastic and visionary illustrations in *The Golden Book of Springfield* (1920) and *Going-to-the-stars* (1926). Mr. Lindsay is sometimes mistakenly called a hobo poet. This name he earned by his youthful wanderings as "a preacher of the gospel of beauty." Through the Carolinas, Georgia, and Florida, and afterwards from Illinois to New Mexico by way of Kansas, he went afoot, lecturing in the smaller towns and distributing his *Rhymes to be Traded for Bread* (1912).

Those who have never listened to Mr. Lindsay read from his own works should reserve their judgment of him, for in his poems, more than in most, the oral rendering is a necessary aid to appreciation. It is true that some hearers put him down as a vaudeville performer; but the more critical catch what he is trying to do—to carry over to his audience the contagious sense of rhythm which he himself feels; to make them sing *with* him, not *after* him; to re-exalt poetry to its place of communal chant, the music of the folk. The "folk," in the modern instance, being slangy, boisterous, jazzy, flamboyant Americans, it is natural that his poetry should try to translate the American rhythm into terms of slang and jazz, or, as the mode was in 1913-1914, ragtime. In the earlier books, *General William Booth Enters into Heaven* (1913), *The Congo and Other Poems* (1914), *The Chinese Nightingale* (1917), and to a less extent in *The Golden Whales of California* (1920), he is often successful in his method.

When successful, there is a barbaric vitality in his raucous rimes and insistent rhythms. It is not easy to forget the uncanny singsong of the witch-men in "The Congo":

> Walk with care, walk with care,
> Or Mumbo-Jumbo, God of the Congo,

And all of the other gods of the Congo,
Mumbo-Jumbo will hoo-doo you.

Or the explosive discord of a thousand automobiles racing westward
in "The Santa Fe Trail":

Listen to the iron horns, ripping, racking,
Listen to the quack horns, slack and clacking! . . .

But this is only the more obvious half of Vachel Lindsay. Ever in
the background is a haunting music, ineffably lyrical. "The Santa
Fe Trail" ends in the languorous "whisper of the prairie fairies":

"Sweet, sweet, sweet, sweet!
Love and glory,
Stars and rain,
Sweet, sweet, sweet, sweet!"

And one of the most successfully musical of American lyrics is "The
Chinese Nightingale." In 1928 *Poetry* announced an award of honor
of five hundred dollars "for the high distinction of his best work."

Unfortunately, some unevenness is evident in Mr. Lindsay's later
work: *Going-to-the-sun* (1923), *Going-to-the-stars* (1926), and *The Candle
in the Cabin* (1926). His *Collected Poems* (1923) seems to betray a
want of self-judgment. Perhaps he has shot his bolt, and it is returning to earth, but its flight was splendid enough.

KANSAS*

Vachel Lindsay

Oh, I have walked in Kansas
Through many a harvest field,
And piled the sheaves of glory there,
And down the wild rows reeled;

Each sheaf a little yellow sun,
A heap of hot-rayed gold;
Each binder like Creation's hand
To mold suns, as of old.

Straight overhead the orb of noon
Beat down with brimstone breath;
The desert wind from south and west
Was blistering flame and death.

Yet it was gay in Kansas,
A-fighting that strong sun;
And I and many a fellow-tramp
Defied that wind and won.

And we felt free in Kansas
From any sort of fear,
For thirty thousand tramps like us
There harvest every year.

She stretches arms for them to come,
She roars for helpers then;
And so it is in Kansas
That tramps, one month, are men.

*From *Collected Poems* by Vachel Lindsay. Copyright 1923 by The Macmillan Company.
Reprinted by permission.

We sang in burning Kansas
The songs of Sabbath-School,
The "Day Star" flashing in the East,
The "Vale of Eden" cool.

We sang in splendid Kansas
"The flag that set us free"—
That march of fifty thousand men
With Sherman to the sea.

We feasted high in Kansas
And had much milk and meat.
The tables groaned to give us **power**
Wherewith to save the wheat.

Our beds were sweet alfalfa hay
Within the barn loft wide.
The loft doors opened out upon
The endless wheat-field tide.

I loved to watch the windmills spin
And watch that big moon rise.
I dreamed and dreamed with lids **half-shut,**
The moonlight in my eyes.

For all men dream in Kansas
By noonday and by night,
By sunrise yellow, red, and wild
And moonrise wild and white.

The wind would drive the glittering clouds,
The cottonwoods would croon,
And past the sheaves and through the leaves
Came whispers from the moon.

AMY LOWELL

Amy Lowell was born, in 1874, at Brookline, Massachusetts, into one of the most distinguished families of New England. James Russell Lowell was a cousin of her grandfather; one brother was a distinguished astronomer; another brother is president of Harvard University. Added to the gift of heredity was every advantage of education and travel which wealth could give; and, as in the case of Robert Browning, wealth proved effective nurture for poetic talent. France, Greece, Egypt, and the near East are regions which she visited as a girl and which later reappear in her kaleidoscopic pages.

She was twenty-eight before she had decided that she would become a poet, thirty-six before she published a line, and thirty-eight when her first volume, *A Dome of Many-Coloured Glass* (1912), appeared. In the meantime she had been perfecting her technique with a rigorous thoroughness which only a New England conscience could have imposed.

The first book attracted no great attention, for it merely copied the Tennysonian mode; but on its heels appeared *Sword Blades and Poppy Seeds* (1914), a work of such arresting originality that it was apparent that her long apprenticeship had justified itself. This book enjoyed extraordinary publicity, because it was America's first taste of the imagist doctrines that had been storming the citadel of British poetry. Miss Lowell had been living in England, had fallen in with Ezra Pound, John Gould Fletcher, and other rebels, had caught the infection, and had returned to America at a fortunate juncture. For America was then ripe to be aroused into poetic enthusiasm, and Miss Lowell was the one to do just this. A woman of masculine aggressiveness—not to say pugnacity, on occasion—she descended upon her native land with an irresistible flood of imagism, polyphonic prose, and *vers libre* which was sufficient to shock a settled complacency into a lively and sometimes acrimonious discussion of poetic theory.

In the critical battle that ensued, Miss Lowell was always in the front rank, giving lusty blows to her skeptical opponents and leading the fight for recognition which the "new poetry" was obliged to make. Now that the dust has settled, it is apparent that the new poetry was not so revolutionary after all. (See Introduction, pages 32-38.) But out of the battle came a series of notable volumes: *Men, Women and*

Ghosts (1916); *Can Grande's Castle* (1918), four long narratives in polyphonic prose; *Pictures of the Floating World* (1919), in which the high exuberance of the preceding books gives way to a subtler mood of suggestion, restraint, and nuance. The period of excited experimentation yields to a maturity of power, a certainty of touch which mark the finished craftsman.

In her later years Miss Lowell wrote *Legends* (1921), a series of eleven narratives; *Fir-Flower Tablets* (1921), translations from Chinese poetry; *A Critical Fable* (1922); and her posthumous volumes, *What's O'Clock* (1925), *East Wind* (1926), and *Ballads for Sale* (1927). *Selected Poems* (1928) was edited by John Livingston Lowes.

Amy Lowell may not be remembered for any particular poems. In spite of her productiveness, her brilliance, and her versatility, there is comparatively little that sings itself into the memory or that touches an answering emotion in the reader. The emotion, if it is there, is constricted by the defiant pride of a woman who would not wear her heart on her sleeve but hid her feelings behind a storm of words. Of intellectual power there is fullest measure, a power that seeks to comprehend all life, all beauty, all outward appearances of color, movement, physical shape. On the other hand, there is little of the radiant warmth of a tender emotion. It may be that her own inhibitions are symbolized in her most famous poem, "Patterns." Every student of Amy Lowell should be familiar with its carefully measured cadences descriptive of the woman who could not break through the patterns of her existence, and its startling last line, which, as hearers of Miss Lowell's readings remember, boomed forth to the sudden slamming shut of her book.

Some commentators predict that Miss Lowell's fame as a poet will be less enduring than her fame as a critic. Certainly her *Tendencies in Modern American Poetry* (1917) helped to give direction to a period of literary change. And if her monumental study, *John Keats* (1925), which appeared shortly before her death and which enshrined the enthusiasm of a lifetime, should outlast her poems, perhaps she would not have had it otherwise.

LILACS

Amy Lowell

Lilacs,
False blue,
White,
Purple,
Color of lilac,
Your great puffs of flowers
Are everywhere in this my New England.
Among your heart-shaped leaves
Orange orioles hop like music-box birds and sing
Their little weak soft songs;
In the crooks of your branches
The bright eyes of song sparrows sitting on spotted eggs
Peer restlessly through the light and shadow
Of all springs.
Lilacs in dooryards
Holding quiet conversations with an early moon;
Lilacs watching a deserted house
Settling sideways into the grass of an old road;
Lilacs, wind-beaten, staggering under a lopsided shock of
     bloom
Above a cellar dug into a hill.
You are everywhere.
You were everywhere.
You tapped the window when the preacher preached his sermon,
And ran along the road beside the boy going to school.
You stood by pasture-bars to give the cows good milking,
You persuaded the housewife that her dishpan was of silver
And her husband an image of pure gold.
You flaunted the fragrance of your blossoms
Through the wide doors of customhouses—
You, and sandalwood, and tea,
Charging the noses of quill-driving clerks

When a ship was in from China.
You called to them: "Goose-quill men, goose-quill men,
May is a month for flitting,"
Until they writhed on their high stools
And wrote poetry on their letter sheets behind the propped-up
   ledgers.
Paradoxical New England clerks,
Writing inventories in ledgers, reading the "Song of Solomon"
   at night,
So many verses before bedtime,
Because it was the Bible.
The dead fed you
Amid the slant stones of graveyards.
Pale ghosts who planted you
Came in the nighttime
And let their thin hair blow through your clustered stems.
You are of the green sea,
And of the stone hills which reach a long distance.
You are of elm-shaded streets with little shops where they sell
   kites and marbles,
You are of great parks where everyone walks and nobody is
   at home.
You cover the blind sides of greenhouses
And lean over the top to say a hurry-word through the glass
To your friends, the grapes, inside.

Lilacs,
False blue,
White,
Purple,
Color of lilac,
You have forgotten your Eastern origin,
The veiled women with eyes like panthers,
The swollen, aggressive turbans of jeweled pashas.
Now you are a very decent flower,

A reticent flower,
A curiously clear-cut, candid flower
Standing beside clean doorways,
Friendly to a house-cat and a pair of spectacles,
Making poetry out of a bit of moonlight
And a hundred or two sharp blossoms.

Maine knows you,
Has for years and years;
New Hampshire knows you,
And Massachusetts
And Vermont.
Cape Cod starts you along the beaches to Rhode Island;
Connecticut takes you from a river to the sea.
You are brighter than apples,
Sweeter than tulips,
You are the great flood of our souls
Bursting above the leaf-shapes of our hearts,
You are the smell of all summers,
The love of wives and children,
The recollection of the gardens of little children;
You are state houses and charters
And the familiar treading of the foot to and fro on a road it
    knows.
May is lilac here in New England,
May is a thrush singing "Sun up!" on a tip-top ash-tree,
May is white clouds behind pine trees
Puffed out and marching upon a blue sky.
May is green as no other,
May is much sun through small leaves,
May is soft earth,
And apple blossoms,
And windows open to a south wind.
May is a full light wind of lilac
From Canada to Narragansett Bay.

Lilacs,
False blue,
White,
Purple,
Color of lilac,
Heart-leaves of lilac all over New England,
Roots of lilac under all the soil of New England,
Lilac in me because I am New England,
Because my roots are in it,
Because my leaves are of it,
Because my flowers are for it,
Because it is my country
And I speak to it of itself
And sing of it with my own voice
Since certainly it is mine.

PATTERNS

Amy Lowell

I walk down the garden paths,
And all the daffodils
Are blowing, and the bright blue squills.
I walk down the patterned garden paths
In my stiff, brocaded gown.
With my powdered hair and jeweled fan,
I, too, am a rare
Pattern.   As I wander down
The garden paths.

My dress is richly figured,
And the train
Makes a pink and silver stain
On the gravel, and the thrift
Of the borders.

Just a plate of current fashion,
Tripping by in high-heeled, ribboned shoes.
Not a softness anywhere about me,
Only whalebone and brocade.
And I sink on a seat in the shade
Of a lime tree.   For my passion
Wars against the stiff brocade.
The daffodils and squills
Flutter in the breeze
As they please.
And I weep;
For the lime tree is in blossom
And one small flower has dropped upon my bosom.

And the plashing of waterdrops
In the marble fountain
Comes down the garden paths.
The dripping never stops.
Underneath my stiffened gown
Is the softness of a woman bathing in a marble basin,
A basin in the midst of hedges grown
So thick, she cannot see her lover hiding,
But she guesses he is near,
And the sliding of the water
Seems the stroking of a dear
Hand upon her.
What is summer in a fine brocaded gown!
I should like to see it lying in a heap upon the ground.
All the pink and silver crumpled up on the ground.

I would be the pink and silver as I ran along the paths,
And he would stumble after,
Bewildered by my laughter.
I should see the sun flashing from his sword-hilt and the buckles
    on his shoes.

I would choose
To lead him in a maze along the patterned paths,
A bright and laughing maze for my heavy-booted lover.
Till he caught me in the shade,
And the buttons of his waistcoat bruised my body as he
     clasped me,
Aching, melting, unafraid.
With the shadows of the leaves and the sundrops,
And the plopping of the waterdrops,
All about us in the open afternoon—
I am very like to swoon
With the weight of this brocade,
For the sun sifts through the shade.

Underneath the fallen blossom
In my bosom
Is a letter I have hid.
It was brought to me this morning by a rider from the Duke.
"Madam, we regret to inform you that Lord Hartwell
Died in action Thursday se'nnight."
As I read it in the white, morning sunlight,
The letters squirmed like snakes.
"Any answer, Madam?" said my footman.
"No," I told him.
"See that the messenger takes some refreshment.
No, no answer."

And I walked into the garden,
Up and down the patterned paths,
In my stiff, correct brocade.
The blue and yellow flowers stood up proudly in the sun,
Each one.
I stood upright, too,
Held rigid to the pattern
By the stiffness of my gown;

Up and down I walked,
Up and down.
In a month he would have been my husband.
In a month, here, underneath this lime,
We would have broke the pattern;
He for me, and I for him,
He as Colonel, I as Lady,
On this shady seat.
He had a whim
That sunlight carried blessing.
And I answered, "It shall be as you have said."
Now he is dead.

In summer and in winter I shall walk
Up and down
The patterned garden paths
In my stiff, brocaded gown.
The squills and daffodils
Will give place to pillared roses, and to asters, and to snow.
I shall go
Up and down
In my gown.
Gorgeously arrayed,
Boned, and stayed.
And the softness of my body will be guarded from embrace
By each button, hook, and lace.
For the man who should loose me is dead,
Fighting with the Duke in Flanders,
In a pattern called a war.
Christ! What are patterns for?

DAVID McCORD

David (Thompson Watson) McCord was born in New York City, in 1897, a descendant of Dr. John Morgan, first Surgeon-General of the Revolutionary Army. Six years of his boyhood were spent in Oregon, three of them on a ranch. After secondary schooling in Portland, Oregon, and Princeton, New Jersey, he entered Harvard University and received his A. B. degree in 1921, A. M. in 1922. For several years he was engaged in editorial work; since 1923 he has been a member of the staff of the *Boston Transcript*, writing on drama and music.

His first book, *Oddly Enough* (1926), is a collection of short, familiar essays that are genuinely hilarious. *Floodgate* (1927) is a book of poems, not so heavy as to be ponderous, not so light as to be frivolous. Building on a foundation of seriousness, Mr. McCord combines a simple metrical felicity with a care for the peculiar and adequate word in order to erect an attractive lyrical structure.

BATTERY PARK[1]

David McCord

On a windy day, for a lark, a lark,
They took me down to Battery Park;
On a windy day when the harbor boats
Whistled their long and lovely notes,
On a windy day that would rock the ark,
They took me down to Battery Park.

The ships were for and the ships were from,
But they took me to the Aquarium;
They held me up against the glass
To see the simple shiners pass;
They held me up to see, they said,
An artificial ocean bed
With shells and gravel, slick and weeds,
And extra things a minnow needs.
But all I cared about a rub
Was one big turtle in a tub—

A lazy turtle in a tank,
Who alternately rose and sank,
And warped about with flippered ease
Upon his calm and tiley seas;
A giant turtle, old as sin,
With room and room to paddle in.

"Come here," they said, "and look at these";
But I wouldn't go if they asked me *please;*
Not all the sharks and all the fish
Are worth a turtle in a dish.
So *I* hung over the edge to see
His marvelous solemnity.

---

[1]*Battery Park*, the southern end of Manhattan Island.

On a windy day, for a lark, a lark,
They took me down to Battery Park;
On a windy day when the harbor boats
Whistled their long and lovely notes,
On a windy day that would rock the ark,
They took me down to Battery Park.

MILDRED E. MARCETTE

Mildred Elizabeth Marcette was born in Providence, Rhode Island, in 1906. After graduation from Pembroke College in Brown University in 1927, she entered Bryn Mawr as a graduate student of English literature. "Query" is reprinted here as an example of the promising poetic material being produced in American colleges.

QUERY

Mildred E. Marcette

I wonder whether it was imagination,
Or rather the lack of it, that was at work
When these Maine farmers named their hamlets.

Did they see, vision-blue in the distance,
The towering spires and myriad-peopled streets
Of cities strong and splendid, past, and yet to be?

Or thumbing some old atlas after a hard day's work in the fields,
Did they pick carelessly, at random,
Eenie, meenie, minie, mo, as children choose?

Athens—
Clear white temples against a glowing cobalt sky—
Half-forgotten tales of Apollo, Zeus, Aphrodite—
Heroes, philosophers, poets, sculptors—
All the wisdom and grace and beauty
Of the shining youth of the world.

(A single elm-lined, dusty roadway—
A few white farmhouses—
A narrow brook, a store, a school.)

Paris—
Web of glowing, scintillating color,
Where the spider Pleasure lurks and lures forever—
And forever linger wistfully in the shadows
The poor vague ghosts of old victims, nobles and queens and
    kings—
Lights, pulsing music, eternal gayety and sorrow.

(A few white farmhouses—
A narrow brook, a store, a school—
A single elm-lined, dusty roadway.)

China—
A magic and a mystery—
Stately silken-robed mandarins,
Sly-eyed, masters of slow, subtle poisonings—
Half-forgotten temples with age-old rites and antique gods—
Spices—incense—the glamour of the unreal and the unknown.

(A narrow brook, a store, a school—
A single elm-lined, dusty roadway—
A few white farmhouses.)

I wonder whether it was imagination,
Or rather the lack of it that was at work
When these Maine farmers named their hamlets.

But for unremembered years they have been at peace,
Sleeping quite soundly in plots tangled, overgrown,
    unremembered.
Who can speak surely of their motives?

JEANETTE MARKS

Jeanette (Augustus) Marks was born in Chattanooga, Tennessee, in 1875. Her whole life has centered in the study and the teaching of English literature. After receiving A.B. and A.M. degrees from Wellesley College, she studied in England. She has been a member of the English Department at Mount Holyoke College since 1901, where her Poetry Shop Talks and her English 26 Playshop have taught students to think of poetry and drama as living and growing forces of literature. Her own example has been a stimulating one, for she has unostentatiously produced a creditable body of plays, short stories, sketches, essays, and a collection of poems under the title of *Willow Pollen* (1921). Much of her work has been inspired by summer walking trips in Wales. In 1911 she won the Welsh National Theater prize for two one-act plays, "Welsh Honeymoon" and "The Merry, Merry Cuckoo."

Of recent years her efforts have been given to the collection of material for *Genius and Disaster* (1925), medico-literary studies of the abnormalities in the lives of Poe, James Thomson, Swinburne, and Francis Thompson. Her theory, which she plans to apply also to De Quincey, Coleridge, Dante Gabriel Rossetti, and Mrs. Browning, seeks to unite literary criticism with the findings of modern medical science in an attempt to place the blame for the ruin which too often attends the highest literary genius.

"White Hair" is typical of Miss Marks's delicate and admirable restraint.

WHITE HAIR

Jeanette Marks

All the warmth has gone out of white hair,
It only answers to the wind
And lifts and stirs like creeping snow
Close to the frozen scalp of earth.
It has no gold of autumn grasses
Or red of beech buds
Or warm brown of tree bark
Or depths of quiet
In which eyes burn like star-flame in a dark night.

Has death white hair
And the cramped empty shoulders of old age?
If he has, I shall be as a child, frightened and trying to hide
    from him.
But if his touch is the touch of warm rain,
If his breath is sweet like the gray-green fruit of the juniper,
If his shoulder is deep and strong like the upheaved root of
    hemlock
And his hair velvet-dusk as a moth's wing,
Then I shall go to him gladly,
And sleep well . . .

DON MARQUIS

Donald (Robert Perry) Marquis was born in Walnut, Illinois, in 1878. He attended Knox College, Galesburg, Illinois, and afterwards studied at the Corcoran School of Art, Washington. Most of his life has been spent in newspaper offices, as reporter, editorial writer, and columnist. His journalistic connections include newspapers in Washington, Philadelphia, Atlanta, and New York; he was also associated with Joel Chandler Harris in editing *Uncle Remus's Magazine.*

His greatest success was attained in "The Sun Dial," his column in *The Sun,* New York, where Hermione, The Old Soak, and archy, the office cockroach, daily beguiled the lives of bored New Yorkers. The Old Soak inspired a successful play by that name.

As a poet, Mr. Marquis is best known for his excellent humorous verse; see *Noah an' Jonah an' Cap'n John Smith* (1922) and *archy and mehitabel* (1927). His ability as a writer of serious poetry is often overlooked. Using both free and conventional forms, he has done some thoughtful and imaginative writing, which may be found in his volumes *Dreams and Dust* (1915), *Poems and Portraits* (1922), and *The Awakening and Other Poems* (1925). It is from the last book that the poem here quoted has been taken.

THOSE THAT COME BACK

Don Marquis

I, too, have heard strange whispers, seen
A stealthy mist rise from the summer's green,
And felt, even in the loud and candid noon,
A central silence and chill secrecy
Laid close against the human heat of me;
But never under sun nor moon,
Nor through the choked, ambiguous utterance of the rain,
Has any presence made his meaning plain . . .
Perhaps these ghosts are helpless ghosts and weak,
Or, when they see us, grow too sad to speak.

EDGAR LEE MASTERS

Edgar Lee Masters was born of pioneer stock at Garnett, Kansas, in 1869. His boyhood was passed there and in Lewiston, Illinois, both small country towns where life sometimes lies more bare than in cities. He was graduated from Knox College, studied law in his father's office, and established his own law practice in Chicago. Though a busy and successful attorney he found time to write poetry, and the inclination to do so was seldom wanting.

Between 1895 and 1914, the year when *Spoon River Anthology*[1] began to appear in *Reedy's Mirror*, Mr. Masters produced hundreds of poems, several plays, and a book of essays—all of them undistinguished, because their author had not been able to break away from conventional influences and because he had not learned to look about him for his best source of material. But *Spoon River Anthology* (1915) brought him a swift fame. A collection of 244 "epitaphs" of past residents of a Middle Western town of whom "All, all are sleeping, sleeping, sleeping on the hill," it tells with devastating candor the truths that these dead could not reveal during their lifetimes. They speak, for the most part, in the first person; and their stories intertwine with all the complexity of an ingrowing town life. One should read as a group, for example, "Benjamin Pantier," "Mrs. Benjamin Pantier," "Reuben Pantier," "Emily Sparks," "Trainor, the Druggist," "A. D. Blood," "Oscar Hummel," "Dora Williams," and "Mrs. Williams." The general effect of the book is sordid. Sin is more sensational than goodness, and though Mr. Masters mixes his ingredients fairly, the impression that remains after reading the book is "of broken hearts and battered brains, . . . of inexorable fatality."

The New Spoon River (1924) continues the method of the earlier book but lacks something of the driving force of its fresh inventiveness. The author intrudes more into the lives and opinions of his creatures; the illusion of spontaneous generation is less convincing. *The New Spoon River* carries over some names from the *Spoon River Anthology*, and the links in the human chain are illustrated by such poems as the two reprinted here: Lucinda Matlock, in love with life at ninety-

---

[1] Spoon River is a river in central Illinois; the country thereabout is described in the *Journal of the Illinois State Historical Society* of October, 1921-January, 1922.

six; Rita Matlock Gruenberg, a suicide at forty-nine, truly one of the "degenerate sons and daughters" of her grandmother's words.

Mr. Masters has written an imposing quantity of verse since *Spoon River Anthology*, but none of it has caught the public interest with the same sudden appeal. Yet these other books contain many a fine lyric, fated to be overshadowed by the sheer mass of the longer poems to which Mr. Masters now devotes his art. Besides the two Spoon River volumes, he has published *Songs and Satires* (1916), *The Great Valley* (1916), *Toward the Gulf* (1918), *Starved Rock* (1919), *Domesday Book* (1920), *Open Sea* (1921).

LUCINDA MATLOCK*

Edgar Lee Masters

I went to the dances at Chandlerville,
And played snap-out at Winchester.
One time we changed partners,
Driving home in the moonlight of middle June,
And then I found Davis.
We were married and lived together for seventy years,
Enjoying, working, raising the twelve children,
Eight of whom we lost
Ere I had reached the age of sixty.
I spun, I wove, I kept the house, I nursed the sick,
I made the garden, and for holiday
Rambled over the fields where sang the larks,
And by Spoon River gathering many a shell,
And many a flower and medicinal weed—
Shouting to the wooded hills, singing to the green valleys.
At ninety-six I had lived enough, that is all,
And passed to a sweet repose.
What is this I hear of sorrow and weariness,
Anger, discontent, and drooping hopes?
Degenerate sons and daughters,
Life is too strong for you—
It takes life to love Life.

RITA MATLOCK GRUENBERG

Edgar Lee Masters

Grandmother! You who sang to green valleys,
And passed to a sweet repose at ninety-six,
Here is your little Rita at last
Grown old, grown forty-nine;

*From *Spoon River Anthology* by Edgar Lee Masters. Copyright 1915 by The Macmillan Company. Reprinted by permission.

Here stretched on your grave under the winter stars,
With the rustle of oak leaves over my head;
Piecing together strength for the act,
Last thoughts, memories, asking how I am here!
After wandering afar, over the world,
Life in cities, marriages, motherhood—
(They all married, and I am homeless, alone.)
Grandmother! I have not lacked in strength,
Nor will, nor courage. No! I have honored you
With a life that used these gifts of your blood.
But I was caught in trap after trap in the years.
At last the cruelest trap of all.
Then I fought the bars, pried open the door,
Crawled through—but it suddenly sprang shut,
And tore me to death as I used your courage
To free myself!
Grandmother! Fold me to your breast again.
Make me earth with you for the blossoms of spring—
Grandmother!

EDNA ST. VINCENT MILLAY

Edna St. Vincent Millay, she of the dactylic name, was born in Rockland, Maine, in 1892. She was graduated from Vassar College in 1917 and is married to Eugene Boissevain. A woman of piquant personality and a charming reader of her own works, she is popular with artistic circles in New York City, where she now makes her home.

Her finest poem, "Renascence," is an unaccountable freak of genius, perhaps the product of one of those glimpses into the reality beyond the temporal which, according to Wordsworth, are clearest in childhood. For Miss Millay was scarcely more than a child, nineteen years of age, when she wrote this amazing account of such a mystic experience as it is given only to children and poets to know. This and other early poems were published in 1917 under the title of *Renascence*. This was followed by *A Few Figs from Thistles* (1920), in which Puck all but gets the better of the philosopher and leads her to indulge in all manner of gay and frivolous whimsies. In *Aria da Capo* (1920), a poetic play, the changelessness of existence is "the dominant's persistence" underneath the foolery.

In *Second April* (1921) and *The Harp-Weaver and Other Poems* (1924) the soberly philosophical side of Miss Millay's nature is brought forward. In the firm thinking of the sonnets in the latter volume she proves herself entitled to rank among the foremost women lyricists of America—Emily Dickinson, Sara Teasdale, and H. D. And many critics would not hestitate to place her name at the lead of this list.

For a while her health was seriously menaced and she retired to Santa Fe to fight the disease which threatened her. Apparently the indomitable spirit of her own poem, "The Poet and His Book," carried her through, for in the spring of 1927 she returned to New York to receive her share of the applause which greeted *The King's Henchman*, an opera by Deems Taylor for which she provided the libretto. In 1928 *The Buck in the Snow* appeared.

GOD'S WORLD*

Edna St. Vincent Millay

O world, I cannot hold thee close enough!
    Thy winds, thy wide gray skies!
    Thy mists, that roll and rise!
Thy woods, this autumn day, that ache and sag
And all but cry with color!   That gaunt crag
To crush!   To lift the lean of that black bluff!
World, world, I cannot get thee close enough!

Long have I known a glory in it all,
    But never knew I this;
    Here such a passion is
As stretcheth me apart—Lord, I do fear
Thou'st made the world too beautiful this year;
My soul is all but out of me—let fall
No burning leaf; prithee, let no bird call.

RECUERDO†¹

Edna St. Vincent Millay

We were very tired, we were very merry—
We had gone back and forth all night on the ferry.
It was bare and bright, and smelled like a stable—
But we looked into a fire, we leaned across a table,
We lay on a hilltop underneath the moon;
And the whistles kept blowing, and the dawn came soon.

We were very tired, we were very merry—
We had gone back and forth all night on the ferry;
And you ate an apple, and I ate a pear,
From a dozen of each we had bought somewhere;

*From *Renascence*, published by Harper and Brothers. Copyright 1917 by Edna St. Vincent Millay.

†From *A Few Figs from Thistles*, published by Harper and Brothers. Copyright 1922 by Edna St. Vincent Millay.

¹*Recuerdo* (Spanish), a memory.

And the sky went wan, and the wind came cold,
And the sun rose dripping, a bucketful of gold.

We were very tired, we were very merry—
We had gone back and forth all night on the ferry.
We hailed, "Good-morrow, mother!" to a shawl-covered head,
And bought a morning paper, which neither of us read;
And she wept, "God bless you!" for the apples and pears,
And we gave her all our money but our subway fares.

JOURNEY*

Edna St. Vincent Millay

Ah, could I lay me down in this long grass
And close my eyes, and let the quiet wind
Blow over me—I am so tired, so tired
Of passing pleasant places! All my life,
Following Care along the dusty road,
Have I looked back at loveliness and sighed;
Yet at my hand an unrelenting hand
Tugged ever, and I passed. All my life long
   Over my shoulder have I looked at peace,
   And now I fain would lie in this long grass
   And close my eyes.
             Yet onward!
                  Catbirds call
Through the long afternoon, and creeks at dusk
Are guttural. Whippoorwills wake and cry,
Drawing the twilight close about their throats.
Only my heart makes answer. Eager vines
Go up the rocks and wait; flushed apple trees
Pause in their dance and break the ring for me;
Dim, shady wood-roads, redolent of fern

*From *Second April and Other Poems,* published by Harper and Brothers. Copyright 1921 by Edna St. Vincent Millay.

And bayberry, that through sweet bevies thread
Of round-faced roses, pink and petulant,
Look back and beckon ere they disappear.
Only my heart, only my heart responds.
Yet, ah, my path is sweet on either side
All through the dragging day—sharp underfoot,
And hot, and like dead mist the dry dust hangs—
But far, oh, far as passionate eye can reach,
And long, ah, long as rapturous eye can cling,
The world is mine: blue hill, still silver lake,
Broad field, bright flower, and the long white road.
A gateless garden, and an open path:
My feet to follow, and my heart to hold.

RUTH COMFORT MITCHELL

Ruth Comfort Mitchell (Mrs. William Sanborn Young) was born in San Francisco, California. Her whole life has been spent in her native state, where she now lives on a ranch at Los Gatos, in the Santa Cruz Mountains. She has, however, traveled widely in the United States, Mexico, and Europe. "The Travel Bureau," from *Narratives in Verse* (1923), is her best known poem. Her poems are light and happy and make pleasant reading.

THE TRAVEL BUREAU

Ruth Comfort Mitchell

All day she sits behind a bright brass rail,
　　Planning proud journeyings in terms that bring
　　Far places near; high-colored words that sing,
"The Taj Mahal at Agra," "Kashmir's Vale,"
Spanning wide spaces with her clear detail,
　　"Sevilla or Fiesole in spring,
　　Through the fiords in June." Her words take wing,
She is the minstrel of the great out-trail.

At half-past five she puts her maps away,
　　Pins on a gray, meek hat, and braves the sleet,
A timid eye on traffic. Dully gray
　　The house that harbors her in a gray street,
　　The close, sequestered, colorless retreat
Where she was born, where she will always stay.

HARRIET MONROE

Harriet Monroe, whose name is closely identified with the literary life of the Middle West, was born in Chicago and still lives there. She is a graduate of the Visitation Academy, Georgetown, D. C.

Miss Monroe's greatest contribution to the cause of modern American poetry is *Poetry: A Magazine of Verse*, which she founded, in October, 1912, and has ably edited to the present time. Her personal enthusiasm was chiefly responsible for the financing of this periodical —never a profit-making venture—and the establishing of various prizes for the encouragement of unknown poets. With a liberal concept of poetry, she has opened her pages to young experimenters of many shades. Some have proved only flashes in the pan. Others have been later cause for pride, since Miss Monroe introduced to the American public the early work of Carl Sandburg, Vachel Lindsay, Robert Frost, Lew Sarett, H. D., and others.

As co-editor with Alice Corbin Henderson of *The New Poetry* (1917; enlarged edition, 1923) she has compiled the most exhaustive anthology of the younger, chiefly American, poets. Her critical contributions to *Poetry* are her most valuable work. Her best poems are gathered in *You and I* (1914) and *The Difference and Other Poems* (1924).

THE PINE AT TIMBERLINE*

Harriet Monroe

What has bent you,
Warped and twisted you,
Torn and crippled you?—
What has embittered you,
O lonely tree?

You search the rocks for a footing, dragging scrawny roots;
You bare your thin breast to the storms, and fling out wild
    arms behind you;
You throw back your witch-like head, with wisps of hair string-
    ing the wind.

You fight with the snows,
You rail and shriek at the tempests;
Old before your time, you challenge the cold stars.

Be still, be satisfied!
Stand straight like your brothers in the valley,
The soft green valley of summer down below.

Why front the endless winter of the peak?
Why seize the lightning in your riven hands?
Why cut the driven wind and shriek aloud?

Why tarry here?

*From *The Difference and Other Poems,* by Harriet Monroe. Copyright 1924 by The Macmillan
Company. Reprinted by permission.

CHRISTOPHER MORLEY

Readers of Christopher (Darlington) Morley do not need to be told that he was born (in 1890) at Haverford, near Philadelphia, Pennsylvania, and attended both Haverford College and Oxford, for his writings are full of affectionate references to these places. "Parsons' Pleasure" is especially rich in the reminiscences of the young Rhodes Scholar dreaming pleasantly of his Quaker college days, all in the mellow atmosphere of an Oxford afternoon. This poem presents an interesting contrast to Rupert Brooke's "The Old Vicarage, Grantchester."

Mr. Morley has turned his nimble genius to many ends—conductor of "The Bowling Green" of the *New York Evening Post* and now of *The Saturday Review of Literature*, essayist, playwright, travel writer, novelist (*Where the Blue Begins* and *Thunder on the Left*), jingler, parodist, poet, anthologist—in all these fields he labors under the stimulus and the curse of being at heart a newspaper man. In consequence his work exhibits a good deal of unevenness, hasty and careless scribbling standing side by side with some of the subtlest and most human writing of our day. Nowhere is this unevenness more evident than in his poetry. Much of *Songs for a Little House* (1917) and *Chimneysmoke* (1921) is frankly sentimental; but his later books of poetry, *Translations from the Chinese* (1922) and *Parsons' Pleasure* (1923), are written with less deference to the tastes of a newspaper audience and more for his own artistic satisfaction. His wit, sometimes fantastic, sometimes gently satiric, and always lively, is never long absent from any of his pages.

Most of all, Mr. Morley is notable for the engaging personality which savors all his writings—at once whimsical, scholarly, sane, and intensely, heartily human.

The Haverford Edition of the Books of Christopher Morley, in twelve volumes, was published in 1927.

NURSERY RHYMES FOR THE TENDER-HEARTED

Christopher Morley

I

Scuttle, scuttle, little roach—
How you run when I approach:
Up above the pantry shelf
Hastening to secrete yourself.

Most adventurous of vermin,
How I wish I could determine
How you spend your hours of ease,
Perhaps reclining on the cheese.

Cook has gone, and all is dark—
Then the kitchen is your park.
In the garbage heap that she leaves
Do you browse among the tea leaves?

How delightful to suspect
All the places you have trekked.
Does your long antenna whisk its
Gentle tip across the biscuits?

Do you linger, little soul,
Drowsing in our sugar bowl?
Or, abandonment most utter,
Shake a shimmy on the butter?

Do you chant your simple tunes
Swimming in the baby's prunes?
Then, when dawn comes, do you slink
Homeward to the kitchen sink?

Timid roach, why be so shy?
We are brothers, thou and I.

In the midnight, like yourself,
I explore the pantry shelf!

II

Rock-a-bye, insect, lie low in thy den,
Father's a cockroach, mother's a hen.
And Betty, the maid, doesn't clean up the sink,
So you shall have plenty to eat and to drink.

Hush-a-bye, insect, behind the mince pies:
If the cook sees you her anger will rise;
She'll scatter poison, as bitter as gall,
Death to poor cockroach, hen, baby, and all.

III

There was a gay hen roach, and what do you think,
She lived in a cranny behind the old sink—
Eggshells and grease were the chief of her diet;
She went for a stroll when the kitchen was quiet.

She walked in the pantry and sampled the bread,
But when she came back her old husband was dead:
Long had he lived, for his legs they were fast,
But the kitchen maid caught him and squashed him at last.

IV

I knew a black beetle, who lived down a drain,
And friendly he was though his manners were plain;
When I took a bath he would come up the pipe,
And together we'd wash, and together we'd wipe.

Though mother would sometimes protest with a sneer
That my choice of a tub-mate was wanton and queer,
A nicer companion I never have seen:
He bathed every night; so he must have been clean.

Whenever he heard the tap splash in the tub
He'd dash up the drain-pipe and wait for a scrub,
And often, so fond of ablution was he,
I'd find him there floating and waiting for me.

But nurse has done something that seems a great shame:
She saw him there, waiting, prepared for a game:
She turned on the hot and she scalded him sore,
And he'll never come bathing with me any more.

PARSONS' PLEASURE

CHRISTOPHER MORLEY

To breed a poet, let him grow
First, settled in one place, to know
One coign of ground pluperfectly;
Until, subconscious and instinct,
Familiar sights and sounds are linked:
Her bend of soil, her smell of air
Bottom the clearness of his mind,
Make a deep shining there, and pass
To inmost in; as mercury behind
A lucid pane, makes looking-glass—
It matters very little where:
His heart has taken quickroot there.

Heart planted thus, then let him be
Tossed and transported to and fro;
Angered, frightened: ecstasy
And idiot anguish, ribald mirth,
Shall salt him to the carnal earth.
Bravely elated, let him vex

Inscrutables—viz., God or sex—
(A subject that I will not touch:
I'd say too little, or too much.)

Two breeding places I have known
Where germinal my heart was sown;
Two places from which I inherit
The present business of my spirit:
Haverford, Oxford, quietly
May make a poet out of me.

O Quaker college! every tree,
Each slope and hollow of her lawn,
How inerasably is drawn
Upon my tender memory.
There, where the broad green cricket field
Lies like a polished convex shield
The breakfast light, on those flat curves,
Gilds something brighter than mere turves!
There's mystic pureness in her scene:
Life indescribably serene
Befits the calmest of all creeds.
What was her placid secret? Was it
The dropping flit of maple seeds
(Coat-hangers for a fairy's closet),
The darkly-lustered copper beeches,
And through the room where GUMMERE[1] teaches
Sweet grassy air of May astir,
The lawnmower's drowsy turning whir,
The hourly flux of feet along the ways . . .

Or leafsmoke of mild autumn days,
The campus dimmed in pungent haze;
Beyond the opal western hill

---

[1] *Gummere*, Francis B. Gummere (1855-1919), philologist and professor of English at Haverford College.

Clear *Darby* waters brownly flow
With amberlucent sudden chill:
Roosting warm fence rails, there beside
The sunny meadow, till we dried—
Then to the griping Cider Mill!
Old FOUNDERS bell, with gentle clang;
Clatter of plates; the songs we sang—
Sweet sentimental, simple youths,
Our notebooks full of harmless truths
(Nor guessed the traps life gets you in,
So much more puzzling than mere sin).

Oxford . . . two rivers and four hills
(*Shotover, Wytham, Cumnor, Boar's*)—
Isis, threshed by riming oars;
Cher, in an aisle of trees and meadows
Where willows sieve thin water-shadows,
And, in the dapple, sliding through,
The chuckling punt, the still canoe.
Of all the rivers that there are,
None so immortal as the Cher!
Wide sunny stretches edged with reeds;
The supper-hampers on the meads;
The tea, brewed with a spirit-lamp;
The cushions, to subfend the damp;
The punt-pole's dripping downward slither,
The lingering dusk of English weather—
But most, of all the mind can treasure,
The swimming pool called PARSONS' PLEASURE.

A greengloom sideloop of the creek,
A sodden place of twilight smell:
Clear dayshine did not often touch
That water; and a moldy hutch
For the convenience of undressing.

An ancient, far from prepossessing,
Offered uncandid towels (eschewed
By most).

       There men's white bodies, nude,
Unconscious, comely, gallant, Greek,
Stretched, tingled cool, shone sleek, lived well
In the one patch where sunwarm fell.
The slow curve of those bodies diving
And, after all these years, surviving
In my mind only: that flash, seen
Against the willows' roofing green
When they were reckless, young, and clean,
That, in my secret mind, must be
Their pitiful immortality.
Indeed, one may so furiously cherish
Moments, that they cannot perish;
And this is not irrelevant:
The poet's reason, which I bade you plant
In one parochial soil, grows fecund
More richly than you reckoned—
Scorns to count first or second
In its general treasury of glee,
And, humbly spored,
Spreads infinite trellis toward
The truth, its only lord.
This, then, be sign and token,
And I have spoken:
Save as he has quickened and been moved
By that irrational agonizing fit
That teaches him to love all life, and honor it—
Dreadful tenderness that goes deep, deep,
Like the downward gaze upon a child asleep—
This, if he does not know it,
He is not poet;
He is not poet, for he has not loved.

DAVID MORTON

David Morton was born in Elkton, Kentucky, in 1886. After graduation in 1909 from Vanderbilt University, he was a newspaper man for a number of years, then a high-school teacher of English, and since 1924 a member of the English Department at Amherst College. He has chosen to limit his writing of verse to the sonnet, and by this concentration has reached a high degree of skill in a difficult medium. At the same time one may question whether *Ships in Harbor and Other Poems* (1921), *Harvest* (1924), and *Nocturnes and Autumnals* (1928) might not be more generally read if their contents were not so limited as to form. But they are pleasant books to pick up when one seeks "long, blue moods of quiet," country fields at evening, "the smell of ruin in the autumn air," twilight on snowy hills, and "red coals glowing through the bars" at the day's end—all familiar, friendly things graciously remembered.

WINTER TWILIGHT

DAVID MORTON

Let us be still where this blue twilight falls
   With crumbling shadows on the hills of snow,
For here, within these thin and wavering walls,
   There is a quiet that our hearts would know.
These stars are older and the dusk more wide
   Than any little day we call our own,
And twilight passes like a moving tide
   That leaves us hushed, so strangely and alone.

And we will turn, now, though the hills be calling,
   And look below us where the dusk sifts down,
For there is naught more lovely than this falling
   Of noiseless shadows through the steepled town,
This gathered stillness in the listening air,
   And stars like tender words, they are so fair.

WHO SHAPES THE CARVEN WORD

DAVID MORTON

Who shapes the carven word, the lean, true line,
And builds with syllable and chiseled phrase,
To rear a sheltering temple and a shrine
To house a dream through brief and meager days
Must know that time wears words away like stone,
And blurs the sharpness of the clean, straight thought;
A ghost will wander out and leave alone
And tenantless the temple that he wrought.

This will be ruins for another day,
Of lichen-bitten stone and empty tower,
A tumbled shrine whose god has moved away . . .
Yet late-comers, in some moon-hushed hour,
May find a strange light haunting still the shade,
And footprints that no mortal feet had made.

JOHN G. NEIHARDT

John Gneisenau Neihardt was born in Sharpsburg, Illinois, in 1881. He earned his way through Nebraska State Normal College, where he made a brilliant record, especially in literature. From 1901 to 1907 he lived among the Omaha Indians, for the purpose of studying them at first hand. Later this knowledge was used in the writing of his epics of early days in the Missouri Valley.

His first poems, however, were lyrics; the best of them may be found in *The Quest* (1916). His style is strictly conventional and would not of itself attract attention to his poetry. But the substantial character of his ideas gives his work a weight and dignity not frequently found in modern poetry. His own conception of the nature of poetic content is vigorously expressed in "O Lyric Master!"

His epics, each of book length, are *The Song of Hugh Glass* (1915), *The Song of Three Friends* (1919), and *The Song of the Indian Wars* (1925). In these, and in similar poems only projected as yet, will be found a careful historical account of various episodes in the settlement of the West by the pioneers.

Mr. Neihardt's *Collected Poems* appeared in 1926.

O LYRIC MASTER!*

John G. Neihardt

Out of thy pregnant silence, brooding and latent so long,
Burst on the world, O Master, sing us the great man-song!
Have we not piled up cities, gutted the iron hills,
Schooled with our dream the lightning and steam, giving them
    thoughts and wills?
We are the poets of matter.   Latent in steel and stone,
Latent in engines and cities and ships, see how our songs have
    grown!
Long have we hammered and chiseled, hewn and hoisted, until
Lo, 'neath the wondering noon of the world, the visible Epic of
    Will!

Breathless we halt in our labor; shout us a song to cheer;
Something that's swift as a saber, keen for the mark as a spear;
Full of the echoes of battle—souls crying up from the dust.
Hungry we cried to our singers—our singers have flung us a
    crust!
Choked with the smoke of the battle, staggering, weary with
    blows,
We cried for a flagon of music—they gave us the dew of a rose!
Gewgaw goblets they gave us, jeweled and crystalline,
But filled with the tears of a weakling.   Better a gourd—and
    wine!

O imminent Lyric Master, thou who hast felt us build,
Molding the mud with our sweat and blood into a thing we
    willed;
Soon shall thy brooding be over, the dream shall be ripened—
    and then,
Thunderous out of thy silence, hurl us the Song of Men!

DOROTHY PARKER

Dorothy (Rothschild) Parker, (Mrs. Edwin Pond Parker), was born in West End, New Jersey, in 1893. She was educated at Miss Dana's School, Morristown, New Jersey, and the Blessed Sacrament Convent, New York. Between 1916 and 1920 she served on the editorial staffs, first of *Vogue*, then of *Vanity Fair*, resigning the latter position to become a free lance. Her contributions to *Life*, *Vanity Fair*, "The Conning Tower" of the *New York World*, and other publications are gathered in *Enough Rope* (1927), a volume wherein airily graceful love lyrics are elbowed by *vers de société* at once impudent, witty, cynical, and occasionally profane. *Sunset Gun* (1928) continues the enviable reputation of *Enough Rope*.

BIOGRAPHIES

Dorothy Parker

I

Now this is the story of Lucy Brown,
A glittering jewel in virtue's crown.
From earliest youth, she aspired to please.
She never fell down and dirtied her knees;
She put all her pennies in savings banks;
She never omitted her "please" and "thanks";
She swallowed her spinach without a squawk;
And patiently listened to Teacher's talk;
She thoughtfully stepped over worms and ants;
And earnestly watered the potted plants;
She didn't dismember expensive toys;
And never would play with the little boys.
And when to young womanhood Lucy came
Her mode of behavior was just the same.
She always was safe in her home at dark;
And never went riding around the park;
She wouldn't put powder upon her nose;
And petticoats sheltered her spotless hose;
She knew how to market and mend and sweep;
By quarter-past ten, she was sound asleep;
In presence of elders, she held her tongue—
The way that they did when the world was young.
And people remarked, in benign accord,
"You'll see that she gathers her just reward."

Observe, their predictions were more than fair.
She married an affluent millionaire
So gallant and handsome and wise and gay,
And rated in Bradstreet at Double A.
And she lived with him happily all her life,
And made him a perfectly elegant wife.

II

Now Marigold Jones, from her babyhood,
Was bad as the model Miss Brown was good.
She stuck out her tongue at her grieving nurse;
She frequently rifled her Grandma's purse;
She banged on the table and broke the plates;
She jeered at the passing inebriates;
And tore all her dresses and ripped her socks,
And shattered the windows with fair-sized rocks;
The words on the fences she'd memorize;
She blackened her dear little brother's eyes;
And cut off her sister's abundant curls;
And never would play with the little girls.
And when she grew up—as is hardly strange—
Her manner of life underwent no change
But faithfully followed her childhood plan.
And once there was talk of a married man!
She sauntered in public in draperies
Affording no secrecy to her knees;
She constantly uttered what was not true;
She flirted and petted, or what have you;
And, tendered advice by her kind Mamma,
Her answer, I shudder to state, was "Blah!"
And people remarked, in sepulchral tones,
"You'll see what becomes of Marigold Jones."

Observe, their predictions were more than fair.
She married an affluent millionaire
So gallant and handsome and wise and gay,
And rated in Bradstreet at Double A.
And she lived with him happily all her life,
And made him a perfectly elegant wife.

JOSEPHINE PRESTON PEABODY

Josephine Preston Peabody (Mrs. Lionel S. Marks) was born in Brooklyn, New York, in 1874. She early went to live in Boston, Massachusetts, where, after her father's death, the family had to struggle with poverty. Furthermore, she was handicapped by ill health, so that she could not complete her course at the Girls' Latin School, Boston, and attended Radcliffe College only as a special student; also she was obliged to resign an instructorship in English Literature at Wellesley College after two years. Her life was none the less ruled by the urge to poetic expression; in fact, she had already begun to turn herself to writing at the age of thirteen. Some of her earlier lyrics are collected in *The Wayfarers* (1898) and *The Singing Leaves* (1903).

In 1906 she married Lionel S. Marks, Professor of Mechanical Engineering at Harvard University. The ensuing years with husband and children, in which constant literary production was varied by foreign travel, are reflected in her published diary and letters as a period of idyllic happiness. In 1916 she fell victim to the disease which halted her writing and made an invalid of her until her death in 1922, but could not break her gallant and cheerful spirit.

Her best poems are her simplest. In *The Singing Man* (1911) and *Harvest Moon* (1916) there are many short lyrics in which mingle the joys of home life, the ecstasy of love, and the realization of motherhood. In these lyrics, tender, wholesome, sincere, her art essays nothing beyond her powers. But when she turns spokesman for downtrodden womankind or preaches against war, she is apt to show that propaganda and poetry do not readily mix. *Collected Poems* was published in 1927.

Mrs. Marks is probably remembered most widely for her poetic drama *The Piper* (1910), which won the Stratford Play Competition and was produced at the Stratford Memorial Theater. The soliloquy of the Piper before the image of the Silent Man is one of her most moving passages. The influence of her early interest in Elizabethan drama, miracle plays, and morality plays is apparent in *The Piper*. Other of her poetic dramas are *Marlowe* (1901) and *The Wolf of Gubbio* (1913), all of them being gathered in *Collected Plays* (1927).

CRADLE SONG

JOSEPHINE PRESTON PEABODY

I

Lord Gabriel, wilt thou not rejoice
When at last a little boy's
  Cheek lies heavy as a rose,
  And his eyelids close?

Gabriel, when that hush may be,
This sweet hand all heedfully
  I'll undo, for thee alone,
  From his mother's own.

Then the far blue highways, paven
With the burning stars of heaven,
  He shall gladden with the sweet
  Hasting of his feet—

Feet so brightly bare and cool,
Leaping, as from pool to pool;
  From a little laughing boy
  Splashing rainbow joy!

Gabriel, wilt thou understand
How to keep his hovering hand—
  Never shut, as in a bond,
  From the bright beyond?

Nay, but though it cling and close
Tightly as a clinging rose,
  Clasp it only so—aright,
  Lest his heart take fright.

(*Dormi, dormi, tu.*[1]
The dusk is hung with blue.)

II

Lord Michael, wilt not thou rejoice
When at last a little boy's
   Heart, a shut-in murmuring bee,
   Turns him unto thee?

Wilt thou heed thine armor well—
To take his hand from Gabriel,
   So his radiant cup of dream
   May not spill a gleam?

He will take thy heart in thrall,
Telling o'er thy breastplate, all
   Colors, in his bubbling speech,
   With his hand to each.

(*Dormi, dormi, tu,*
Sapphire is the blue;
Pearl and beryl, they are called,
Chrysoprase and emerald,
Sard and amethyst.
Numbered so, and kissed.)

Ah, but find some angel-word
For thy sharp, subduing sword!
   Yea, Lord Michael, make no doubt
   He will find it out:

(*Dormi, dormi, tu!*)
   His eyes will look at you.

---

[1] *Dormi, dormi, tu,* Sleep, thou, sleep.

III

Last, a little morning space,
Lead him to that leafy place
   Where Our Lady sits awake,
   For all mothers' sake.

Bosomed with the Blessed One,
He shall mind her of her Son,
   Once so folded from all harms,
   In her shining arms.

(In her veil of blue,
Dormi, dormi, tu.)

   So—and fare thee well.
   Softly—Gabriel . . .
When the first faint red shall come,
Bid the day-star lead him home—
   For the bright world's sake—
   To my heart, awake.

EDWIN FORD PIPER

Edwin Ford Piper writes with authority of the middle border, for he was born of pioneer parents at Auburn, Nebraska, in 1871, before the West was wholly tamed. He attended the University of Nebraska and Harvard University, but the real preparation for his work as poet was the life of the range as he lived it in boyhood. See his poem "The Boy on the Prairie." From 1899 to 1905 he taught English at the University of Nebraska; since then he has been a member of the English Department at the University of Iowa.

Mr. Piper's best poems are eloquent of the West beloved by all who have known it and fallen under its spell. It is true that he does not always attempt the lyrical magic of "Low Voices," but often writes the blunter speech of rancher, tramp, gambler, cowboy, gunman. He is, however, essentially a lyricist, even when he is telling a story. His metrical patterns are generally admirable. He writes free verse with an adequate sense of its possibilities; he also employs blank verse and rime.

His two books, *Barbed Wire and Wayfarers* (1924) and *Paintrock Road* (1927), are important items in the growing literature of the West.

LOW VOICES*

Edwin Ford Piper

Beat against me no more,
Thoughts of my West,
Lying along low hills and river valleys.
I remember four-footed things
With heads poised, listening;
And red children at play in the sun,
And windy rain
Over unfurrowed land,
And lovers singing.

Bruise me no more, beat against me no more—
The wings of your wild birds bruise my dreams.
While moth and firefly fan the dusk
I remember the easy riders,
The loping ponies, the creak of leather,
And campfire light on boyish faces,
And low voices, low voices
Of windy rain in the long deep grass,
And lovers singing.

*From *Barbed Wire and Wayfarers* by Edwin Ford Piper. Copyright 1924 by The Macmillan Company. Reprinted by permission.

DUDLEY POORE

Dudley (Greene) Poore, born in 1893 in Cedar Rapids, Iowa, prepared for college at Phillips Academy, Andover, Massachusetts. He was graduated from Harvard University in the class of 1917. While an undergraduate he contributed with distinction to the *Harvard Monthly* and was a member of the literary group which collaborated in *Eight Harvard Poets* (1917). He served in France during the War. Since 1918 he has spent most of his time in European travel, and has lived much in Rome, Paris, and Madrid. With John Dos Passos, the author of *Manhattan Transfer*, he made a walking trip through Spain. When in America he lives either in New York City or in the Central New York village of Skaneateles. "Some shadow of the latter place," he writes "or of the orchards and lakes and white steeples and red barns of Onandaga County, appears in 'Marigold Pendulum'—if that poem reflects any world outside myself." Mr. Poore's work has been further influenced by his love of music and by his roving acquaintance with Latin Europe and its literature.

From time to time Mr. Poore contributes poems to *The Dial*. "Marigold Pendulum," reprinted in slightly abridged form from the pages of *The Dial*, is an admirable example of imagist technique. The method appears at its best in Parts IV, V, and VIII. The magic of Part I depends largely on the use of names suggesting far lands and dim figures of history; exact meaning is nothing, connotation everything.

MARIGOLD PENDULUM

DUDLEY POORE

I

Dear, with this tawny marigold
I send you Ophir,

I send you Spain,
high galleons from Peru
wallowing slow in parrot-green water,

I send you the gold house of Nero on the Aventine,
the throne of Babur, the bed of Semiramis,

I send you the dromedaries of Zenobia,
the beryl jaguars of Domitian,
the yellow desert beyond Baalbek,
fresh-minted drachmae of Heliopolis,
rugs of Sultanabad, amber and green.

Love, look with favor on the gift,
and the rest of my wealth shall be yours
by the next caravan.

IV

Who tethered that white balloon
to the hilltop grainfield?
How it bellies and tugs,
whipping the guy ropes,
bending the oak-tree pegs,
swelling rounder and higher,
crowding the very swallows out of heaven!

Knee deep in the hayrick
the sun at rest on his pitchfork,
in overalls stitched from a double breadth
of blue sky denim,

watches the glistening bag of silk
that fills and fills
with mounting vapor of ripe meadows.

Oh, love, to climb with you
into the wicker basket of the wheatfield.
Oh, to loose the straining ropes of twisted sunlight
that tie the white cloud to the hillcrest,
and rise and sail
dazzlingly over houses and steeples,
to see red barns and zigzag fences,
pastures shouldering green elm parasols,
rumbling carts that yellow dust clouds lope behind,
dangling thirsty tongues,
chugging engines that pant
sweating up long hills in nodding bonnets
of curled ostrich or aigrette,
snaky rivers striped with bridges
writhing across the haze of level plains
till the sea sets an icy green heel
on their envenomed heads,
while swarming houses run to crowd the wharves
and dabble their toes in the surf,
where the sailing ships
clap shining hands on the horizon,
and steamers toss dark windy hair.

Then at evening to rise yet higher,
rung after rung up the laddered atmosphere,
through emptiness like a hollow dish
to the highest shelf of thunder,
and there above cockcrow, above canon,
peeping over the world's tanned shoulder
down the pale abyss where the sun stables at night
to brighten his rusting harness,

and the stars polish their silver cups by day,
to loose a pigeon of lightning
from a hamper of storm.

V

On the barn's peak the moon sits washing her whiskers.
Now she blinks a green eye, slowly arches her back,
and walking along the gable on satin pads
glares at me hungrily.
All day she looked so demure!
When I lay on my back in the deep grass,
watching her prowl the sky eaves, and leap
over fences of blue,
I never guessed she could show so thirsty a tooth.
Tonight I am afraid of her.
I wish she had not seen me here at tne window
observing her antics.
She is not nearly so attractive as by day,
sly creature, rusted with mange,
and one ear gone, I see, in the fight she had
with the orange leopard that owns the morning.

VII

Summer's gold pendulum slowlier swinging
gleams through the fog-dimmed glass
of the year's tall clock.
Come with me, love, wrap your bright shoulders
warm in the swallow's cloak, and fly with me
over the brown stubble of reaped fields,
to rest side by side on a telephone wire
watching the loaded hay carts crawl important
like fat caterpillars down a leaf blade of road,
or at evening to bend against the silver trance
of still pools where the sunset holds
long and long

the print of our wing tips,
till we find a lost blue key
that winds the intricate spring
behind a red pumpkin moon
and a nipped marigold sun.

VIII

They are all yours:
images plucked with the wild Turk's-cap lily
in deep reedy meadows guarded
by the darting regiment
of dragonflies in burnished cuirass.

Yours the songs I make
when weary with searching
I come with the tang of salt winds on my lips
and the beating of moth wings in my blood,
to hold my joy in the blue leaping world
and the tall dancing sun with yellow hair
against the wheel of my mind,
as the Greek cutter wrought
in the hard translucence
of sard or of jasper
the body of Eros.

Yours because all loveliness
is a polished shield in whose hollow
I see your eyes.

And my poems are a fire
lighted on the brink of night and death
where I hurl like driftwood
moon, stars, and sun,
kingdoms, galleons, caravans,
with hell and God and the four archangels,
the better to see your face.

EZRA POUND

Incredible as it may seem, Ezra (Loomis) Pound, aesthete and ultra-sophisticate of Montparnasse, began life in the pioneer wilds of Idaho, where he was born, in 1885, at Hailey. It would be stretching significance too far to say that this fact in any way accounts for the pioneer independence of his artistic notions, but it does at least illustrate the devious ways by which genius comes into the world. For Mr. Pound, at his best, has been something of a genius—erratic almost to the point of irrationality, but possessed of the power of originating ideas which in steadier hands have been carried to maturity. Mr. Pound himself has practically disappeared as a critical influence, but his earlier books, *Personae* (1909), *Exultations* (1909), and *Ripostes* (1912), furnished much of the inspiration for the imagist movement which produced such dependable craftsmen as H. D., John Gould Fletcher, and Amy Lowell. Mr. Pound, however, has increasingly emphasized in his work a weakness inherent in imagism and indeed all "experimental" poetry, a solicitude for technique and form at the expense of weight and substance. In consequence, his later books, *Poems* (1913), *Lustra* (1916), *Poems* (1921), and others, display a steady dissipation of his earlier brilliance. In 1927 Mr. Pound gathered the best of his poems in a volume under the earlier title, *Personae*.

FURTHER INSTRUCTIONS

Ezra Pound

Come, my songs, let us express our baser passions.
Let us express our envy for the man with a steady job and no
   worry about the future.

You are very idle, my songs;
I fear you will come to a bad end.

You stand about the streets.
You loiter at the corners and bus-stops,
You do next to nothing at all.
You do not even express our inner nobilities;
You will come to a very bad end.

And I? I have gone half cracked.
I have talked to you so much
      that I almost see you about me,
Insolent little beasts! Shameless! Devoid of clothing!

But you, newest song of the lot,
You are not old enough to have done much mischief.
I will get you a green coat out of China
With dragons worked upon it.
I will get you the scarlet silk trousers
From the statue of the infant Christ at Santa Maria Novella[1];
Lest they say we are lacking in taste,
Or that there is no caste in this family.

THE RIVER-MERCHANT'S WIFE: A LETTER[2]

Ezra Pound

While my hair was still cut straight across my forehead
I played about the front gate, pulling flowers,

[1] *Santa Maria Novella*, a church in Florence.
[2] Translated from the Chinese of Li Po (705-762), perhaps the most popular poet of the T'ang
Dynasty.

You came by on bamboo stilts, playing horse;
You walked about my seat, playing with blue plums.
And we went on living in the village of Chokan:
Two small people, without dislike or suspicion.

At fourteen I married My Lord you.
I never laughed, being bashful.
Lowering my head, I looked at the wall.
Called to, a thousand times, I never looked back.

At fifteen I stopped scowling;
I desired my dust to be mingled with yours
Forever and forever, and forever.
Why should I climb the look-out?

At sixteen you departed,
You went into far Ku-to-Yen, by the river of swirling eddies,
And you have been gone five months.
The monkeys make sorrowful noise overhead.
You dragged your feet when you went out.
By the gate now, the moss is grown, the different mosses,
Too deep to clear them away!
The leaves fall early this autumn, in wind.
The paired butterflies are already yellow with August
Over the grass in the west garden—
They hurt me.
I grow older.
If you are coming down through the narrows of the river Kiang
Please let me know beforehand,
And I will come out to meet you,
        As far as Cho-fu-Sa.

LIZETTE WOODWORTH REESE

The uneventful serenity of Lizette Woodworth Reese's long life is reflected in the eloquent simplicity of her verse. She has drawn from her years such powers of discernment and creation as come from the adventures of her inner life, a life wherein the dominant delights are the beauty of the Maryland countryside, the labor of literary artistry, and the study of her fellows.

Born in Baltimore, Maryland, in 1856, Miss Reese has spent her life in that city. She taught, until her retirement in 1921, in the Western High School. In her first book, *A Branch of May* (1887), she adopted the terse, salty style which has ever since been characteristic of her. It was a singular style for those sentimental, flowery days; but Miss Reese, like Emily Dickinson in this country and A. E. Housman in England, anticipated the change which was to give us poetry of more honest values. These three writers have many qualities in common: emotional restraint, rigid compression, a fine feeling for the exact word. With Miss Dickinson, Miss Reese shares an intuitive good sense; with A. E. Housman, she writes of lanes and hedgerows and the fugitive loveliness of human life.

A Handful of Lavender (1891), *A Quiet Road* (1896), and *A Wayside Lute* (1909) suggest books of tenuous content, but the titles are misleading. These books are no less solid in body and no less modern in spirit than her most recent works, *Spicewood* (1920), *Wild Cherry* (1923), and *Little Henrietta* (1927). An amazing artistic consistency throughout the long span of her production springs from her sure knowledge of what she has to say and her unshakable devotion to standards of style long since defined by the works of Herrick and his contemporaries.

An excellent group of Miss Reese's lyrics was published in 1926 as *Selected Poems*.

OLD SAUL

LIZETTE WOODWORTH REESE

I cannot think of any word
  To make it plain to you,
How white a thing the hawthorn bush
  That delicately blew

Within a crook of Tinges Lane;
  Each May Day there it stood;
And lit a flame of loveliness
  For the small neighborhood.

So fragile-white a thing it was,
  I cannot make it plain;
Or the sweet fumbling of the bees,
  Like the break in a rain.

Old Saul lived near.   And this his life—
  To cobble for his bread;
To mourn a tall son lost at sea;
  A daughter worse than dead.

And so, in place of all his lack,
  He set the hawthorn tree;
Made it his wealth, his mirth, his god,
  His Zion to touch and see.

Born English he.   Down Tinges Lane
  His lad's years came and went;
He saw out there behind his thorn,
  A hundred thorns of Kent.

At lovers slipping through the dusk
    He shook a lover's head;
Grudged them each flower. It was too white
    For any but the dead.

Once on a blurred, wet, silver day
    He said to two or three:
"Folks, when I go, pluck yonder bloom
    That I may take with me."

But it was winter when he went,
    The road wind-drenched and torn;
They laid upon his coffin lid
    A wreath made all of thorn.

TEARS

Lizette Woodworth Reese

When I consider Life and its few years—
A wisp of fog betwixt us and the sun;
A call to battle, and the battle done
Ere the last echo dies within our ears;
A rose choked in the grass; an hour of fears;
The gusts that past a darkening shore do beat;
The burst of music down an unlistening street—
I wonder at the idleness of tears.
Ye old, old dead, and ye of yesternight,
Chieftains, and bards, and keepers of the sheep,
By every cup of sorrow that you had,
Loose me from tears, and make me see aright
How each hath back what once he stayed to weep:
Homer his sight, David his little lad!

LOLA RIDGE

Lola Ridge is a native of Dublin, Ireland, but spent her childhood in Australia and New Zealand. In 1907 she came to the United States. As a writer of fiction and advertising copy, an illustrator, and a factory worker, she managed to earn a living and at the same time store up experiences of American life which were to receive vivid expression in her poetry. Recognition came suddenly in 1918 with the publication, in *The New Republic*, of "The Ghetto," a powerful and comprehending study of East Side New York. Unfortunately, it is too long to be quoted here in full. The selection has been made with Miss Ridge's advice, but the poem should be read in its entirety if one would appreciate its true stature.

Miss Ridge's first volume, *The Ghetto and Other Poems* (1918), contains several short pieces in which the zeal for social change does not obscure the artistic outlines. She uses free verse so skillfully that it seems the only logical medium for her liberal and sometimes radical ideas. At times, too, it shows her indebtedness to the rhythms of the Old Testament. Her method is generally descriptive, but the picture presented always stands for something more than a mere appearance. In *Sun-Up* (1920) she continues the same practice as in the earlier volume, with somewhat greater latitude in artistic experiments and a more outspoken social propaganda.

THE GHETTO*

Lola Ridge

IV

Calicoes and furs,
Pocket-books and scarfs,
Razor strops and knives
(Patterns in check . . .)

Olive hands and russet head,
Pickles red and coppery,
Green pickles, brown pickles,
(Patterns in tapestry . . .)

Coral beads, blue beads,
Beads of pearl and amber,
Gewgaws, beauty pins—
Bijoutry for chits—
Darting rays of violet,
Amethyst, and jade . . .
All the colors out to play,
Jumbled iridescently . . .
(Patterns in stained glass
Shivered into bits!)

Nooses of gay ribbon
Tugging at one's sleeve,
Dainty little garters
Hanging out their sign . . .
Here a pout of frilly things—
There a sonsy[1] feather . . .
(White beards, black beards
Like knots in the weave . . .)

[1]*sonsy*, jolly-looking.

And ah, the little babies—
Shiny black-eyed babies—
(Half a million pink toes
Wriggling all together.)
Baskets full of babies
Like grapes on a vine.

Mothers waddling in and out,
Making all things right—
Picking up the slipped threads
In Grand Street[2] at night—
Grand Street like a great bazaar,
Crowded like a float,
Bulging like a crazy quilt
Stretched on a line.

But nearer seen
This litter of the East
Takes on a garbled majesty.

The herded stalls
In dissolute array . . .
The glitter and the jumbled finery
And strangely juxtaposed
Cans, paper, rags,
And colors decomposing,
Faded like old hair,
With flashes of barbaric hues
And eyes of mystery . . .
Flung
Like an ancient tapestry of motley weave
Upon the open wall of this new land.

Here, a tawny-headed girl . . .
Lemons in a greenish broth

---

[2]*Grand Street*, a street on the East Side of New York.

And a huge earthen bowl
By a bronzed merchant
With a tall black lamb's wool cap upon his head . . .
He has no glance for her.
His thrifty eyes
Bend—glittering, intent,
Their hoarded looks
Upon his merchandise,
As though it were some splendid cloth
Or sumptuous raiment
Stitched in gold and red . . .

He seldom talks
Save of the goods he spreads—
The meager cotton with its dismal flower—
But with his skinny hands
That hover like two hawks
Above some luscious meat,
He fingers lovingly each calico,
As though it were a gorgeous shawl,
Or costly vesture
Wrought in silken thread,
Or strange bright carpet
Made for sandaled feet . . .

Here an old gray scholar stands.
His brooding eyes—
That hold long vistas without end
Of caravans and trees and roads,
And cities dwindling in remembrance—
Bend mostly on his tapes and thread.
What if they tweak his beard—
These raw young seed of Israel
Who have no backward vision in their eyes—
And mock him as he sways
Above the sunken arches of his feet—
They find no peg to hang their taunts upon.

His soul is like a rock
That bears a front worn smooth
By the coarse friction of the sea,
And, unperturbed, he keeps his bitter peace.

What if a rigid arm and stuffed blue shape,
Backed by a nickel star,
Does prod him on,
Taking his proud patience for humility . . .
All gutters are as one
To that old race that has been thrust
From off the curbstones of the world . . .
And he smiles with the pale irony
Of one who holds
The wisdom of the Talmud stored away
In his mind's lavender.

But this young trader,
Born to trade as to a caul,
Peddles the notions of the hour.
The gestures of the craft are his
And all the lore
As when to hold, withdraw, persuade, advance . . .
And be it gum or flags,
Or clean-all or the newest thing in tags,
Demand goes to him as the bee to flower.
And he—appraising
All who come and go
With his amazing
Sleight-of-mind and glance
And nimble thought
And nature balanced like the scales at nought—
Looks westward where the trade-lights glow,
And sees his vision rise—
A tape-ruled vision,
Circumscribed in stone—
Some fifty stories to the skies.

EDWIN ARLINGTON ROBINSON

Edwin Arlington Robinson was born in 1869 at Head Tide, Maine, where the first two or three years of his life were spent. Then his father, a grain merchant, took the family to live in the larger town of Gardiner, Maine, a place which became eventually the "Tilbury Town" of Mr. Robinson's poems. For, despite the outlandish names which he bestows on his characters and the fact that they never speak with the Yankee accents of Robert Frost's people, the men and women of Tilbury Town bear the print of a New England heritage. That they are not just provincials is owing to Mr. Robinson's power to make them a part of universal humanity and their lives a part of universal experience. From 1891 to 1893 Mr. Robinson attended Harvard University, leaving before completion of his course, because of his father's business difficulties. For the next twenty years he followed various occupations to earn a livelihood, though his real occupation was the writing of poetry. Yet during these years he was practically unknown.

His first book, *The Torrent and the Night Before* (1896), was a mere pamphlet, privately printed, with the whimsical notice, "This book is dedicated to any man, woman, or critic who will cut the edges of it—I have done the top." Though it made no stir, it at least drew the remark from one critic that "his humor is of a grim sort, and the world is not beautiful to him, but a prison-house"—a remark which elicited from Mr. Robinson a reply memorable for its precise formulation of the central idea to which he has ever since held faithful: "The world is not a 'prison-house,' but a kind of spiritual kindergarten, where millions of bewildered infants are trying to spell *God* with the wrong blocks."

In the following year appeared *The Children of the Night* (1897), which, reprinted in 1905, drew the attention of President Roosevelt and caused him to give the struggling poet a position in the New York Customhouse. This position he held for several years but eventually resigned in order to devote himself wholly to writing, the MacDowell Colony having furnished him the opportunity to work at leisure. This early volume contained some of the shorter poems which were to become among his best known—"John Evereldown," "Luke Havergal," "Richard Corey"—as well as some thirty sonnets which proved his command of this exacting form; but the book attracted little comment by the critics.

The next two volumes went similarly unnoticed. Although *Captain Craig* (1902) is a poem much too long for the average reader's patience, it has many passages richly rewarding to those who make their way through it. *The Town down the River* (1910) contains examples of the keenly-etched portraiture for which, perhaps, Mr. Robinson has come to be most admired.

With *The Man against the Sky* (1916) at last came recognition and, in the inner circle, fame. Here was certainly poetry of a high order, and when readers now turned back to the earlier volumes they found that Mr. Robinson had been producing work of equal quality all along. That his art showed few signs of "development" was not to his discredit; few poets have had so little need to outgrow their beginnings. Not only did he early determine his austere technique, but he adopted certain ideas which he has not found it necessary to abandon. In *The Man against the Sky* are, for instance, his earlier doubts of a rational explanation of the universe. He puts these doubts into Shakespeare's mouth, in the poem in which "Ben Jonson Entertains a Man from Stratford." *The Man against the Sky* is also remarkable for the title poem, which begins with a passage of somberly splendid exaltation, but ends on the old questioning of Fate.

Spurred by recognition, Mr. Robinson produced with increasing rapidity: *Merlin* (1917), *The Three Taverns* (1920), *Lancelot* (1920), *Avon's Harvest* (1921), *Collected Poems* (1921), *Roman Bartholow* (1923), *The Man Who Died Twice* (1924), *Dionysus in Doubt* (1925), *Tristram* (1927)—a remarkable record which yet involves no thinning of the artist's power. *Collected Poems of Edwin Arlington Robinson* appeared in a five-volume edition in 1927. *Sonnets*, a collection of all of his poetry in this form, was published in 1928.

For all his widely accredited skill as technician, analyst, dramatist, and philosopher, Mr. Robinson cannot be called a popular poet. His intellectual subtleties are too hard for unthinking readers, and even the most perceptive will sometimes find him needlessly enigmatic. True, his ideas are difficult ones, but a supreme poet would rise above their difficulty and cast a sudden illumination over them. With this reservation, however, Mr. Robinson's work must take very high place in contemporary poetry on both sides of the Atlantic.

FOR A DEAD LADY

Edwin Arlington Robinson

No more with overflowing light
Shall fill the eyes that now are faded,
Nor shall another's fringe with night
Their woman-hidden world as they did.
No more shall quiver down the days
The flowing wonder of her ways,
Whereof no language may requite
The shifting and the many-shaded.

The grace, divine, definitive,
Clings only as a faint forestalling;
The laugh that love could not forgive
Is hushed, and answers to no calling;
The forehead and the little ears
Have gone where Saturn keeps the years;
The breast where roses could not live
Has done with rising and with falling.

The beauty, shattered by the laws
That have creation in their keeping,
No longer trembles at applause,
Or over children that are sleeping;
And we who delve in beauty's lore
Know all that we have known before
Of what inexorable cause
Makes Time so vicious in his reaping.

LUKE HAVERGAL

EDWIN ARLINGTON ROBINSON

Go to the western gate, Luke Havergal—
There where the vines cling crimson on the wall—
And in the twilight wait for what will come.
The wind will moan, the leaves will whisper some—
Whisper of her, and strike you as they fall;
But go, and if you trust her she will call.
Go to the western gate, Luke Havergal—
Luke Havergal.

No, there is not a dawn in eastern skies
To rift the fiery night that's in your eyes;
But there, where western glooms are gathering,
The dark will end the dark, if anything:
God slays himself with every leaf that flies,
And hell is more than half of paradise.
No, there is not a dawn in eastern skies—
In eastern skies.

Out of a grave I come to tell you this—
Out of a grave I come to quench the kiss
That flames upon your forehead with a glow
That blinds you to the way that you must go.
Yes, there is yet one way to where she is—
Bitter, but one that faith can never miss.
Out of a grave I come to tell you this—
To tell you this.

There is the western gate, Luke Havergal,
There are the crimson leaves upon the wall.
Go—for the winds are tearing them away—
Nor think to riddle the dead words they say,
Nor any more to feel them as they fall;
But go! and if you trust her she will call.
There is the western gate, Luke Havergal—
Luke Havergal.

THE POOR RELATION*

Edwin Arlington Robinson

No longer torn by what she knows
And sees within the eyes of others,
Her doubts are when the daylight goes,
Her fears are for the few she bothers.
She tells them it is wholly wrong
Of her to stay alive so long;
And when she smiles her forehead shows
A crinkle that had been her mother's.

Beneath her beauty, blanched with pain,
And wistful yet for being cheated,
A child would seem to ask again
A question many times repeated;
But no rebellion has betrayed
Her wonder at what she has paid
For memories that have no stain,
For triumph born to be defeated.

To those who come for what she was—
The few left who know where to find her—
She clings, for they are all she has;
And she may smile when they remind her,
As heretofore, of what they know
Of roses that are still to blow
By ways where not so much as grass
Remains of what she sees behind her.

They stay awhile, and having done
What penance or the past requires,
They go, and leave her there alone

*From *The Man against the Sky* by Edwin Arlington Robinson. Copyright 1916 by The
Macmillan Company. Reprinted by permission.

To count her chimneys and her spires.
Her lip shakes when they go away,
And yet she would not have them stay;
She knows as well as anyone
That Pity, having played, soon tires.

But one friend always reappears,
A good ghost, not to be forsaken;
Whereat she laughs and has no fears
Of what a ghost may reawaken,
But welcomes, while she wears and mends
The poor relation's odds and ends,
Her truant from a tomb of years—
Her power of youth so early taken.

Poor laugh, more slender than her song
It seems; and there are none to hear it
With even the stopped ears of the strong
For breaking heart or broken spirit.
The friends who clamored for her place,
And would have scratched her for her face,
Have lost her laughter for so long
That none would care enough to fear it.

None live who need fear anything
From her, whose losses are their pleasure;
The plover with a wounded wing
Stays not the flight that others measure;
So there she waits, and while she lives,
And death forgets, and faith forgives,
Her memories go foraging
For bits of childhood song they treasure.

And like a giant harp that hums
On always, and is always blending

The coming of what never comes
With what has passed and had an ending,
The City trembles, throbs, and pounds
Outside, and through a thousand sounds
The small intolerable drums
Of Time are like slow drops descending.

Bereft enough to shame a sage
And given little to long sighing,
With no illusion to assuage
The lonely changelessness of dying—
Unsought, unthought-of, and unheard,
She sings and watches like a bird,
Safe in a comfortable cage
From which there will be no more flying.

JAMES RORTY

James Rorty was born in 1890 at Middletown, New York, of Irish-Spanish and New England stock. He was graduated from Tufts College in 1913, since when he has crowded a variety of occupations into a few years: newspaper reporter, social worker, advertising copy writer, California rancher, editor of *New Masses*, choir singer, vaudeville artist, stretcher-bearer in France for two years, publicity man, "ghost writer" (one who writes speeches, articles, and books to bear another man's name as author), playwright, and play-adapter—surely here is a poet who should have much to say when he is ready to turn his experience to literary account. Except for the privately printed *What Michael Said to the Census Taker* (1923), his first book is *Children of the Sun* (1926). This volume contains rimed as well as free verse.

REMEMBERING THE MOUNTAINS*

JAMES RORTY

Remembering the mountains, I was still.
Will you be quiet, my friends—will you gather close, you who
strive so hard to do, and do?
See, I bring you gifts of silence, and cool snows,
I tell you of tall pines, erect and motionless, pointing at the sky.
I deal treacherously with your desires. I bleach your hearts.
I confront your troubled faces with the old faces of the rocks.
I give your strained ears only silence, and the zoom of the
nighthawk.
I take the greed of the merchant, the pride of the soldier, the
terror of the driven worker, and drop them one by one into
the lake.
Will you be quiet, my friends—will you gather close, you who
strive so hard to do, and do?
See, I bring you gifts of silence and cool snows.

*From *Children of the Sun* by James Rorty. Copyright 1926 by The Macmillan Company.
Reprinted by permission.

CARL SANDBURG

Carl Sandburg, the truest interpreter that the Middle West has yet had, was born at Galesburg, Illinois, on the edge of the prairies, in 1878. His parents were illiterate, hard-working, Swedish immigrants; there was in them the stamina of a vigorous peasant stock, and this they gave their son. His boyhood was hard, with little chance for schooling. At thirteen he was driving a milk wagon. In succession he held jobs as porter, brickyard laborer, scene shifter, pottery laborer. At seventeen he traveled westward into Kansas, worked in the harvest fields, washed dishes in Kansas City, Omaha, and Denver, sold stove polish, carpentered, painted houses; and finally he went back to Galesburg and the milk wagon—all this before he was twenty!

Service as a Spanish War volunteer left him with one hundred dollars, and he decided to go to college. In spite of the shortcomings in his academic preparation, he entered Lombard College, in his home town, and quickly displayed a maturity of character which made his presence felt in the college life. He was already a personality, even though he was doing janitor work to pay his way. When he left college he was no longer a mere healthy roustabout, but a thoughtful and purposeful man, eager to give expression to his restless ideas and sworn to the cause of the great undistinguished mass of common humanity above which he had risen. Newspaper work gave him his first opportunity, though all accounts are that he was too erratic to make a satisfactory reporter. For a while he turned advertising copy writer. Then he entered public affairs as organizer for the Social Democratic party of Wisconsin, as secretary to the mayor of Milwaukee, and as labor editor of the *Milwaukee Journal*.

His appearance as a poet was spectacular: in 1914 his poem "Chicago" received the Helen Haire Levinson prize for its startling originality. Perhaps it was not a wholly propitious introduction, for many readers never got beyond the first lines, never caught the picture of the city "with lifted head singing so proud to be alive . . . laughing with white teeth . . . as a young man laughs." For them Mr. Sandburg was the man who had written poetry about hog-butchering, and there was an end of him.

But those who have followed with understanding the many poems in his several volumes—*Chicago Poems* (1916), *Cornhuskers* (1918), *Smoke and Steel* (1920), *Slabs of the Sunburnt West* (1923), and *Good Morning, America* (1928)—know that there are two sides to his genius, and that one of them is no less tender and sensitive and lyrical than the other is tough and powerful and terribly realistic. At one time he is compelled by the ardor of his social indignation to write:

> When I, the People, learn to remember, when I,
> the People, use the lessons of yesterday and
> no longer forget who robbed me last year, who
> played me for a fool—then there will be no
> speaker in all the world say the name: "The
> People," with any fleck of a sneer in his voice
> or any far-off smile of derision.
> The mob—the crowd—the mass—will arrive then.

Or again, he is only describing things as they appear to him, in the only way that he can veraciously describe them:

> Omaha, the roughneck, feeds armies,
> Eats, and swears from a dirty face.
> Omaha works to get the world a breakfast.

But quite as often—more often, in fact, in his later work—Mr. Sandburg's indignation turns to pity:

> And then one day I got a true look at the Poor,
> millions of the Poor, patient and toiling; more
> patient than crags, tides, and stars; innumerable,
> patient as the darkness of night—and all
> broken, humble ruins of nations.

And the raw colors of reality are refined by the magic of his poet's vision:

> Under the harvest moon,
> When the soft silver
> Drips shimmering
> Over the garden nights . .

In *The Atlantic Monthly* for March, 1923, Mr. Sandburg published thirty-eight definitions of poetry. In them will be found plentiful support for those who maintain that he is a student of the elusive and intangible: "Poetry is an echo asking a shadow dancer to be a partner," or again, "Poetry is the report of a *nuance* between two moments, when people say, 'Listen!' and 'Did you see it? Did you hear it? What was it?'" Nor does he leave wholly out of account the other side of his artistic theory: "Poetry is the achievement of the synthesis of hyacinths and biscuits." To understand this cryptic definition one must be reminded of the Persian proverb, "If I had two loaves of bread I would sell one to buy white hyacinths to feed my soul"—to which Mr. Sandburg dryly adds, "But let us not forget the reverse of that. I have two baskets of white hyacinths, and I wish to God I could sell one and buy some bread." There is his poetic philosophy complete.

In *Rootabaga Stories* (1922) and *Rootabaga Pigeons* (1923), Mr. Sandburg has, according to Harry Hansen, "crystallized the whimsy, the fantasy, the quaint musings, of the child heart of a nation that has skyscrapers for its castles, policemen for captains, railroads for knightly cavalcades, prairies of waving corn, silver-blue lakes like blue porcelain breakfast plates—the magic that you can conjure up any day from your bedroom window."

Selected Poems was published in 1926, with an introduction by Rebecca West. In 1928, partly in recognition of Mr. Sandburg's half-poetical masterpiece of biography, *Abraham Lincoln: The Prairie Years* (1926), Knox College, in his native town, conferred upon him the degree of Doctor of Letters. In the same year there appeared *Good Morning, America*, a volume which illustrates all the qualities for which Mr. Sandburg's poetry is notable.

CHICAGO

Carl Sandburg

Hog Butcher for the World,
Tool Maker, Stacker of Wheat,
Player with Railroads, and the Nation's Freight
Handler;
Stormy, husky, brawling,
City of the Big Shoulders:

They tell me you are wicked and I believe them, for I have
seen your painted women under the gas lamps luring the
farm boys.
And they tell me you are crooked and I answer: Yes, it is true
I have seen the gunman kill and go free to kill again.
And they tell me you are brutal and my reply is: On the faces
of women and children I have seen the marks of wanton
hunger.
And having answered so, I turn once more to those who sneer
at this my city, and I give them back the sneer and say to
them:
Come and show me another city with lifted head singing so
proud to be alive and coarse and strong and cunning.
Flinging magnetic curses amid the toil of piling job on job,
here is a tall bold slugger set vivid against the little
soft cities;
Fierce as a dog with tongue lapping for action, cunning as a
savage pitted against the wilderness,
Bareheaded,
Shoveling,
Wrecking,
Planning,
Building, breaking, rebuilding.
Under the smoke, dust all over his mouth, laughing with white
teeth,

Under the terrible burden of destiny laughing as a young man
     laughs,
Laughing even as an ignorant fighter laughs who has never lost
     a battle,
Bragging and laughing that under his wrist is the pulse, and
     under his ribs the heart, of the people,
                         Laughing!
Laughing the stormy, husky, brawling laughter of Youth, half-
     naked, sweating, proud to be Hog Butcher, Tool Maker,
     Stacker of Wheat, Player with Railroads, and Freight
     Handler to the Nation.

FOUR PRELUDES ON PLAYTHINGS
OF THE WIND

"The Past Is a Bucket of Ashes."[1]

CARL SANDBURG

1

The woman named Tomorrow
sits with a hairpin in her teeth
and takes her time
And does her hair the way she wants it
and fastens at last the last braid and coil
and puts the hairpin where it belongs
and turns and drawls: Well, what of it?
My grandmother, Yesterday, is gone.
What of it? Let the dead be dead.

2

The doors were cedar
and the panels strips of gold
and the girls were golden girls
and the panels read and the girls chanted:

[1]From Mr. Sandburg's "Prairie."

We are the greatest city,
and the greatest nation:
nothing like us ever was.
The doors are twisted on broken hinges.
Sheets of rain swish through on the wind
    where the golden girls ran and the panels read:
    We are the greatest city,
    the greatest nation:
    nothing like us ever was.

3

It has happened before.
Strong men put up a city and got
    a nation together,
And paid singers to sing and women
    to warble: We are the greatest city,
        the greatest nation:
        nothing like us ever was.

And while the singers sang
and the strong men listened
and paid the singers well,
and felt good about it all,
    there were rats and lizards who listened
    . . .   and the only listeners left now
    . . .   are . . .   the rats . . .   and the lizards.

And there are black crows
crying, "Caw, caw,"
bringing mud and sticks
building a nest
over the words carved
on the doors where the panels were cedar
and the strips on the panels were gold
and the golden girls came singing:

We are the greatest city,
the greatest nation:
nothing like us ever was.

The only singers now are crows crying, "Caw, caw,"
And the sheets of rain whine in the wind and doorways.
And the only listeners now are . . . the rats . . . and the
lizards.

4

The feet of the rats
scribble on the door sills;
the hieroglyphs of the rat footprints
chatter the pedigrees of the rats
and babble of the blood
and gabble of the breed
of the grandfathers and the great-grandfathers
of the rats.

And the wind shifts
and the dust on a door sill shifts
and even the writing of the rat footprints
tells us nothing, nothing at all
about the greatest city, the greatest nation,
where the strong men listened
and the women warbled: Nothing like us ever was.

PRAYERS OF STEEL

Carl Sandburg

Lay me on an anvil, O God.
Beat me and hammer me into a crowbar.
Let me pry loose old walls.
Let me lift and loosen old foundations.

Lay me on an anvil, O God.
Beat me and hammer me into a steel spike.
Drive me into the girders that hold a skyscraper together.
Take red-hot rivets and fasten me into the central girders.
Let me be the great nail holding a skyscraper through blue
    nights into white stars.

From SLABS OF THE SUNBURNT WEST

CARL SANDBURG

Into the night, into the blanket of night,
Into the night rain gods, the night luck gods,
Overland goes the overland passenger train.

   Stand up, sandstone slabs of red,
Tell the overland passengers who burnt you.

Tell 'em how the jacks and screws loosened you.
Tell 'em who shook you by the heels and stood you on your
    heads,
Who put the slow pink of sunset mist on your faces.

Panels of the cold gray open night,
Gates of the Great American Desert,
   Skies keeping the prayers of the wagon men,
   The riders with picks, shovels, and guns,
On the old trail, the Santa Fe trail,[1] the Raton pass
Panels, skies, gates, listen tonight while we send up our prayers
    on the Santa Fe trail.

          (A colossal bastard frog
           squats in stone.

---

[1]*Santa Fe trail*, the route followed by early traders between St. Louis, Missouri, and Mexico; Santa Fe, New Mexico, was the main station on this route. *Raton Pass*, a point on the Santa Fe trail just south of the Colorado-New Mexico border.

Once he squawked.
Then he was frozen and
shut up forever.)

Into the night the overland passenger train,
Slabs of sandstone red sink to the sunset red,
Blankets of night cover 'em up.
Night rain gods, night luck gods, are looking on.

March on, processions.
Tie your hat to the saddle and ride, O Rider.
Let your ponies drag their navels in the sand.
Go hungry; leave your bones in the desert sand.
When the desert takes you the wind is clean.
The winds say so on a noisy night.

The fingerbone of a man
lay next to the handle of a frying pan
and the footbone of a horse.
"Clean, we are clean," the winds whimper on a noisy night.

Into the night the overland passenger train,
And the engineer with an eye for signal lights,
And the porters making up berths for passengers,
And the boys in the diner locking the icebox—
And six men with cigars in the buffet car mention
    "civilization," "history," "God."

Into the blanket of night goes the overland train,
Into the black of the night the processions march,
    The ghost of a pony goes by,
    A hat tied to the saddle,
    The wagon tongue of a prairie schooner
    And the handle of a Forty-niner's pickax
    Do a shiver dance in the desert dust,

In the coyote gray of the alkali dust.
And—six men with cigars in the buffet car mention
  "civilization," "history," "God."

Sleep, O wonderful hungry people.
Take a shut-eye, take a long old snooze,
  and be good to yourselves;
Into the night the overland passenger train
And the sleepers cleared for a morning sun
  and the Grand Canyon of Arizona.

From THE WINDY CITY

Carl Sandburg

Winds of the Windy City, come out of the prairie,
  all the way from Medicine Hat.
Come out of the inland sea-blue water, come where they
  nickname a city for you.

Corn wind in the fall, come off the black lands,
  come off the whisper of the silk hangers,
  the lap of the flat spear leaves.

Blue-water wind in summer, come off the blue miles
  of lake, carry your inland sea-blue fingers,
  carry us cool, carry your blue to our homes.

White spring winds, come off the bag-wool clouds,
  come off the running melted snow, come white
  as the arms of snow-born children.

Gray fighting winter winds, come along on the tearing
  blizzard tails, the snouts of the hungry
  hunting storms, come fighting gray in winter.

Winds of the Windy City,
Winds of corn and sea blue,
Spring wind white and fighting winter gray,
Come home here—they nickname a city for you.

The wind of the lake shore waits and wanders.
The heave of the shore wind hunches the sand piles.
The winkers of the morning stars count out cities
And forget the numbers.

LEW SARETT

With the possible exception of Carl Sandburg, no living American poet has had a more varied life than Lew Sarett or has built the structure of his creative talents more completely upon his own experiences and contacts. If it be true that discouragement and hardship are fruitful influences in the making of a poet, Mr. Sarett could hardly have escaped his calling. Born in Chicago in 1888 of immigrant parents, one French, the other of Lithuanian and Polish descent, he spent his early childhood in Marquette, Michigan, in the Lake Superior region, where he acquired the love of outdoor life and the appreciation of its beauty that became the directing passion of his life and writing.

But when he returned to Chicago at twelve years of age, family misfortunes forced upon him the support of himself and his mother, and years of poverty amid sordid surroundings followed. His education began with night classes at Hull House; with the return of his family to Michigan he progressed to high school and college. From Beloit College he went to Harvard University and then to the University of Illinois, where he received a law degree in 1916. He remained at the University of Illinois as a teacher until 1920, when he went to the Cumnock School of Oratory at Northwestern University.

However, his formal education played only a slight part in the development of the poet. In order to earn his way through school, Mr. Sarett worked in summer camps, becoming a guide, a woodsman, a United States Forest Ranger, and a friend and companion of Indians in the Rockies and the Canadian woods. His understanding of the truly religious nature of the Indians made him long to interpret it to the white man. In 1920 this desire took the form of a book of poems of the wilderness, *Many, Many Moons*. The following year he was awarded, by *Poetry*, the Helen Haire Levinson Prize for "The Box of God," a deeply religious—and pagan—poem lamenting the conversion of an Indian to Christianity.

The Box of God became the title of another volume of poems published in 1922, a book full of Indian sounds and songs. In *Slow Smoke* (1925) Mr. Sarett expresses his deep pity for the wild and hunted animals of the woods.

Mr. Sarett now spends but half of the college year in teaching and lecturing, reading from his poems. The rest of the time he lives in the North Woods of Wisconsin.

TO A WILD GOOSE OVER DECOYS

Lew Sarett

O lonely trumpeter, coasting down the sky,
Like a winter leaf blown from the bur-oak tree
By whipping winds, and flapping silverly
Against the sun—I know your lonely cry.

I know the worn wild heart that bends your flight
And circles you above this beckoning lake,
Eager of neck, to find the honking drake
Who speaks of reedy refuge for the night.

I know the sudden rapture that you fling
In answer to our friendly gander's call—
Halloo! Beware decoys!—or you will fall
With a silver bullet whistling in your wing!

Beat on your weary flight across the blue!
Beware, O traveler, of our gabbling geese!
Beware this weedy counterfeit of peace!—
Oh, I was once a passing bird like you.

FOUR LITTLE FOXES

Lew Sarett

Speak gently, Spring, and make no sudden sound;
For in my windy valley, yesterday, I found
New-born foxes squirming on the ground—
            Speak gently.

Walk softly, March, forbear the bitter blow;
Her feet within a trap, her blood upon the snow,
The four little foxes saw their mother go—
            Walk softly.

Go lightly, Spring, oh, give them no alarm;
When I covered them with boughs to shelter them from harm,
The thin blue foxes suckled at my arm—
          Go lightly.

Step softly, March, with your rampant hurricane;
Nuzzling one another, and whimpering with pain,
The new little foxes are shivering in the rain—
          Step softly.

I HAVE A RENDEZVOUS WITH DEATH

ALAN SEEGER

I have a rendezvous with Death
At some disputed barricade,
When Spring comes back with rustling shade
And apple blossoms fill the air.
I have a rendezvous with Death

ALAN SEEGER

Alan Seeger was born in New York City in 1888, and lived during his boyhood on Staten Island. A little later his family took him to Mexico, and the exotic richness of that country is reflected in his earlier verse. He attended the Horace Mann School, New York, and was graduated from Harvard University in 1910. In 1913 he went to Paris to follow a literary career. There he found himself when the World War broke in August, 1914; before the end of the month he had enlisted in the Foreign Legion. He served constantly and with gallantry on several fronts for almost two years, and fell in action on July 4, 1916.

Unlike some of the British "soldier poets" Seeger wrote little during his military life. His preparation for poetry was romantic, and he must have realized that it was inadequate to the grim subject of war. One fine and unforgetable poem, however, was struck out from his experience. Although his book, *Poems* (1916), contains no other equal to this one poem, "I Have a Rendezvous with Death" is sufficient to insure that Seeger will be remembered.

but I've a rendezvous with Death

I HAVE A RENDEZVOUS WITH DEATH

Alan Seeger

I have a rendezvous with Death
At some disputed barricade,
When Spring comes back with rustling shade
And apple blossoms fill the air—
I have a rendezvous with Death
When Spring brings back blue days and fair.

It may be he shall take my hand
And lead me into his dark land
And close my eyes and quench my breath—
It may be I shall pass him still.
I have a rendezvous with Death
On some scarred slope of battered hill,
When Spring comes round again this year,
And the first meadow flowers appear.

God knows 'twere better to be deep
Pillowed in silk and scented down,
Where love throbs out in blissful sleep,
Pulse nigh to pulse, and breath to breath,
Where hushed awakenings are dear . . .
But I've a rendezvous with Death
At midnight in some flaming town,
When Spring trips north again this year;
And I to my pledged word am true,
I shall not fail that rendezvous.

FRANCES SHAW

Frances (Wells) Shaw (Mrs. Howard V. Shaw) was born in Chicago, Illinois, in 1872, of New England parentage. She studied at the Dearborn Seminary, Chicago, and at the Farmington School in Connecticut. Extensive foreign travel has added to her store of experiences. Her published volumes are entitled *Ragdale Book of Verse* (1911) and *Songs of a Baby's Day* (1917, revised 1928); a collection of later verse will be published as *Who Loves the Rain*, the title poem, reprinted here, being her best known. Suggestive of contentment and an untroubled spirit, this poem gives one much the same sense of peace as does the Twenty-third Psalm.

WHO LOVES THE RAIN

Frances Shaw

Who loves the rain,
And loves his home,
And looks on life with quiet eyes,
Him will I follow through the storm;
And at his hearth-fire keep me warm;
Nor hell nor heaven shall that soul surprise,
Who loves the rain,
And loves his home,
And looks on life with quiet eyes.

WILBERT SNOW

Wilbert Snow is a native of the state which furnishes the *locale* for most of his poems—Maine. More accurately speaking, the setting for his poetry is formed by the rocky inlets and picturesque islands of the Maine shoreline, which he knew as a youth and has remembered in his poetic maturity. *Maine Coast* (1923) and *The Inner Harbor* (1926) exploit this comparatively untouched field. Like Robert Frost, he understands the advantage of working intensively the ground which he knows best. In style he has caught, too, something of the calculated informality of Mr. Frost.

Mr. Snow was a student at Bowdoin College and Columbia University. He has followed many and strangely various callings: lobsterman, book agent, district-school teacher, Eskimo and Reindeer Agent for the Department of the Interior in Alaska, artillery officer in the World War, and college instructor in English. He is at present connected with Wesleyan University, Middletown, Connecticut.

"Taking away the Banking" describes an annual rite which only those who have wintered in a snug farmhouse can fully appreciate.

TAKING AWAY THE BANKING

Wilbert Snow

When March winds carried prophecies of June,
And gray days were no longer winter-killed,
We all went out and worked till afternoon
To take the spruce-limb banking off, and filled
The air with shouts, heaping what soon would be
A bonfire blazing by the willow tree.

We tugged at big ends of the bottom brush,
The small ends as reluctant to let go
As winter was himself, although the rush
Of warmth, once started, was an overflow
Of sunny days, bluebirds, and brooklets racing
Like children from worn mothers, tired of chasing.

We found that spring already underneath
Had started on his work, the light-brown grasses
Were flaunting spots of green, the little teeth
Of mice and snouts of worms had chiseled passes—
Worms we sent wriggling as a tempting cud
For hungry flounders coming out of mud.

Oh, there were ugly days enough to come,
With rain and sleet and April fluffs of snow,
Big winds that moaned and made the wires hum,
And neighbors calling out, "We told you so";
But looking on it now I think the days
We coaxed the spring along, and felt the rays

Of March intensify the balsam smell
In those green boughs, and saw the underpinning
Exposed once more, and children run pell-mell
To hunt for crocuses, set fancies spinning
More rapidly than blooming hours of May
When all the hills of God kept holiday.

GEORGE STERLING

Born in Sag Harbor, New York, in 1869, and a student in St. Charles College, Maryland, George Sterling moved to the Pacific Coast when he was twenty-six, and lived there until his death in 1926. His work was very popular among Californians and he was generally regarded as the state poet. Removed from frequent contact with any considerable group of fellow poets, he wrote independently of modernist schools, satisfying himself with a classical style which too frequently became merely rhetorical. To some extent he outgrew his fondness for ornament, and his later poetry is his simplest and best. Such a poem as "The Last Days" may have been the outgrowth of his natural development, but it has many of the qualities of the so-called "new poetry." Sterling's first book, *The Testimony of the Suns* (1903), was followed by ten more volumes, the best of his work having been gathered in *Selected Poems* (1923).

THE LAST DAYS

George Sterling

The russet leaves of the sycamore
Lie at last on the valley floor—
By the autumn wind swept to and fro
Like ghosts in a tale of long ago.
Shallow and clear the Carmel glides
Where the willows droop on its vine-walled sides.

The bracken-rust is red on the hill;
The pines stand brooding, somber and still;
Gray are the cliffs, and the waters gray,
Where the sea gulls dip to the sea-born spray.
Sad November, lady of rain,
Sends the goose-wedge over again.

Wilder now, for the verdure's birth,
Falls the sunlight over the earth;
Kildees call from the fields where now
The banding blackbirds follow the plow;
Rustling poplar and brittle weed
Whisper low to the river-reed.

Days departing linger and sigh:
Stars come soon to the quiet sky;
Buried voices, intimate, strange,
Cry to body and soul of change;
Beauty, eternal fugitive,
Seeks the home that we cannot give.

SARA TEASDALE

Sara Teasdale (Mrs. Ernst B. Filsinger) was born in St. Louis, Missouri, in 1884. Her education was gained in private schools and in European travel. Since 1916 she has lived in New York City. Her important books are *Rivers to the Sea* (1915), *Love Songs* (1917), *Flame and Shadow* (1920), and *Dark of the Moon* (1926). While the reader will note in these books a steady maturing of the poet's powers, the substance of all four is much the same. The love declarations of men have been the familiar subject of poets through all generations, but the answering song of the beloved has but rarely made itself heard. The fragments of Sappho and Elizabeth Barrett Browning's *Sonnets from the Portuguese* immediately come to mind. Miss Teasdale's poems, though less robust, are of this company.

We must grant that a poet should know, better than anyone else, the limitations of her interest, and if Miss Teasdale has largely confined her exquisite talents to a somewhat narrow field, we can still find ample offering of beauty in what she has given us. The earlier poems are marked by a Venetian glass fragility, a hesitancy to explore the deeper and darker places of the heart. Miss Teasdale's pen hints of passion as lightly as the moth's wing brushes the rose. Indeed she writes, in these earlier poems, of romance rather than love; and a quick dexterity sometimes interferes with her sincerity. In the succeeding years her poems take on greater depth: the tone is more thoughtful, the mood occasionally somber.

Always, whether she follows the classical manner or experiments with the newer forms of verse, Miss Teasdale is a conscientious and impeccable artist. Her verse is polished without being self-conscious, technically flawless without suffering detraction from its easy grace. Her mastery of verse-forms will repay careful study.

The question of who is the leading woman lyricist in America today can be answered only by a choice between Miss Teasdale and Miss Millay. It is a choice which must be governed largely by personal taste.

SPRING NIGHT*

Sara Teasdale

The park is filled with night and fog,
    The veils are drawn about the world,
The drowsy lights along the paths
    Are dim and pearled.

Gold and gleaming the empty streets,
    Gold and gleaming the misty lake;
The mirrored lights, like sunken swords,
    Glimmer and shake.

Oh, is it not enough to be
Here with this beauty over me?
My throat should ache with praise, and I
Should kneel in joy beneath the sky.
Oh, beauty, are you not enough?
Why am I crying after love
With youth, a singing voice, and eyes
To take earth's wonder with surprise?
Why have I put off my pride,
Why am I unsatisfied—
I, for whom the pensive night
Binds her cloudy hair with light—
I, for whom all beauty burns
Like incense in a million urns?
Oh, beauty, are you not enough?
Why am I crying after love?

EUNICE TIETJENS

Eunice (Hammond) Tietjens was born in Chicago in 1884; she was educated in Europe. In 1904 she married Paul Tietjens. She is now the wife of Cloyd Head, but continues to write under the name of her first husband. She was an associate editor of *Poetry: A Magazine of Verse* during its early days, went to France as war correspondent for the *Chicago Daily News*, and traveled extensively in the interior of China. *Profiles from China* (1917), born of the last-named experience, contains lively pictures of Oriental life as it came under her keen observation, rendered most readable by a successful free-verse style. *Body and Raiment* (1919) and *Profiles from Home* (1925) concern more familiar themes and are less notable in their handling of free verse.

THE SHOP[1]

EUNICE TIETJENS

The master of the shop is a pious man, in good odor with the
    priests.
He is old and honorable, and his white mustache droops below
    his chin.
Mencius[2], I think, looked so.

The shop behind him is a mimic world, a world of pieties and
    shams—the valley of remembrance—the dwelling-place of
    the unquiet dead.
Here on his shelves are ranged the splendor and the panoply
    of life—silk in smooth gleaming rolls, silver in ingots, carv-
    ing and embroidery and jade, a scarlet bearer-chair, a pipe
    for opium . . .
Whatever life has need of, it is here,
And it is for the dead.

Whatever life has need of, it is here. Yet it is here in sham, in
    effigy, in tortured compromise.
The dead have need of silk. Yet silk is dear, and there are living
    backs to clothe.
The rolls are paper . . . Do not look too close.
The dead, I think, will understand.
The carvings, too, the bearer-chair, the jade—yes, they are
    paper; and the shining ingots, they are tinsel.
Yet they are made with skill and loving care!
And if the priest knows—surely he must know!—when they
    are burned they'll serve the dead as well as verities,
So living mouths can feed.

[1] The articles sold here are to be burned at funerals for the use of the dead in the spirit world.
(Author's note.)
[2] *Mencius* (died 289 B.C.), the Latinized form of Mang-tsze, the name of a Chinese moral
teacher esteemed second only to Confucius.

The master of the shop is a pious man. He has attained much
  honor, and his white mustache droops below his chin.
"Such an one," he said, "I burned for my own father. And
  such an one my son will burn for me. For I am old, and
  half my life already dwells among the dead."

And, as he speaks, behind him in the shop I feel the presence of
  a hovering host, the myriads of the immortal dead, the
  rulers of the spirit in this land. . . .
For in this kingdom of the dead they who are living cling with
  fevered hands to the torn fringes of the mighty past.
  And if they fail a little, compromise. . . .

The dead, I think, will understand.

RIDGELY TORRENCE

(Frederic) Ridgely Torrence was born in Xenia, Ohio, in 1875. After preparation under private tutors he attended Miami and Princeton Universities. Between 1897 and 1903 he was successively librarian of the Astor Library and the Lenox Library, New York. He has since held editorial positions on the *Cosmopolitan Magazine* and *The New Republic*. As an author Mr. Torrence is known in two fields, the drama and the lyric. He has published three volumes of plays, the best known being his group of plays for a negro theater: *Granny Maumee*, *The Rider of Dreams*, and *Simon the Cyrenian* (1917).

In *Hesperides* (1925) Mr. Torrence has put the lyrics of twenty-five years' writing into a small volume of even distinction. In a period when much triviality finds its way into verse, Mr. Torrence chooses only important themes. His clear perception of the tragic undercurrents of life receives a nobility of treatment in which the spiritual quality is conspicuous. His method is shown at its best in his "Eye-Witness," a poem too long for reproduction here. "The Son" illustrates, in highly compressed form, the same ability to uncover depths of experience. A close study of these few lines will show that they describe the bitter frustration of a lifetime.

THE SON*

(Southern Ohio Market Town)

RIDGELY TORRENCE

I heard an old farm-wife,
Selling some barley,
Mingle her life with life
And the name "Charley."

Saying: "The crop's all in,
We're about through now;
Long nights will soon begin,
We're just us two now.

"Twelve bushels at sixty cents,
It's all I carried—
He sickened making fence;
He was to be married—

"It feels like frost was near—
His hair was curly.
The spring was late that year,
But the harvest early."

---

*From *Hesperides* by Ridgely Torrence. Copyright 1925 by The Macmillan Company.
Reprinted by permission.

CHARLES HANSON TOWNE

Charles Hanson Towne was born in Louisville, Kentucky, in 1877. He was educated privately and at the College of the City of New York. His work as writer and magazine editor has caused him to make his home in New York. His most important volumes of poetry are *The Quiet Singer* (1908), *Manhattan* (1909), and *Beyond the Stars and Other Poems* (1912). The dignity and sobriety which mark his work are seen at their best in "Manhattan," a poem which also illustrates his conservative preference in style.

MANHATTAN—XI

CHARLES HANSON TOWNE

Man's greatest miracle is accomplished here.
Steeple and dome he hurls high in the air,
Until, like dreams in marble and in stone,
They lift their wonder to a world amazed.

Behind the poem is the poet's soul;
Behind the canvas throbs the artist's heart;
Behind all music lie unfathomed tones
Known only dimly to one Master mind.
So here, when visions of new beauty rise,
Behind them float the dreams of cities old,
Fallen now to silence, with the dust of kings.
Who wrought these granite ghosts, saw more than we
May ever see. He saw pale, tenuous lines
On some age-mellowed shore where cities rose
Proudly as Corinth or imperial Rome;
He saw, through mists of vision, Bagdad leap
To immaterial being, and he sought
To snatch one curve from her elusive domes;
He saw lost Nineveh, and Babylon,
And Tyre, and all the golden dreams of Greece,
Columns and fanes that cannot be rebuilt,
Ev'n as Shakespearian lines can never sing
Again on any poet's resplendent page.
But the vague Source of these most lovely things
Was his for one high instant; and he caught
Their spirit and their glory for all time.
These are the shadows of far nobler walls,
The wraiths of ancient pomp and glittering days,
Set here by master minds and master souls,
Almost as wonderful as mountains are,
Mysterious as the petals of a flower.

JEAN STARR UNTERMEYER

Jean Starr Untermeyer was born in 1886, at Zanesville, Ohio. After attending the Putnam Seminary in Zanesville she went at the age of sixteen to New York City, where she did some work at Columbia University. She is the wife of Louis Untermeyer, poet and anthologist. Her first book, *Growing Pains* (1918), was the product of extremely careful and self-critical writing over a period of eight years. *Dreams Out of Darkness* (1921) and *Steep Ascent* (1927) maintain the same standards of perfection; in contrast to the earlier volume, they are examples almost entirely of conventional forms of verse. She maintains, even in moods of deep emotion, a characteristic austerity and intellectuality. This is apparent in "Clay Hills" and "Sinfonia Domestica," the poems reprinted here, which reveal intensity of feeling beneath precise and well-considered modes of expression.

CLAY HILLS*

Jean Starr Untermeyer

It is easy to mold the yielding clay.
And many shapes grow into beauty
Under the facile hand.
But forms of clay are lightly broken;
They will lie shattered and forgotten in a dingy corner.

Yet underneath the slipping clay
Is rock . . .
I would rather work in stubborn rock
All the years of my life,
And make one strong thing
And set it in a high, clean place,
To recall the granite strength of my desire.

SINFONIA DOMESTICA†

Jean Starr Untermeyer

When the white wave of a glory that is hardly I
    Breaks through my mind and washes it clean,
I know at last the meaning of my ecstasy,
    And know at last my wish and what it can mean.

To have sped out of life that night—to have vanished
    Not as a vision, but as something touched, yet grown
Radiant as moonlight, circling my naked shoulder;
    Wrapped in a dream of beauty, longed for, but never known!

*From *Growing Pains* by Jean Starr Untermeyer. Copyright 1918 by B. W. Huebsch, Inc.
New York: The Viking Press, Inc.
    †From *Dreams out of Darkness* by Jean Starr Untermeyer. Copyright 1921 by B. W. Huebsch,
Inc. New York: The Viking Press, Inc.

For how with our daily converse, even the sweet sharing
   Of thoughts, of food, of home, of common life,
How shall I be that glory, that last desire,
   For which men struggle? Is Romance a wife?

Must I bend a heart that is bowed to breaking
   With a frustration, inevitable and slow,
And bank my flame to a low hearth-fire, believing
   You'll come for warmth and life to its tempered glow?

Shall I mold my hope anew, to one of service,
   And tell my uneasy soul "Behold, this is good,"
And meet you (if we do meet) even at heaven's threshold
   With ewer and basin, with clothing, and with food?

LOUIS UNTERMEYER

Louis Untermeyer was born in New York City in 1885. He attended the DeWitt Clinton High School without graduating and, in his own words, "boasts that he is the least educated writer in America." Formal education he evidently did not need, for he has reached his present distinction as poet, critic, and editor without college training and in spite of twenty years devoted to business. At seventeen he went into his father's jewelry factory in Newark; he was successively designer, factory manager, and vice-president. In 1923 he resigned his connection with the firm to devote his whole time to writing and study.

Challenge (1914) is his first considerable book of verse. Here there is sometimes more power than felicity, the author's social indignations driving him to write poetry which in style seems unnecessarily strident, though in thought it expresses a courageous protest. Through his succeeding volumes, *These Times* (1917), *The New Adam* (1920), *Roast Leviathan* (1923), and *Burning Bush* (1928), there is evident a steadily bettering fusion of matter and technique, resulting, especially in the last three volumes, in a body of poetry at once graceful and significant. The note of protest is not missing, but it has become subtler and more persuasive. An important item in these later poems is Mr. Untermeyer's wholesome pride in his racial heritage; he is a defender of the Jew in the modern world.

As parodist, Mr. Untermeyer has contributed to the gayety of life, as well as to the exposure of his victims, in four volumes, later gathered into *Collected Parodies* (1926). Here his metrical cleverness, united with his critical acumen, has fashioned the laughable counterfeits of many poets both ancient and contemporary.

Among the other products of a busy career are translations— *Poems of Heinrich Heine* (1917); literary criticism—*American Poetry Since 1900* (1923); and anthologies—*Modern American Poetry* and *Modern British Poetry* (revised 1925) and *This Singing World* (1923).

PORTRAIT OF A MACHINE

Louis Untermeyer

What nudity is beautiful as this
Obedient monster purring at its toil;
These naked iron muscles dripping oil
And the sure-fingered rods that never miss.
This long and shining flank of metal is
Magic that greasy labor cannot spoil;
While this vast engine that could rend the soil
Conceals its fury with a gentle hiss.

It does not vent its loathing, does not turn
Upon its makers with destroying hate.
It bears a deeper malice; lives to earn
Its master's bread and laughs to see this great
Lord of the earth, who rules but cannot learn,
Become the slave of what his slaves create.

REBELS

Louis Untermeyer

Stiff in midsummer green, the stolid hillsides
    March with their trees, dependable and stanch,
Except where here and there a lawless maple
    Thrusts to the sky one red, rebellious branch.

You see them standing out, these frank insurgents,
    With that defiant and arresting plume;
Scattered, they toss the flame like some old signal,
    Calling their comrades to a brilliant doom.

What can it mean—this strange, untimely challenge;
    This proclamation of an early death?

Are they so tired of earth they fly the banner
  Of dissolution or a bleeding faith?

Rebellious or resigned, they flaunt their color;
  A sudden torch, a burning battle-cry.
"Light up the world," they wave to all the others,
  "Swiftly we live, and splendidly we die."

ROBERT FROST RELATES

"THE DEATH OF THE TIRED MAN"[1]

Louis Untermeyer

There were two of us left in the berry patch;
Bryan O'Lin and Jack had gone to Norwich.—
They called him Jack a' Nory, half in fun
And half because it seemed to anger him.
So there we stood and let the berries go,
Talking of men we knew and had forgotten.
A sprawling, humpbacked mountain frowned on us
And blotted out a smoldering sunset cloud
That broke in fiery ashes. "Well," he said,
"Old Adam Brown is dead and gone; you'll never
See him any more. He used to wear
A long brown coat that buttoned down before.
That's all I ever knew of him; I guess that's all
That anyone remembers. Eh?" he said,
And then, without a pause to let me answer,
He went right on.
            "How about Dr. Foster?"
"Well, how *about* him?" I managed to reply.
He glared at me for having interrupted.

---

[1] See "The Death of the Hired Man," Robert Frost. Under the heading of "The Modern Nursery" Mr. Untermeyer executes a "drastic revision" of the Mother Goose rimes in the manners of certain modern poets.

And stopped to pick his words before he spoke,
Like one who turns all personal remarks
Into a general survey of the world.
Choosing his phrases with a finicky care
So they might fit some vague opinions,
Taken, third-hand, from last year's *New York Times*
And jumbled all together into a thing
He thought was his philosophy.
                    "Never mind;
There's more in Foster than you'd understand.
But," he continued, darkly as before,
"What do you make of Solomon Grundy's case?
You know the gossip when he first came here.
Folks said he'd gone to smash in Lunenburg,
And four years in the State Asylum there
Had almost finished him. It was Sanders' job
That put new life in him. A clear, cool day;
The second Monday in July it was.
'Born on a Monday,' that is what they said.
Remember the next few days? I guess you don't.
That was before your time. Well, Tuesday night
He said he'd go to church; and just before the prayer
He blurts right out, 'I've come here to get christened.
If I am going to have a brand-new life
I'll have a new name, too.' Well, sure enough,
They christened him, though I've forgotten what;
And Etta Stark (you know, the pastor's girl),
Her head upset by what she called romance,
She went and married him on Wednesday noon.
Thursday the sun or something in the air
Got in his blood and right off he took sick.
Friday the thing got worse, and so did he;
And Saturday at four o'clock he died.
Buried on Sunday with the town decked out
As if it was a circus-day. And not a soul

Knew why they went or what he meant to them
Or what he died of. What would be *your* guess?"

"Well," I replied, "it seems to me that he,
Just coming from a sedentary life,
Felt a great wave of energy released,
And tried to crowd too much in one short week.
The laws of physics teach—"

"No, not at all.
He never knew 'em. He was just tired," he said.

MARK VAN DOREN

Mark Van Doren was born at Hope, Illinois, in 1894. He attended the University of Illinois and Columbia University and became a teacher of English in the latter institution. As literary editor of *The Nation* he has held one of the most responsible positions in American literary criticism. His poetry has been published under the title *Spring Thunder and Other Poems* (1924). "Marriage" presents an interesting contrast to "Sinfonia Domestica," a poem on the same subject. See page 301. Mrs. Untermeyer finds only frustrated ecstasy in the "low hearth-fire" of domestic life; Mr. Van Doren foregoes romantic adventure for the assured peace of the commonplace.

MARRIAGE

Mark Van Doren

No wandering any more where the feet stumble
Upon a sudden rise, or sink in deep
Marsh grasses. No uncertain following on
With nothing there to follow—a sure bird,
A fence, a farmhouse. No adventuring now
Where motion that is yet not motion dies.
Circles have lost their magic, and the voice
Comes back upon itself . . . The road is firm.
It runs, and the dust is not too deep, and the end
Never can heave in sight—though one is there.
It runs in a straight silence, and evening falls
At an expected inn, whose barest room
Cannot be lonely if a hand is reached
To touch another hand, the walls forgotten. . . .
Morning is laughter, and the road resumes. . . .
Adventurous, it never will return.

JOHN V. A. WEAVER

There is little in the early life and education of John Van Alstyne Weaver to explain his choice of the lives of common people as the stuff out of which to make his poetry. He was born in Charlotte, North Carolina, in 1893, and received his preparatory education in Chicago. After graduation from Hamilton College he went for further study to Harvard University and Columbia University. Until the World War he was on the staff of the *Chicago Daily News*, and after several years of army service went to live in New York City. He later became literary editor of the *Brooklyn Daily Eagle*, resigning in 1924 to give all his time to writing.

He has published four volumes of verse: *In American* (1921), *Finders* (1923), *More in American* (1926), and *To Youth* (1928). Like Orrick Johns and other experimenters he has adopted the American vernacular as the language of much of his poetry, but with greater success. He seldom allows the superficial matter of diction to obscure the genuinely poetic impulse at the heart of his writing. "Legend" is a good example of his skill in giving voice to the sensitive but inarticulate imaginings of the uneducated man. Only the narrowest definition would deny this the title of poetry, for the emotion clearly rises above the mere words. In his longer narrative poems, Mr. Weaver is always energetic and dramatic, more often serious than humorous, occasionally sentimental, with always a fine understanding of the workingman and working woman and their tragic limitations.

LEGEND

JOHN V. A. WEAVER

I wonder where it could of went to;
   I know I seen it just as plain:
A beautiful, big fairy city
   Shinin' through the rain.

Rain it was, not snow—in winter!
   Special-order April weather
Ticklin' at our two faces
   Pressed up close together.

Not a single soul was near us
   Standin' out there on the bow;
When we passed another ferry
   He says, sudden, "Now!"

Then I looked where he was pointin'. . . .
   I seen a magic city rise. . . .
Gleamin' windows, like when fields is
   Full of fireflies.

Towers and palaces in the clouds, like,
   Real as real, but nice and blurred.
"Oh!"—I starts in—but he wispers
   "Hush! Don't say a word!

"Don't look long, and don't ast questions,
   Elset you make the fairies sore.
They won't let you even see it
   Never any more.

"Don't you try to ever go there—
 It's to dream of, not to find.
Lovely things like that is always
 Mostly in your mind."

Somethin' made me say, "It's Jersey!" . . .
 Somethin' mean. . . . He hollers, "Hell!
Now you done it, sure as shootin',
 Now you bust the spell!"

Sure enough, the towers and castles
 Went like lightnin' out of sight. . . .
Nothin' there but filthy Jersey
 On a drizzly night.

TO YOUTH

John V. A. Weaver

This I say to you.
Be arrogant! Be true!
True to April lust that sings
Through your veins. These sharp springs
Matter most . . . Afteryears
Will be time enough for sleep . . .
Carefulness . . . and tears.

Now, while life is raw and new,
Drink it clear, drink it deep!
Let the moonlight's lunacy
Tear away your cautions. Be
Proud, and mad, and young, and free!
Grasp a comet! Kick at stars
Laughingly! Fight! Dare!

Arms are soft, breasts are white,
Magic's in the April night—
Never fear.   Age will catch you,
Slow you down, ere it dispatch you
To your long and solemn quiet . . .

What will matter then the riot
Of the lilacs in the wind?
What will mean—then—the crush
Of lips at hours when birds hush?

Purple, green, and flame will end
In a calm, gray blend.
Only . . . graven in your soul
After all the rest is gone
There will be the ecstasies . . .
Those alone . . .

MARIE DE L. WELCH

San Francisco and Paris have played nearly equal parts in the development of Marie de Laveaga Welch. Born in San Francisco in 1905 of parents who had been born there, too, and brought up in a house overlooking the Golden Gate, Miss Welch comes naturally enough by a passionate love of her native city. Her grandparents went to California, about 1870, from France, Spain, and Scotland. A considerable portion of her life has been spent in Paris. Her education began at home, where she and her sister "pleasantly frayed a long string of governesses." High school in San Francisco was followed by college, where she went expecting "to learn philosophy and how to write short stories, and not learning," and where she edited a literary magazine "that died the usual pauper's death."

Miss Welch's poetry has appeared in *Poetry*, *The Nation*, and other magazines. It is characterized by a candor of thought and a sincerity of feeling which demand a clear and forthright expression. Hence the pretty-artificial finds no place in Miss Welch's work; mere sensuousness yields to a reflective intelligence and a just emotion. The product is strong and sweet and firm.

SHE NEVER FOUND COMFORT

MARIE DE L. WELCH

She never found comfort
When a friend told her
To weep her pain away,
And offered a shoulder;

But a thin tan lizard
Lying on a boulder,
Indifferent and delicate,
Greatly consoled her.

ONLY THIS COUNSEL

MARIE DE L. WELCH

Save your wisdom, since your friend,
In love and hunger, thought and pain
Will too easily attain
Wisdom himself, and at the end
When his heart and hands and eyes
Are very tired, he will need
A comrade who is wise indeed
To comfort him for being wise.

FOR A FALLEN STAR

MARIE DE L. WELCH

Learn, dark-hearted,
Lost lover, learn
How surely the moon
And the stars burn,

Though the heart's light
Is dimmed and gone
That once was brighter
Than stars or moon.

Learn, lover, how little
To moon and star
The fine fires
Of the heart are,
How little is touched
By the heart's light
The cold and shining
Heart of night.

JOHN HALL WHEELOCK

John Hall Wheelock was born at Far Rockaway, Long Island, New York. He was graduated from Harvard University and afterwards studied at the Universities of Göttingen and Berlin. His first book, *The Human Fantasy* (1911), bears the stamp of a fresh and powerful inspiration. Successive volumes are *The Beloved Adventure* (1912), *Love and Liberation* (1913), and *Dust and Light* (1919). In *The Black Panther* (1922) he reaches some of his best achievement by combining substantial and careful workmanship with honesty of feeling. The two poems quoted are from this volume. *The Bright Doom* (1927) explores the vast issues of life and death with a sober and courageous thoughtfulness.

THE BLACK PANTHER

John Hall Wheelock

There is a panther caged within my breast;
　　But what his name, there is no breast shall know
　　Save mine, nor what it is that drives him so,
Backward and forward, in relentless quest—
That silent rage, baffled but unsuppressed,
　　The soft pad of those stealthy feet that go
　　Over my body's prison to and fro,
Trying the walls forever without rest.

All day I feed him with my living heart;
　　But when the night puts forth her dreams and stars,
　　The inexorable Frenzy reawakes;
　　His wrath is hurled upon the trembling bars,
The eternal passion stretches me apart,
　　And I lie silent—but my body shakes.

THE FISH-HAWK

John Hall Wheelock

On the large highway of the awful air that flows
　　Unbounded between sea and heaven, while twilight screened
The sorrowful distances, he moved and had repose;
　　On the huge wind of the Immensity he leaned
His steady body in long lapse of flight—and rose

Gradual, through broad gyres of ever-climbing rest,
　　Up the clear stair of the eternal sky, and stood
Throned on the summit! Slowly, with his widening breast,
　　Widened around him the enormous solitude,
From the gray rim of ocean to the glowing west.

Headlands and capes forlorn of the far coast, the land
   Rolling her barrens toward the south, he, from his throne
Upon the gigantic wind, beheld; he hung—he fanned
   The abyss for mighty joy, to feel beneath him strewn
Pale pastures of the sea, with heaven on either hand—

The world with all her winds and waters, earth and air,
   Fields, folds, and moving clouds. The awful and adored
Arches and endless aisles of vacancy, the fair
   Void of sheer heights and hollows hailed him as her lord
And lover in the highest, to whom all heaven lay bare!

Till from that tower of ecstasy, that baffled height,
   Stooping, he sank; and slowly on the world's wide way
Walked, with great wing on wing, the merciless, proud might,
   Hunting the huddled and lone reaches for his prey
Down the dim shore—and faded in the crumbling light.

Slowly the dusk covered the land. Like a great hymn
   The sound of moving winds and waters was; the sea
Whispered a benediction, and the west grew dim
   Where evening lifted her clear candles quietly . . .
Heaven, crowded with stars, trembled from rim to rim.

MARGARET WIDDEMER

Margaret Widdemer was born at Doylestown, Pennsylvania; she was graduated from the Drexel Institute Library School in 1909. Although a writer of short stories, novels, and, more recently, of parody, she is known chiefly for her poems on behalf of the overworked and under-privileged classes. She gained sudden notice for her first published poem, which later became the title poem of *Factories with Other Lyrics* (1915). Her *The Old Road to Paradise* (1918) shared the Columbia Poetry Prize for 1918 with Mr. Sandburg's *Cornhuskers*. Her poems of social protest remain her strongest and most original work. Her latest volume, *Ballads and Lyrics* (1925), treats of lighter subjects. "Teresina's Face" is the sort of poem she does most happily. *Collected Poems of Margaret Widdemer* was published in 1928.

TERESINA'S FACE

MARGARET WIDDEMER

He saw it last of all before they herded in the steerage,
  Dusk against the sunset where he lingered by the hold—
The tear-stained, dusk-rose face of her, the little Teresina,
  Sailing out to lands of gold.

Ah, his days were long, long days, still toiling in the vineyard,
  Working for the gold to set him free to go to her,
Where gay there glowed the flower-face of little Teresina,
  Where all joy and riches were.   .   .   .

Hard to find one rose-face where the dark rose-faces cluster,
  Where the outland laws are strange, and outland voices
    hum—
Only one lad's hoping, and the word of Teresina,
  Who would wait for him to come:

          .   .   .   .

God grant he may not find her, since he may not win her freedom
  Nor yet be great enough to love, in such marred, captive guise,
The patient, painted face of her, the little Teresina,
  With its cowed, all-knowing eyes!

ELINOR WYLIE

Elinor (Hoyt) Wylie (Mrs. William Rose Benét) was born in Somerville, New Jersey, of old American stock. Her girlhood was spent in Washington, D. C., and in Europe. Although she had written from childhood, her first book of verse, except for an anonymous volume, was *Nets to Catch the Wind* (1921); this was followed by *Black Armour* (1923) and *Trivial Breath* (1928). These three thin volumes comprise her poetic output to date, but they have been more than enough to engage the admiration of discriminating readers. Her nice subtleties and dexterities of technique will never catch the popular ear, nor will they bring her the same regard that the world pays a writer of more human emotions. But as a brilliant fencer with words and ideas she supplies an intellectual delight which is its own justification.

The qualities of her verse are found also in her novels: *Jennifer Lorn* (1923), *The Venetian Glass Nephew* (1925), *The Orphan Angel* (1926), and *Mr. Hodge and Mr. Hazard* (1928).

THE EAGLE AND THE MOLE

Elinor Wylie

Avoid the reeking herd,
Shun the polluted flock,
Live like that stoic bird,
The eagle of the rock.

The huddled warmth of crowds
Begets and fosters hate;
He keeps, above the clouds,
His cliff inviolate.

When flocks are folded warm,
And herds to shelter run,
He sails above the storm,
He stares into the sun.

If in the eagle's track
Your sinews cannot leap,
Avoid the lathered pack,
Turn from the steaming sheep.

If you would keep your soul
From spotted sight or sound,
Live like the velvet mole;
Go burrow underground.

And there hold intercourse
With roots of trees and stones,
With rivers at their source,
And disembodied bones.

II

BRITISH POETS

A. E.

(GEORGE WILLIAM RUSSELL)

George William Russell, universally known by his pseudonym, A. E., was born in 1867 in Lurgan, County Armagh, in the North of Ireland. His family moved to Dublin while he was a boy, and the remainder of his life has been closely identified with the capital of the Free State. After attending a school at Rathmines, he studied at the School of Art, Dublin, where he met the poet W. B. Yeats. As assistant secretary of the Irish Agricultural Organization Society, he worked enthusiastically to organize coöperative societies and agricultural banks, under the direction of Sir Horace Plunkett. At the same time he was developing into a prolific writer of poetry, plays, essays, and articles on agricultural reform, so that he presently found himself one of the leaders of the Irish literary renascence, in association with Mr. Yeats, J. M. Synge, Lady Gregory, Dr. Douglas Hyde, and others (see Introduction, page 44). He was a promoter of the Irish Literary Theater in 1899. His home has long been a gathering-place for writers, artists, and thinkers. His influence upon younger men has been great and good.

His many poems have been gathered in *Collected Poems* (1914). They are powerfully imbued with mysticism; constantly the poet identifies himself with the Earth Spirit or Earth Mother which embraces all things.

BY THE MARGIN OF THE GREAT DEEP

A. E.

(George William Russell)

When the breath of twilight blows to flame the misty skies,
All its vaporous sapphire, violet glow, and silver gleam'
With their magic flood me through the gateway of the eyes;
    I am one with the twilight's dream.

When the trees and skies and fields are one in dusky mood,
Every heart of man is rapt within the mother's breast;
Full of peace and sleep and dreams in the vasty quietude,
    I am one with their hearts at rest.

From our immemorial joys of hearth and home and love
Strayed away along the margin of the unknown tide,
All its reach of soundless calm can thrill me far above
    Word or touch from the lips beside.

Aye, and deep and deep and deeper let me drink and draw
From the olden fountain more than light or peace or dream,
Such primeval being as o'erfills the heart with awe,
    Growing one with its silent stream.

RECONCILIATION

A. E.

(George William Russell)

I begin through the grass once again to be bound to the Lord;
    I can see, through a face that has faded, the face full of rest
Of the earth, of the mother, my heart with her heart in accord.
    As I lie 'mid the cool green tresses that mantle her breast
I begin with the grass once again to be bound to the Lord.

By the hand of a child I am led to the throne of the King,
    For a touch that now fevers me not is forgotten and far,
And His infinite sceptered hands that sway us can bring
    Me in dreams from the laugh of a child to the song of a star.
On the laugh of a child I am borne to the joy of the King.

RICHARD ALDINGTON

Richard Aldington was born in Hampshire, England, in 1892. He acquired his formal education at Dover College and London University. As an editor of *The Egoist* he has published much of his work in its pages. He has always been devoted to the translation of Greek poetry; both in subject-matter and in spirit, Mr. Aldington reflects, though indirectly, an attentuated classicism. His quality of chaste restraint is perhaps his most important contribution to modern poetry, a contribution which he must share with his wife, the American-born H. D.

During the height of the imagist experiment, he was a leading rebel, first of the group brought together by Ezra Pound in 1914 and later of the group gathered by Amy Lowell in the three annuals, *Some Imagist Poets, 1915, 1916, 1917.* In this school were also to be found H. D., F. S. Flint, D. H. Lawrence, and John Gould Fletcher.

The essential idea of the Imagists was to present the concrete thing seen in an instant of time, in hard, definite, direct outlines, avoiding abstractions. The vogue of imagism was transitory, and its exponents have in most cases turned back to more conventional principles. But imagism performed the valuable service, both in England and in America, of stimulating poets to seek the vivid, living word with the ring of good coin newly minted, in place of mechanical phrases sanctioned by custom which fall upon the ear with the dull thud of counterfeits. The poems which follow are examples of good imagist writing.

Mr. Aldington's books are: *Images Old and New* (1915), *War and Love* (1918), *Images of War* (1919), *Images of Desire* (1920), *Exile and Other Poems* (1923).

THE FAUN SEES SNOW FOR THE FIRST TIME[1]

RICHARD ALDINGTON

Zeus,
Brazen-thunder-hurler,
Cloud-whirler, son-of-Kronos,[2]
Send vengeance on these Oreads[3]
Who strew
White frozen flecks of mist and cloud
Over the brown trees and the tufted grass
Of the meadows, where the stream
Runs black through shining banks
Of bluish white.

Zeus,
Are the halls of heaven broken up
That you flake down upon me
Feather-strips of marble?

Dis and Styx![4]
When I stamp my hoof
The frozen-cloud-specks jam into the cleft
So that I reel upon two slippery points. . . .

Fool, to stand here cursing
When I might be running!

---

[1] Mr. Aldington preserves, in general, the Greek spelling of proper names. "Kronos," for example, is more commonly transliterated "Chronos."
[2] *Kronos*, ruler of heaven and earth, deposed by his son Zeus.
[3] *Oreads*, nymphs of the hills.
[4] *Dis and Styx!* an oath.

CHORICOS[1]

RICHARD ALDINGTON

The ancient songs
Pass deathward mournfully.
Cold lips that sing no more, and withered wreaths,
Regretful eyes, and drooping breasts and wings—
Symbols of ancient songs
Mournfully passing
Down to the great white surges,
Watched of none
Save the frail sea-birds
And the lithe pale girls,
Daughters of Okeanos[2].

And the songs pass
From the green land
Which lies upon the waves as a leaf
On the flowers of hyacinth;
And they pass from the waters,
The manifold winds, and the dim moon,
And they come,
Silently winging through soft Kimmerian[3] dusk,
To the quiet level lands
That she keeps for us all,
That she wrought for us all for sleep
In the silver days of the earth's dawning—
Proserpina[4], daughter of Zeus.

And we turn from the Kuprian's[5] breasts,
And we turn from thee,
Phoibos Apollon[6],

[1] *Choricos*, a song for a choral dance.
[2] *Okeanos*, the ocean-god.
[3] *Kimmerian*, pertaining to a mythical land in the farthest West, wrapped in mists and darkness.
[4] *Proserpina*, wife of Pluto, god of the underworld.
[5] *the Kuprian*, Aphrodite of Cyprus, goddess of love.
[6] *Phoibos Apollon*, god of light.

And we turn from the music of old
And the hills that we loved and the meads,
And we turn from the fiery day,
And the lips that were over-sweet;
For silently
Brushing the fields with red-shod feet,
With purple robe
Searing the flowers as with a sudden flame,
Death,
Thou hast come upon us.

And of all the ancient songs
Passing to the swallow-blue halls
By the dark streams of Persephone,[7]
This only remains:
That we turn to thee,
Death,
That we turn to thee, singing
One last song.

O Death,
Thou art an healing wind
That blowest over white flowers
A-tremble with dew;
Thou art a wind flowing
Over dark leagues of lonely sea;
Thou art the dusk and the fragrance;
Thou art the lips of love mournfully smiling;
Thou art the pale peace of one
Satiate with old desires;
Thou art the silence of beauty,
And we look no more for the morning
We yearn no more for the sun,
Since with thy white hands,

---

[7] *Persephone*, same as Proserpina.

Death,
Thou crownest us with the pallid chaplets,
The slim colorless poppies
Which in thy garden alone
Softly thou gatherest.
And silently,
And with slow feet approaching,
And with bowed head and unlit eyes,
We kneel before thee:
And thou, leaning toward us,
Caressingly layest upon us
Flowers from thy thin cold hands,
And, smiling as a chaste woman
Knowing love in her heart,
Thou sealest our eyes,
And the illimitable quietude
Comes gently upon us.

ANONYMOUS

The typically Irish piece of impudence entitled "Ambition in Cuffe Street" is reprinted from a book of poems by various authors, collected by Miss Susan L. Mitchell, herself a poet, under the title *Secret Springs of Dublin Song*.

Inquiry of the publishers as to whether James Stephens might have written this poem brought a disclaimer of knowledge of its authorship and the cryptic admission: "We know it is not by Miss Susan Mitchell, and you will do no harm in ascribing it to James Stephens." Further inquiry from an authoritative source elicited the assurance that the poem was *not* written by Mr. Stephens. Beyond that it is not permitted to say.

AMBITION IN CUFFE STREET[1]

ANONYMOUS

When I grow big I'll smoke and swear
And drink like my old fellow there;
I'll smoke till all the air is thick,
I'll drink five pints and not feel sick,
And use bad language to my fill,
   I will!

On a high stool for hours I'll sit,
Or lean against the door and spit;
I'll drink each pint to the last sup,
And tell the man to hurry up,
Till I have had five tankards, yes,
   No less!

I'll talk with Jemmy Cassidy—
He'll have grown old and fat like me—
We'll talk of women and everything,
And then perhaps we'll start to sing,
We'll start to sing and fight and shout,
'Twill take three men to chuck us out,
By God, the things that I could do—
   Whew!

[1]*Cuffe Street*, a thoroughfare near Stephen's Green, Dublin.

MARTIN ARMSTRONG

Martin (Donisthorpe) Armstrong was born near Newcastle-on-Tyne, Northumberland, in 1882. He was graduated from the Charterhouse School and received the B. A. degree from Pembroke College, Cambridge. His work has been, to some extent, influenced by his residence for awhile in Italy, and his five years' fighting experience on the western front in the World War, as first a private, then a lieutenant, and finally a captain in the British Infantry.

Beginning as a poet, he has lately turned his attention to short stories and novels. His best poems will be found in *The Buzzards and Other Poems* (1921). Since that year, he has published three volumes of short stories and two novels, *At the Sign of the Goat and Compasses*, 1925, and *Desert*, 1926. The knack of the story-teller is apparent in the delightful character sketch of Miss Thompson which is reprinted here.

MISS THOMPSON GOES SHOPPING

Martin Armstrong

In her lone cottage on the downs,
With winds and blizzards and great crowns
Of shining cloud, with wheeling plover   *Miss Thompson*
And short grass sweet with the small white clover, *at Home*
Miss Thompson lived, correct and meek,
A lonely spinster, and every week
On market-day she used to go
Into the little town below,
Tucked in the great downs' hollow bowl
Like pebbles gathered in a shoal.

So, having washed her plates and cup   *She goes a-*
And banked the kitchen-fire up,   *Marketing.*
Miss Thompson slipped upstairs and dressed,
Put on her black (her second best),
The bonnet trimmed with rusty plush,
Peeped in the glass with simpering blush,
From camphor-smelling cupboard took
Her thicker jacket off the hook,
Because the day might turn to cold.
Then, ready, slipped downstairs and rolled
The hearthrug back; then searched about,
Found her basket, ventured out,
Snecked[1] the door, and paused to lock it
And plunge the key in some deep pocket.
Then as she tripped demurely down
The steep descent, the little town
Spread wider till its sprawling street
Inclosed her, and her footfalls beat
On hard stone pavement, and she felt
Those throbbing ecstasies that melt

---

[1] *snecked*, latched.

Through heart and mind, as, happy, free,
Her small, prim personality
Merged into the seething strife
Of auction-marts and city life.

Serenely down the busy stream   *She Visits the*
Miss Thompson floated in a dream.   *Bootmaker,*
Now, hovering, bee-like, she would stop
Entranced before some tempting shop,
Getting in people's way and prying
At things she never thought of buying;
Now wafted on without an aim,
Until in course of time she came
To Watson's bootshop. Long she pries
At boots and shoes of every size—
Brown football-boots with bar and stud
For boys that scuffle in the mud,
And dancing-pumps with pointed toes
Glossy as jet and dull black bows;
Slim ladies' shoes with two-inch heel
And sprinkled beads of gold and steel—
"How anyone can wear such things!"
On either side the doorway springs
(As in a tropic jungle loom
Masses of strange thick-petaled bloom
And fruits misshapen) fold on fold
A growth of sand-shoes[2] rubber-soled,
Clambering the doorposts, branching, spawning,
Their barbarous bunches like an awning
Over the windows and the doors.
But, framed among the other stores,
Something has caught Miss Thompson's eye
(O worldliness! O vanity!),
A pair of slippers—scarlet plush.

---

[2]*sand-shoes*, sneakers.

Miss Thompson feels a conscious blush
Suffuse her face, as though her thought
Had ventured further than it ought.
But Oh, that color's rapturous singing
And the answer in her lone heart ringing!
She turns (O Guardian Angels, stop her
From doing anything improper!)
She turns; and see, she stoops and bungles
In through the sand-shoes' hanging jungles,
Away from light and common sense,
Into the shop dim-lit and dense
With smells of polish and tanned hide.

Soon from a dark recess inside   *Mrs. Watson.*
Fat Mrs. Watson comes slip-slop
To mind the business of the shop.
She walks flat-footed with a roll—
A serviceable, homely soul,
With kindly, ugly face like dough,
Hair dull and colorless as tow.
A huge Scotch pebble[3] fills the space
Between her bosom and her face.
One sees her making beds all day.
Miss Thompson lets her say her say:
"So chilly for the time of year.
It's ages since we saw you here."
Then, heart a-flutter, speech precise,
Describes the shoes and asks the price.
"Them, Miss? Ah, them is six-and-nine."
Miss Thompson shudders down the spine
(Dream of impossible romance).
She eyes them with a wistful glance,   *Wrestles with a*
Torn between good and evil. Yes,   *Temptation;*
For half-a-minute and no less

[3]*Scotch pebble*, agate.

Miss Thompson strives with seven devils,
Then, soaring over earthly levels,
Turns from the shoes with lingering touch—
"Ah, six-and-nine is far too much.
Sorry to trouble you. Good day!"   *And Is Saved.*

A little farther down the way
Stands Miles's fish-shop, whence is shed   *She Visits the*
So strong a smell of fishes dead   *Fishmonger,*
That people of a subtler sense
Hold their breath and hurry thence.
Miss Thompson hovers there and gazes:
Her housewife's knowing eye appraises
Salt and fresh, severely cons
Kippers bright as tarnished bronze;
Great cods disposed upon the sill,
Chilly and wet, with gaping gill,
Flat head, glazed eye, and mute, uncouth,
Shapeless, wan, old-woman's mouth.
Next a row of soles and plaice
With querulous and twisted face,
And red-eyed bloaters, golden-gray;
Smoked haddocks ranked in neat array;
A group of smelts that take the light
Like slips of rainbow, pearly bright;
Silver trout with rosy spots,
And coral shrimps with keen black dots
For eyes, and hard and jointed sheath
And crisp tails curving underneath.
But there upon the sanded floor,
More wonderful in all that store
Than anything on slab or shelf,
Stood Miles, the fishmonger, himself.

Foursquare he stood and filled the place.   *Mr. Miles.*
His huge hands and his jolly face

Were red. He had a mouth to quaff
Pint after pint, a sounding laugh,
But wheezy at the end, and oft
His eyes bulged outward, and he coughed.
Aproned he stood from chin to toe.
The apron's vertical long flow
Warped grandly outwards to display
His hale, round belly hung midway,
Whose apex was securely bound
With apron-strings wrapped round and round.
Outside, Miss Thompson, small and staid,
Felt, as she always felt, afraid
Of this huge man who laughed so loud
And drew the notice of the crowd.
Awhile she paused in timid thought,
Then promptly hurried in and bought
"Two kippers, please. Yes, lovely weather."
"Two kippers? Sixpence altogether."
And in her basket laid the pair
Wrapped face to face in newspaper.

Then on she went, as one half blind,   *Relapses into*
For things were stirring in her mind;   *Temptation;*
Then turned about with fixed intent
And, heading for the boot shop, went
Straight in and bought the scarlet slippers   *And Falls.*
And popped them in beside the kippers.

So much for that. From there she tacked,   *She Visits the*
Still flushed by this decisive act,   *Chemist,*
Westward, and came without a stop
To Mr. Wren the chemist's shop,
And stood awhile outside to see
The tall, big-bellied bottles three—

Red, blue, and emerald, richly bright,
Each with its burning core of light.
The bell chimed as she pushed the door.
Spotless the oilcloth on the floor,
Limpid as water each glass case,
Each thing precisely in its place.
Rows of small drawers, black-lettered each
With curious words of foreign speech,
Ranked high above the other ware.
The old strange fragrance filled the air,
A fragrance like the garden pink,
But tinged with vague medicinal stink
Of camphor, soap, new sponges, blent
With chloroform and violet scent.

And Wren the chemist, tall and spare,   *Mr. Wren.*
Stood gaunt behind his counter there.
Quiet and very wise he seemed,
With skull-like face, bald head that gleamed;
Through spectacles his eyes looked kind.
He wore a pencil tucked behind
His ear. And never he mistakes
The wildest signs the doctor makes
Prescribing drugs. Brown paper, string,
He will not use for anything,
But all in neat white parcels packs
And sticks them up with sealing-wax.
Miss Thompson bowed and blushed, and then
Undoubting bought of Mr. Wren,
Being free from modern scepticism,
A bottle for her rheumatism;
Also some peppermints to take
In case of wind; an oval cake
Of scented soap; a penny square
Of pungent naphthalene to scare

The moth. And after Wren had wrapped
And sealed the lot, Miss Thompson clapped
Them in beside the fish and shoes;
"Good day," she says, and off she goes.

Belike Miss Thompson, whither next?
Outside, you pause awhile, perplext,
Your bearings lost. Then all comes back
And round she wheels, hot on the track   *Is Led Away*
Of Giles the grocer, and from there   *to the Pleasures*
To Emilie the milliner,   *of the Town,*
There to be tempted by the sight   *Such as*
Of hats and blouses fiercely bright.   *Groceries and*
(O guard Miss Thompson, Powers that Be,   *Millinery, And*
From Crudeness and Vulgarity.)   *Other Allure-*
                                                  ments.

Still on from shop to shop she goes
With sharp bird's-eye, inquiring nose,
Prying and peering, entering some,
Oblivious of the thought of home.
The town brimmed up with deep-blue haze,
But still she stayed to flit and gaze,
Her eyes a-blur with rapturous sights,
Her small soul full of small delights,
Empty her purse, her basket filled.
The traffic in the town was stilled.   *But at Length*
The clock struck six. Men thronged the inns.   *is Convinced of*
Dear, dear, she should be home long since.   *Indiscretion.*

Then as she climbed the misty downs   *And Returns*
The lamps were lighted in the town's   *Home.*
Small streets. She saw them star by star
Multiplying from afar;
Till, mapped beneath her, she could trace
Each street, and the wide square market-place

Sunk deeper and deeper as she went
Higher up the steep ascent.
And all that soul-uplifting stir
Step by step fell back from her,
The glory gone, the blossoming
Shriveled, and she, a small, frail thing,
Carrying her laden basket. Till
Darkness and silence of the hill
Received her in their restful care,
And stars came dropping through the air.

But loudly, sweetly, sang the slippers
In the basket with the kippers;
And loud and sweet the answering thrills
From her lone heart on the hills.

HILAIRE BELLOC

(Joseph) Hilaire (Pierre) Belloc was born in France in 1870. His formal education began at Cardinal Newman's Oratory School, Edgbaston; was interrupted by his return to France to serve his time as a French citizen in the artillery; and was brilliantly completed at Balliol College, Oxford, where he was graduated with high honors in history. His writings cover an astonishing variety of subjects and forms. Primarily he is an essayist and journalist, but he is also a novelist, an historian, and a poet. In the last-named calling he has put into verse his favorite subjects—his home county of Sussex, boats and the sea, the good cheer of old inns, and the exaltations of his Catholic faith. With the exception of the religious pieces, Mr. Belloc's poetry has a thumping vigor which truthfully reflects its author's hearty relish for living. His *Collected Poems* appeared in 1923.

THE SOUTH COUNTRY

HILAIRE BELLOC

When I am living in the Midlands
   That are sodden and unkind,
I light my lamp at evening;
   My work is left behind;
And the great hills of the South Country
   Come back into my mind.

The great hills of the South Country
   They stand along the sea;
And it's there walking in the high woods
   That I could wish to be,
And the men that were boys when I was a boy
   Walking along with me.

The men that live in North England
   I saw them for a day;
Their hearts are set upon the waste fells,
   Their skies are fast and gray;
From their castle walls a man may see
   The mountains far away.

The men that live in West England
   They see the Severn strong,
A-rolling on rough water brown
   Light aspen leaves along.
They have the secret of the rocks,
   And the oldest kind of song.

But the men that live in the South Country
   Are the kindest and most wise,
They get their laughter from the loud surf;
   And the faith in their happy eyes
Comes surely from our sister the Spring

When over the sea she flies;
The violets suddenly bloom at her feet,
　　She blesses us with surprise.

I never get between the pines
　　But I smell the Sussex air;
Nor I never come on a belt of sand
　　But my home is there,
And along the sky the line of the Downs
　　So noble and so bare.

A lost thing could I never find,
　　Nor a broken thing mend:
And I fear I shall be all alone
　　When I get toward the end.
Who will be there to comfort me
　　Or who will be my friend?

I will gather and carefully make my friends
　　Of the men of the Sussex Weald,[1]
They watch the stars from silent folds,
　　They stiffly plow the field.
By them and the God of the South Country
　　My poor soul shall be healed.

If I ever become a rich man,
　　Or if ever I grow to be old,
I will build a house with deep thatch
　　To shelter me from the cold,
And there shall the Sussex songs be sung
　　And the story of Sussex told.

I will hold my house in the high wood
　　Within a walk of the sea,
And the men that were boys when I was a boy
　　Shall sit and drink with me.

[1] *Weald*, a district comprising portions of Sussex, Kent, and Surrey; of very irregular topography; formerly heavily wooded.

HENRY BRYAN BINNS

Henry Bryan Binns was born in 1873 in Ulverston, Lancashire, of Quaker parentage. He attended a Quaker school at Hitchin, Hertfordshire, and the University College, Manchester. His life and thought were much influenced not only by this Quaker background, so apparent in "Injunction," but also by fifteen months spent in the United States when he was twenty-four years of age. The latter circumstance was doubtless responsible for his *A Life of Walt Whitman* (1905), *Abraham Lincoln* (1907), and *Whitman and His Poetry* (1914).

"Injunction" is found in *The Free Spirit* (1914). It is typical of the serious mood and Whitmanian style which mark his work. Binns died in 1923.

INJUNCTION*

Henry Bryan Binns

It is no use pricking up your ears at every step;

Neither the postman nor the telegraph boy will bring you that
for which you wait.

They will bring you news, perhaps; but not that for which you
wait.

And you must go on waiting while you prick your ears up at
their footstep.

For the Divine Companion requires all your attention, and He
is not there.

He is here in the deep quiet of your heart: the quiet that abides
and is content because of Him.

Seek then for quietness.

By your desire, withdraw yourself from the ever-alertness of
your brain, the imprisonment of sick nerves;

Partake of the deep life within your soul;

Turn now away from your delight in that which is without and
in the play of your powers:

Give yourself now to this that waits;

That clamors not nor insists, but waits—

Knowledge of Him and guiding love of Him.

*From *The Free Spirit* by Henry Bryan Binns. Copyright 1914 by B. W. Huebsch, Inc.
New York: The Viking Press, Inc.

EDMUND BLUNDEN

Edmund (Charles) Blunden, born in England in 1896, was educated at Queen's College, Oxford, and served as a lieutenant in the Royal Sussex Regiment during the World War. Until recently he lived in Suffolk, but he is now a professor of English literature in the Imperial University, Tokyo. In 1923 he won the Hawthornden prize for the best work of a young writer.

The contents of Mr. Blunden's two small volumes, *The Waggoner and Other Poems* (1920) and *The Shepherd* (1922), are typical of the country school of poetry which has grown up in England since the War. Not only does Mr. Blunden choose pastoral subjects, but he uses the homely language of the countryside with vigorous effectiveness. Contrast, for example, the opening lines of "The Waggoner" with the polished classicism of Gray's "Elegy Written in a Country Churchyard." Mr. Blunden's picture was not written in the aloofness of the study, for the mud of the barnyard clings to the lines:

> The old wagon drudges through the miry lane
> By the skulking pond where the pollards frown,
> Notched, dumb, surly images of pain;
> On a dulled earth the night droops down.

"The Almswomen" proves that such an utterly conventional verse form as the heroic couplet still has plenty of vitality when applied to fresh material.

Mr. Blunden's *English Poems* (1925), keeps to bucolic subjects for the most part, but adopts a self-conscious, artificial, tortured diction which is far removed from the legitimate difficulties of his earlier style. This new obscurity does not grow out of the uncouthness of country life, but is deliberate and self-imposed.

ALMSWOMEN

EDMUND BLUNDEN

At Quincey's moat the squandering village ends,
And there in the almshouse dwell the dearest friends
Of all the village, two old dames that cling
As close as any trueloves in the spring.
Long, long ago they passed threescore-and-ten,
And in this doll's house lived together then;
All things they have common, being so poor,
And their one fear, Death's shadow at the door.
Each sundown makes them mournful, each sunrise
Brings back the brightness in their failing eyes.

How happy go the rich fair-weather days
When on the roadside folk stare in amaze
At such a honeycomb of fruit and flowers
As mellows round their threshold; what long hours
They gloat upon their steepling hollyhocks,
Bee's balsams, feathery southernwood, and stocks,
Fiery dragon's-mouths, great mallow leaves
For salves, and lemon-plants in bushy sheaves,
Shagged Esau's-hands with five green finger-tips.
Such old sweet names are ever on their lips.
As pleased as little children where these grow,
In cobbled pattens and worn gowns they go,
Proud of their wisdom when on gooseberry shoots
They stuck eggshells to fright from coming fruits
The brisk-billed rascals; pausing still to see
Their neighbor owls saunter from tree to tree,
Or in the hushing half-light mouse the lane,
Long-winged and lordly.
                                    But when those hours wane,
Indoors they ponder, scared by the harsh storm
Whose pelting saracens on the window swarm,

And listen for the mail to clatter past
And church clock's deep bay withering on the blast;
They feed the fire that flings a freakish light
On pictured kings and queens grotesquely bright,
Platters and pitchers, faded calendars
And graceful hour-glass trim with lavenders.

Many a time they kiss and cry, and pray
That both be summoned in the selfsame day,
And wiseman linnet tinkling in his cage
End too with them the friendship of old age,
And all together leave their treasured room
Some bell-like evening when the may's in bloom.

ROBERT BRIDGES

Robert (Seymour) Bridges, Poet Laureate of England since 1913, was born in 1844 at Walmer, on the Kentish coast; he was a student at Eton and at Corpus Christi College, Oxford. After achieving distinction for his classical scholarship at Oxford, he studied medicine and was for a number of years attached to the staff of St. Bartholomew's Hospital, London. He also found opportunity to travel on the Continent and in the East. In 1882, at the age of thirty-eight, he retired to private life, to devote himself to the study of the classics and the writing of poetry. Dr. Bridges has lived for many years near Oxford. His production has been large, including poetical dramas on classical themes and in the classical manner, critical essays (especially *Milton's Prosody*, 1893, revised 1921), and non-dramatic poetry, issued in a six-volume collected edition, *Poetical Works* (1913), also in a convenient one-volume edition (1914). *October and Other Poems* appeared in 1920.

Much of his poetry will not at once appeal to younger readers, unless they are already pretty thoroughly imbued with the idea of classical restraint. In this restraint is admirable grace and purity but also a chaste austerity which erects a barrier, however impalpable, between poet and reader. The sound scholarship of Dr. Bridges can produce metrical forms of cold and perfect loveliness, but only the stirring of profound emotions can quicken these forms into pulsating life.

A PASSER-BY

Robert Bridges

Whither, O splendid ship, thy white sails crowding,
   Leaning across the bosom of the urgent West,
That fearest nor sea rising, nor sky clouding,
   Whither away, fair rover, and what thy quest?
    Ah! soon, when winter has all our vales opprest,
When skies are cold and misty, and hail is hurling,
   Wilt thou glide on the blue Pacific, or rest
In a summer haven asleep, thy white sails furling?

I there before thee, in the country that well thou knowest,
   Already arrived am inhaling the odorous air:
I watch thee enter unerringly where thou goest,
   And anchor queen of the strange shipping there,
    Thy sails for awnings spread, thy masts bare;
Nor is aught from the foaming reed to the snow-capped grandest
   Peak, that is over the feathery palms, more fair
Than thou, so upright, so stately and still thou standest.

And yet, O splendid ship, unhailed and nameless,
   I know not if, aiming a fancy, I rightly divine
That thou hast a purpose joyful, a courage blameless,
   Thy port assured in a happier land than mine.
    But for all I have given thee, beauty enough is thine,
As thou, aslant with trim tackle and shrouding,
   From the proud nostril curve of a prow's line
In the offing scatterest foam, thy white sails crowding.

WINTER NIGHTFALL[1]

ROBERT BRIDGES

The day begins to droop,
　　Its course is done;
But nothing tells the place
　　Of the setting sun.

The hazy darkness deepens,
　　And up the lane
You may hear, but cannot see,
　　The homing wain.

An engine pants and hums
　　In the farm hard by;
Its lowering smoke is lost
　　In the lowering sky.

The soaking branches drip,
　　And all night through
The dropping will not cease
　　In the avenue.

A tall man there in the house
　　Must keep his chair;
He knows he will never again
　　Breathe the spring air:

His heart is worn with work;
　　He is giddy and sick
If he rise to go as far
　　As the nearest rick.

He thinks of his morn of life,
　　His hale, strong years;
And braves as he may the night
　　Of darkness and tears.

[1]Compare with J. C. Squire's poem of the same title, page 512.

RUPERT BROOKE

Rupert Brooke was born in 1887 at Rugby, where his father was a house-master, and was educated there and at King's College, Cambridge. After his graduation he lived for a time at Grantchester, and his memories of this period, mellowed by exile in Germany, are wistfully expressed in "The Old Vicarage, Grantchester."

He early distinguished himself not only as an enthusiastic student of letters but also as a splendid athlete. He was the finest type of young Englishman, singularly handsome, clean-living, lovable. His sensitiveness to beauty was that of a born poet. Every advantage and encouragement were his. He had the friendship of the leading writers of his time, such as Gibson, De la Mare, Henry James, Thomas, and Flecker. He traveled in Germany, Italy, America, and the South Seas. In 1913 he was elected a Fellow of King's College.

He had published only one small volume, *Poems* (1911), but it was sufficient to justify his friends in expecting the highest poetic achievement of him. On the eve of his fulfilling these expectations, the World War broke out. With characteristic enthusiasm and buoyancy he threw himself into it without reserve. After a brief service in Belgium he was sent in 1915 to the Dardanelles; he died on the way, of blood poisoning, in the harbor of Skyros in the Aegean, and is buried there under the Greek sky which he loved.

His *1914 and Other Poems* (1915), which appeared shortly before his death, contained the strangely accurate prophecy of "The Soldier," a sonnet which, if he had written nothing else, would have won him fame. It is an easy and a futile thing to conjecture what might have been but for the War. Undoubtedly, if Brooke had fulfilled his early promise, he would have been one of the leading poets of our time. But it was not to be, and the world must give thanks that the limited production of his brief life, issued as *Collected Poems* (1915), should comprise infinite riches in a little space. His poetry is admired for its Keats-like perception of sensuous beauty and for its rare zest in vivid and high-spirited living.

THE SOLDIER

Rupert Brooke

If I should die, think only this of me:
That there's some corner of a foreign field
That is forever England. There shall be
In that rich earth a richer dust concealed;
A dust whom England bore, shaped, made aware,
Gave, once, her flowers to love, her ways to roam;
A body of England's, breathing English air,
Washed by the rivers, blest by suns of home.
And think, this heart, all evil shed away,
A pulse in the eternal mind, no less
Gives somewhere back the thoughts by England given;
Her sights and sounds; dreams happy as her day;
And laughter, learnt of friends; and gentleness,
In hearts at peace, under an English heaven.

THE GREAT LOVER

Rupert Brooke

I have been so great a lover: filled my days
So proudly with the splendor of Love's praise,
The pain, the calm, and the astonishment,
Desire illimitable, and still content,
And all dear names men use, to cheat despair,
For the perplexed and viewless streams that bear
Our hearts at random down the dark of life.
Now, ere the unthinking silence on that strife
Steals down, I would cheat drowsy Death so far,
My night shall be remembered for a star
That outshone all the suns of all men's days.

Shall I not crown them with immortal praise
Whom I have loved, who have given me, dared with me
High secrets, and in darkness knelt to see
The inenarrable[1] godhead of delight?
Love is a flame—we have beaconed the world's night.
A city—and we have built it, these and I.
An emperor—we have taught the world to die.
So, for their sakes I loved, ere I go hence,
And the high cause of Love's magnificence,
And to keep loyalties young, I'll write those names
Golden for ever, eagles, crying flames,
And set them as a banner, that men may know,
To dare the generations, burn, and blow
Out on the wind of Time, shining and streaming. . . .

These I have loved:
    White plates and cups, clean-gleaming,
Ringed with blue lines; and feathery, faery dust;
Wet roofs, beneath the lamplight; the strong crust
Of friendly bread; and many-tasting food;
Rainbows; and the blue bitter smoke of wood;
And radiant raindrops couching in cool flowers;
And flowers themselves, that sway through sunny hours,
Dreaming of moths that drink them under the moon;
Then, the cool kindliness of sheets, that soon
Smooth away trouble; and the rough male kiss
Of blankets; grainy wood; live hair that is
Shining and free; blue-massing clouds; the keen
Unpassioned beauty of a great machine;
The benison of hot water; furs to touch;
The good smell of old clothes; and other such—
The comfortable smell of friendly fingers,
Hair's fragrance, and the musty reek that lingers
About dead leaves and last year's ferns. . . .

----

[1] *inenarrable*, indescribable.

                                    Dear names,
And thousand others throng to me! Royal flames;
Sweet water's dimpling laugh from tap or spring;
Holes in the ground; and voices that do sing;
Voices in laughter, too; and body's pain,
Soon turned to peace; and the deep-panting train;
Firm sands; the little dulling edge of foam
That browns and dwindles as the wave goes home;
And washen stones, gay for an hour; the cold
Graveness of iron; moist black earthen mold;
Sleep; and high places; footprints in the dew;
And oaks; and brown horse-chestnuts, glossy-new;
And new-peeled sticks; and shining pools on grass—
All these have been my loves. And these shall pass.
Whatever passes not, in the great hour,
Nor all my passion, all my prayers, have power
To hold them with me through the gate of Death.
They'll play deserter, turn with the traitor breath,
Break the high bond we made, and sell Love's trust
And sacramented covenant to the dust.
—Oh, never a doubt but, somewhere, I shall wake,
And give what's left of love again, and make
New friends, now strangers. . . .
                               But the best I've known
Stays here, and changes, breaks, grows old, is blown
About the winds of the world, and fades from brains
Of living men, and dies.
                         Nothing remains.

O dear my loves, O faithless, once again
This one last gift I give: that after men
Shall know, and later lovers, far-removed
Praise you, "All these were lovely"; say, "He loved."

JOSEPH CAMPBELL

In spite of his later residence in Dublin and association with the Dublin literary group, Joseph Campbell (Seosamh MacCathmhaoil) is an Ulster poet, having been born in Belfast, in 1879, and educated at Saint Malachy's College in that city. This fact colors, to some extent, his pictures of peasant life, for the North of Ireland peasant is not the same as the peasants of J. M. Synge, W. B. Yeats, and their followers. Also, as Thomas Boyd remarks, Mr. Campbell has struck out on an individual path by seeking to interpret Christian beliefs as they are colored by the peasant mind. Such poems as "The Gilly of Christ" are an important and original contribution to Christian folklore.

He served through the Irish revolutionary war, and was held as a military captive by the Irish Free State for a year and a half; his experiences in prison are to be embodied in a book of poetry.

His most famous poem, "I Am the Mountainy Singer," was the opening piece in his early volume of Ulster folk-poetry entitled *The Rushlight* (1906); this book was illustrated by Mr. Campbell, who is artist as well as poet. Later volumes of chief importance are *The Mountainy Singer* (1909), *Irishry* (1913), and *Earth of Cualann* (1917). *Judgment*, a play, was produced by the Abbey Theater, Dublin, in 1912. Since 1925 he has been living in New York as founder and director of the School of Irish Studies.

Mr. Campbell has kindly contributed the notes which accompany the poems.

I AM THE MOUNTAINY SINGER

JOSEPH CAMPBELL

I am the mountainy singer—
  The voice of the peasant's dream,
The cry of the wind on the wooded hill,
  The leap of the fish in the stream.

Quiet and love I sing—
  The carn[1] on the mountain crest,
The cailin[2] in her lover's arms,
  The child at its mother's breast.

Beauty and peace I sing—
  The fire on the open hearth,
The cailleach[3] spinning at her wheel,
  The plow in the broken earth.

Travail and pain I sing—
  The bride on the childing bed,
The dark man laboring at his rimes,
  The ewe in the lambing shed.

Sorrow and death I sing—
  The canker come on the corn,
The fisher lost in the mountain loch,
  The cry at the mouth of morn.

No other life I sing,
  For I am sprung of the stock
That broke the hilly land for bread,
  And built the nest in the rock.

[1]carn, cairn, a heap of stones on a mountain top to mark the burial-place of king or chief.
[2]cailin (căl-yĕn'), a young girl, a colleen.
[3]cailleach (căl'yah), an old woman. Cf. the Cailleach Bheara, the Old Woman of Beare, famous in Gaelic epic.

THE NINEPENNY FIDIL

Joseph Campbell

My father and mother were Irish,
    And I am Irish, too;
I bought a wee fidil for ninepence,
    And it is Irish, too.
I'm up in the morning early
    To meet the dawn of day,
And to the lintwhite's[1] piping
    The many's the tune I play.

One pleasant eve in June time
    I met a lochrie-man:[2]
His face and hands were weazen,
    His height was not a span.
He boored[3] me for my fidil—
    "You know," says he, "like you,
My father and mother were Irish,
    And I am Irish, too!"

He took my wee red fidil,
    And such a tune he turned—
The Glaise[4] in it whispered,
    The Lionan in it m'urned.[5]
Says he, "My lad, you're lucky—
    I wish t' I was like you;
You're lucky in your birth-star,
    And in your fidil, too!"

---

[1] *lintwhite*, the linnet.
[2] *lochrie-man*, an Ulster folk-form of the Gaelic word, leprechaun, one of the solitaries in the Gaelic fairy mythology, shoemaker, and keeper of the sparan sgillinge, or purse of gold.
[3] *boored*, bored, persistently asked for.
[4] *Glaise* (gläsh'ä) *Lionan* (lin'an), mountain streams in County Donegal.
[5] *m'urned*, mourned.

He gave me back my fidil,
  My fidil-stick, also,
And stepping like a mayboy,
  He jumped the Leargaidh Knowe[6].
I never saw him after,
  Nor met his gentle kind;
But, whiles, I think I hear him
  A-wheening in the wind!

My father and mother were Irish,
  And I am Irish, too;
I bought a wee fidil for ninepence,
  And it is Irish, too.
I'm up in the morning early
  To meet the dawn of day,
And to the lintwhite's piping
  The many's the tune I play.

---

[6]*Leargaidh Knowe* (lärg'ē nou), a hillock in County Donegal. Cf. Burns's folk fragment, "Ca' the yowes to the knowes."

PATRICK R. CHALMERS

Patrick Reginald Chalmers, born in 1872 of Scotch parentage, a student at Rugby, and now living in Oxford, is typical of the cultured Britisher who mingles letters with affairs. Although chiefly occupied with his responsibilities as a landowner and a director of the Mercantile Bank of India and other concerns, he yet finds time and inclination to produce occasional lyrics. His poetry is light, graceful, amusing, skillful. He is not an experimenter. His work will be found in *Green Days and Blue Days* (1912), *A Peck of Maut* (1913), *Pipes and Tabors* (1922), and *Pancakes* (1924).

A DREAM

Patrick R. Chalmers

And at night we'd find a town,
  Flat-roofed, by a star-strewn sea,
Where the pirate crew came down
  To a long-forgotten quay,
And we'd meet them in the gloaming,
  Tarry pigtails, back from roaming,
With a pot of pirate ginger for the likes of her and me!

She was small and rather pale,
  Gray-eyed, gray as smoke that weaves,
And we'd watch them stowing sail,
  Forty most attractive thieves;
Propped against the porphyry column,
  She was seven, sweet, and solemn,
And she'd hair blue-black as swallows when they flit beneath
  the eaves.

On the moonlit sands and bare,
  Clamorous, jeweled in the dusk,
There would be an Eastern fair,
  We could smell the mules and musk,
We could see the cressets[1] flaring,
  And we'd run to buy a fairing[2]
Where a black man blew a fanfare on a carven ivory tusk.

And we'd stop before the stall
  Of a grave green-turbaned khan,
Gem or flower—he kept them all—
  Persian cat or yataghan[3];

---

[1]*cressets*, holders for lamps or torches.
[2]*fairing*, a present bought at a fair.
[3]*yataghan*, a Turkish sword.

And I'd pay a golden guinea
   And she'd fill her holland pinny[4]
With white kittens and red roses and blue stone from Turkestan!

London streets have flowers anew,
   London shops with gems are set;
When you've none to give them to,
   What is pearl or violet?
Vain things both and emptinesses,
   So they wait a dream-Princess's
Coming, if she's sweet and solemn with gray eyes and hair of jet!

---

[4]*pinny*, pinafore.

G. K. CHESTERTON

Gilbert Keith Chesterton needs no introduction to most readers, for if they do not know him as a poet they must have met him in the role of essayist, novelist, dramatist, controversialist, critic, or writer of fantastic short stories. Were he not active in so many fields at once, he might be more renowned as a poet; as it happens, his uncanny gift of paradox has won him his most general recognition as an essayist.

He was born in Kensington, London, in 1874, and attended St. Paul's School and the Slade School of Art. He began his literary career as a book reviewer, from which early experience he went on to give the world extended and penetrating studies of Dickens, Browning, and Bernard Shaw. Perhaps his best known book of literary criticism is the wayward and brilliant *Victorian Age in Literature* (1913).

His essays, of which many volumes have been published since *Heretics* (1905), have a disconcerting way of kicking over the conventions with a fine show of iconoclasm, when in reality all his dazzling play of paradox and irony is but a cloak for an essentially orthodox mind. Particularly is this true of his essays on religion, which constitute the ablest *apologia* of the modern Anglo-Catholic Church. Mr. Chesterton has discovered the way to make orthodoxy attractive. Stuart P. Sherman called him "a very sophisticated and exhilarating conservative."

Much of his poetry will be found in *Poems* (1915), from which "Lepanto" is reprinted. *The Ballad of the White Horse* (1911) is a long narrative ballad in his best manner. *Wine, Water and Song* (1915) and *The Ballad of St. Barbara* (1922) are later contributions to the body of high-spirited song which Mr. Chesterton finally brought together in *Collected Poems* (1927). "Lepanto" is universally admired as his greatest achievement in verse—one of the greatest, indeed, of his time. The reader will do well not to dwell too closely on the historical allusions with which the poem is packed, but, reading it aloud, catch the gorgeous color and irresistible swing which make it such a stirring challenge to the imagination.

LEPANTO[1]

GILBERT KEITH CHESTERTON

White founts falling in the courts of the sun,
And the Soldan of Byzantium[2] is smiling as they run;
There is laughter like the fountains in that face of all men
        feared;
It stirs the forest darkness, the darkness of his beard,
It curls the blood-red crescent, the crescent of his lips,
For the inmost sea of all the earth is shaken with his ships.
They have dared the white republics up the capes of Italy,
They have dashed the Adriatic round the Lion of the Sea,[3]
And the Pope has cast his arms abroad for agony and loss,
And called the kings of Christendom for swords about the Cross.
The cold queen of England[4] is looking in the glass;
The shadow of the Valois[5] is yawning at the Mass;
From evening isles fantastical rings faint the Spanish gun,
And the Lord upon the Golden Horn[6] is laughing in the Sun.

Dim drums throbbing, in the hills half heard,
Where only on a nameless throne a crownless prince[7] has stirred;

---

[1] The Battle of Lepanto (October 7, 1571) was notable as the beginning of the decline of Turkish power in the eastern Mediterranean. As in many of the great wars of history, it was superior sea power which finally determined the outcome of the conflict. The Turks, possessed of many ships, had captured Cyprus and menaced the trade routes of Venice and Spain. Under the inspiration of Pope Pius V a great fleet of vessels was collected from the countries of the western Mediterranean and placed under the brilliant leadership of Don John of Austria, half brother of King Philip II of Spain. Although the Christian fleet was outnumbered, it possessed the better equipment and the superior discipline. The victory in the Bay of Lepanto was overwhelming, and the Turkish power was forever broken. Incidentally, this was the last great naval battle in which galleys were employed.

Among the fighters in the Christian ships was Miguel de Cervantes, a youth of twenty-four, who

> " . . . sees across a weary land a straggling road in Spain,
>   Up which a lean and foolish knight forever rides in vain,"

and smiles, according to Mr. Chesterton, as he realizes that Don Quixote, the creature of his brain, will soon laugh from the stage the outmoded tradition of chivalry which Don John romantically exemplifies.

[2] *Soldan of Byzantium*, the sultan of the Byzantine empire, the capital of which was Constantinople, or Byzantium.

[3] *Lion of the Sea*, Venice, chief of the Italian seaport republics, whose Patron Saint, Mark, has a lion as his symbol.

[4] *the cold queen of England*, Elizabeth.

[5] *the shadow of the Valois*, probably Henry of Navarre.

[6] *Golden Horn*, the harbor of Constantinople.

[7] *a crownless prince*, Don John (1545-1578) was the illegitimate son of Philip I of Spain.

Where, risen from a doubtful seat and half-attainted stall,
The last knight of Europe takes weapons from the wall,
The last and lingering troubadour to whom the bird has sung,
That once went singing southward when all the world was
    young.
In that enormous silence, tiny and unafraid,
Comes up along a winding road the noise of the Crusade.
Strong gongs groaning as the guns boom far,
Don John of Austria is going to the war,
Stiff flags straining in the night-blasts cold,
In the gloom black-purple, in the glint old-gold,
Torchlight crimson on the copper kettle-drums,
Then the tuckets,[8] then the trumpets, then the cannon, and he
    comes.
Don John laughing in the brave beard curled;
Spurning of his stirrups like the thrones of all the world,
Holding his head up for a flag of all the free.
Love-light of Spain—hurrah!
Death-light of Africa!
Don John of Austria
Is riding to the sea.

Mahound[9] is in his paradise above the evening star,
(*Don John of Austria is going to the war.*)
He moves a mighty turban on the timeless houri's knees,
His turban that is woven of the sunsets and the seas.
He shakes the peacock gardens as he rises from his ease,
And he strides among the tree-tops and is taller than the
    trees;
And his voice through all the garden is a thunder sent to bring
Black Azrael and Ariel and Ammon on the wing.[10]
Giants and the Genii,
Multiplex of wing and eye,

---

[8]*tucket*, a flourish of trumpets.
[9]*Mahound*, Mahomet.
[10]*Azrael, Ariel, Ammon*, three of the powerful angels who, according to the Mohammedan belief, attend God.

Whose strong obedience broke the sky
When Solomon was king.

They rush in red and purple from the red clouds of the morn,
From the temples where the yellow gods shut up their eyes in
    scorn;
They rise in green robes roaring from the green hells of the sea
Where fallen skies and evil hues and eyeless creatures be,
On them the sea-valves cluster and the gray sea-forests curl,
Splashed with a splendid sickness, the sickness of the pearl;
They swell in sapphire smoke out of the blue cracks of the
    ground—
They gather and then wonder and give worship to Mahound.
And he saith, "Break up the mountains where the hermit-folk
    can hide,
And sift the red and silver sands lest bone of saint abide,
And chase the Giaours[11] flying night and day, not giving rest,
For that which was our trouble comes again out of the west.

We have set the seal of Solomon on all things under sun,
Of knowledge and of sorrow and endurance of things done.
But a noise is in the mountains, in the mountains, and I know
The voice that shook our palaces—four hundred years ago;
It is he that saith not 'Kismet'; it is he that knows not Fate;
It is Richard,[12] it is Raymond, it is Godfrey, at the gate!
It is he whose loss is laughter when he counts the wager worth,
Put down your feet upon him, that our peace be on the earth."
For he heard drums groaning, and he heard guns jar.
(*Don John of Austria is going to the war.*)
Sudden and still—hurrah!
Bolt from Iberia!
Don John of Austria
Is gone by Alcalar.[13]

---

[11]*Giaours*, infidels.
[12]*Richard*, Richard Coeur de Lion, a leader of the Third Crusade. *Raymond*, *Godfrey*, leaders
of the First Crusade.
[13]*Alcalar*, a town near Madrid.

St. Michael's on his Mountain[14] in the sea-roads of the north
(*Don John of Austria is girt and going forth.*)
Where the gray seas glitter, and the sharp tides shift,
And the sea-folk labor, and the red sails lift.
He shakes his lance of iron, and he claps his wings of stone;
The noise is gone through Normandy; the noise is gone alone;
The North is full of tangled things[15] and texts and aching eyes,
And dead is all the innocence of anger and surprise,
And Christian killeth Christian in a narrow, dusty room,
And Christian dreadeth Christ that hath a newer face of doom,
And Christian hateth Mary that God kissed in Galilee—
But Don John of Austria is riding to the sea.
Don John calling through the blast and the eclipse,
Crying with the trumpet, with the trumpet of his lips,
Trumpet that sayeth *Ha!*
Domino gloria![16]
Don John of Austria
Is shouting to the ships.

King Philip's in his closet with the Fleece about his neck[17]
(*Don John of Austria is armed upon the deck.*)
The walls are hung with velvet that is black and soft as sin,
And little dwarfs creep out of it and little dwarfs creep in.
He holds a crystal phial[18] that has colors like the moon,
He touches, and it tingles, and he trembles very soon,
And his face is as a fungus of a leprous white and gray
Like plants in the high houses, that are shuttered from the day,
And death is in the phial and the end of noble work,
But Don John of Austria has fired upon the Turk.
Don John's hunting, and his hounds have bayed—
Booms away past Italy the rumor of his raid.

[14]*St. Michael's on his Mountain,* Michael, the warrior saint, was said to have appeared on a mountainous island off Penzance in Cornwall.
[15]*the North is full of tangled things,* the lines which follow describe the discord of the Reformation.
[16]*Domino gloria!* Glory to God!
[17]*King Philip,* Philip II of Spain, wearing the order of the Golden Fleece.
[18]*a crystal phial,* Philip was suspected of poisoning his enemies.

Gun upon gun, ha! ha!
Gun upon gun, hurrah!
Don John of Austria
Has loosed the cannonade.

The Pope was in his chapel before day or battle broke,
(*Don John of Austria is hidden in the smoke.*)
The hidden room in man's house where God sits all the year,
The secret window whence the world looks small and very dear.
He sees as in a mirror on the monstrous twilight sea
The crescent of his cruel ships whose name is mystery;
They fling great shadows foe-wards, making Cross and Castle[19]
    dark,
They veil the plumed lions on the galleys of St. Mark;[20]
And above the ships are palaces of brown, black-bearded chiefs,
And below the ships are prisons, where with multitudinous
    griefs,
Christian captives sick and sunless, all a laboring race repines
Like a race in sunken cities, like a nation in the mines.
They are lost like slaves that swat,[21] and in the skies of morning
    hung
The stairways of the tallest gods when tyranny was young.
They are countless, voiceless, hopeless as those fallen or fleeing
    on
Before the high kings' horses in the granite of Babylon.
And many a one grows witless in his quiet room in hell
Where a yellow face looks inward through the lattice of his cell,
And he finds his God forgotten, and he seeks no more a sign—
(*But Don John of Austria has burst the battle-line!*)
Don John pounding from the slaughter-painted poop,
Purpling all the ocean like a bloody pirate's sloop,
Scarlet running over on the silvers and the golds,
Breaking of the hatches up and bursting of the holds,

---

[19]*Cross and Castle*, the arms of Aragon and of Castile.
[20]*galleys of St. Mark*, the Venetian ships.
[21]*swat*, sweated.

Thronging of the thousands up that labor under sea,
White for bliss and blind for sun and stunned for liberty.
Vivat Hispania![22]
Domino Gloria!
Don John of Austria
Has set his people free!

Cervantes[23] on his galley sets the sword back in the sheath
(*Don John of Austria rides homeward with a wreath.*)
And he sees across a weary land a straggling road in Spain,
Up which a lean and foolish knight forever rides in vain,
And he smiles, but not as Sultans smile, and settles back the
          blade. . . .
(*But Don John of Austria rides home from the Crusade.*)

---

[22]*Vivat Hispania!* Long live Spain!
[23]*Cervantes* (1547-1616), author of "Don Quixote."

PADRAIC COLUM

Padraic Colum was born in 1881 at Longford, in the very center of Ireland. As all of his poetry shows, he was brought up in intimate contact with Irish peasant life, and the influence of his earlier years still dominates his writing, even though he has lived in the United States since 1916. He was educated only in the schools of County Longford, but grew up in the thick of the new literary movement which centered about the figures of Yeats, Synge, and A. E., in Dublin. When A. E. published the collection of poems by the younger writers entitled *New Songs* (1904), Mr. Colum shared the principal honors with Seumas O'Sullivan. He has developed into one of the outstanding figures of the second generation of Ireland's literary renascence, combining in his poetry and his plays something of the music of Mr. Yeats, much of the earthy tang of Synge, something of A. E.'s mystical vision, and something of Douglas Hyde's faithful rendition of folk accents.

But most of all Padraic Colum is simply himself. The title of his chief volume of poetry, *Wild Earth* (1907, with additional poems 1909 and 1916), asserts the peculiar spirit of his art. For his first preoccupation is with "the proud and hard earth" as the peasant knows it. His poem "The Plougher" opens with the stark, dramatic suddenness of a Hardy novel:

> Sunset and silence! A man: around him earth savage, earth broken;
> Beside him two horses—a plough!

There is the setting, there the protagonist. The same sympathy with those whose lives are close to the soil is evident in his best-known poem, "An Old Woman of the Roads." In *Creatures* (1927), Mr. Colum departs from his more familiar subjects to draw a series of odd animal portraits.

AN OLD WOMAN OF THE ROADS*

Padraic Colum

Oh, to have a little house!
To own the hearth and stool and all!
The heaped-up sods upon the fire,
The pile of turf against the wall!

To have a clock with weights and chains
And pendulum swinging up and down!
A dresser filled with shining delph,
Speckled and white and blue and brown!

I could be busy all the day
Clearing and sweeping hearth and floor,
And fixing on their shelf again
My white and blue and speckled store!

I could be quiet there at night
Beside the fire and by myself,
Sure of a bed and loath to leave
The ticking clock and the shining delph!

Och! but I'm weary of mist and dark,
And roads where there's never a house nor bush,
And tired I am of bog and road,
And the crying wind and the lonesome hush!

And I am praying to God on high,
And I am praying Him night and day,
For a little house—a house of my own—
Out of the wind's and the rain's way.

*From *Wild Earth and Other Poems* by Padraic Colum.   Copyright 1916 by The Macmillan Company.   Reprinted by permission.

FRANCES CORNFORD

Frances (Darwin) Cornford's life has been closely associated with Cambridge, England, for there she was born in 1886, there she married in 1909 Francis Macdonald Cornford, a Fellow of Trinity College, and there she lives with her family of three sons and two daughters. "Autumn Morning at Cambridge" is a pleasant glimpse of the university life which she knows so well. She is a daughter of Sir Francis Darwin, a granddaughter of Charles Darwin.

Her best poetry is contained in *Spring Morning* (1915) and *Autumn Midnight* (1923). Her style is invariably light but sure, deft without stooping to prettiness. Her compact stanzas reflect a personality which has lived quietly and richly.

AUTUMN MORNING AT CAMBRIDGE

FRANCES CORNFORD

I ran out in the morning, when the air was clean and new,
And all the grass was glittering and gray with autumn dew,
I ran out to the apple tree and pulled an apple down,
And all the bells were ringing in the old gray town.

Down in the town, off the bridges and the grass
They are sweeping up the leaves to let the people pass,
Sweeping up the old leaves, golden-reds and browns,
While the men go to lecture with the wind in their gowns.

IN FRANCE

FRANCES CORNFORD

The poplars in the fields of France
Are golden ladies come to dance;
But yet to see them there is none
But I and the September sun.

The girl who in their shadow sits
Can only see the sock she knits;
Her dog is watching all the day
That not a cow shall go astray.

The leisurely, contented cows
Can only see the earth they browse;
Their piebald bodies through the grass
With busy, munching noses pass.

Alone the sun and I behold
Processions crowned with shining gold—
The poplars in the fields of France,
Like glorious ladies come to dance.

W. H. DAVIES

The life of William Henry Davies is in sharp contrast to the somewhat stereotyped careers of most British poets; not for him a sheltered youth in an atmosphere of culture, matriculation at Oxford or Cambridge, travel on the Continent, and eventual launching in London on well-chosen letters of introduction. Mr. Davies was born, in 1870, in a public-house, of humble Welsh parents, in the town of Newport, Monmouthshire; his schooling was negligible in amount and quality; he knocked about from one unimportant job to another, never settling into a fixed vocation, and generally preferring idleness to work—in short, he became a tramp, or, as he has called himself, a "supertramp."

Thanks to a small legacy, he had a sure income, though it was only eight shillings a week. It was enough, at any rate, to take him to America, where for several years he lived the life of any hobo—working a little in orchards or harvest fields when he felt like it, wintering in a comfortable jail, drinking, pilfering, begging—an ordinary and quite disreputable vagabond. He visited England several times by cattle boat, a memory of which trips he has put into "Sheep." Feeling the call of the Klondike gold-rush, he started West, but slipped as he was jumping a moving freight train, and lost a foot.

This accident threatened to put an end to his wanderings. His family sent for him, and he went home; but the vagrant in him would not be still. He set out for London with the unaccountable purpose of being a poet. Perhaps he knew better than anyone else what songs had been stirring within him; but that out of the sordidness of his previous existence should have welled poetry of utterly unaffected naïveté, like the spontaneous singing of a bird, is one of the incredible episodes in the history of English literature. His sweet and simple lyrics, suggestive of Blake or Wordsworth or Herrick, bear no trace of sophistication or disillusionment.

His first book, *The Soul's Destroyer* (1907), was published at his own expense, with money he saved from his legacy while peddling pins for a livelihood. The venture was apparently a complete failure until some lucky publicity in the *Daily Mail* and recognition by Bernard Shaw brought sudden fame. The poet who had thus begun his literary career in the squalor of a London flop-house was, anomalously enough, to become a leader of the country school of poets who find their inspiration in lanes and hedgerows, larks and daisies.

The best of Mr. Davies's prolific production has been gathered in *Collected Poems: First Series* (1916) and *Second Series* (1923). A volume of *Selected Poems* was brought out in 1925. Students of this author will also want to read *The Autobiography of a Super-Tramp* (1906).

A GREETING

WILLIAM H. DAVIES

Good morning, Life—and all
Things glad and beautiful.
My pockets nothing hold,
But he that owns the gold,
The Sun, is my great friend—
His spending has no end.

Hail to the morning sky,
Which bright clouds measure high;
Hail to you birds whose throats
Would number leaves by notes;
Hail to you shady bowers,
And you green fields of flowers.

Hail to you women fair,
That make a show so rare
In cloth as white as milk—
Be't calico or silk:
Good morning, Life—and all
Things glad and beautiful.

THE SLEEPERS

W. H. DAVIES

As I walked down the waterside
  This silent morning, wet and dark;
Before the cocks in farmyards crowed,
  Before the dogs began to bark;
Before the hour of five was struck
By old Westminster's mighty clock.

As I walked down the waterside
　This morning, in the cold damp air,
I saw a hundred women and men
　Huddled in rags and sleeping there:
These people have no work, thought I,
And long before their time they die.

That moment, on the waterside,
　A lighted car came at a bound;
I looked inside, and saw a score
　Of pale and weary men that frowned;
Each man set in a huddled heap,
Carried to work while fast asleep.

Ten cars rushed down the waterside,
　Like lighted coffins in the dark;
With twenty dead men in each car,
　That must be brought alive by work:
These people work too hard, thought I,
And long before their time they die.

GEOFFREY DEARMER

Geoffrey Dearmer was born in London in 1893; his father was an author and professor of art at King's College, his mother a novelist and dramatist. He grew up in London and was educated at Christ Church College, Oxford. He saw service during the World War both at Gallipoli in 1915 and in France in 1916, and remained in the British army until 1921. Many of his poems celebrate some whimsical aspect of the animal kingdom, for Mr. Dearmer has developed his love of animals as his special province in poetry. "The Tailor," which appeared in *The Saturday Review of Literature*, covers the whole subject of his interest and affords an example of his ingenuity as a versifier.

His poems have been published in *Poems* (1918) and *The Day's Delight* (1923).

THE TAILOR

Geoffrey Dearmer

You may call the feminine dog a bitch,
    You may call the pig a pig,
      You may abuse any beast you choose
From the elephants down to the pygmy shrews,
From the elephants up to the crowned hoopoes,
    Tiny or little or big:
  Only you shall not dare
  To abuse the things they wear.
Things which are never too loose or tight
And never too heavy and never too light
    But absolutely
    Oh, so minutely
  Adequate, suitable, right.

  Dresses for Cinderella
  Of silk and satin and cloth
Are not a patch on the bat's umbrella
  Or the powdered fans of the moth;
  Or the frog's green jumping-breeches;
  Or the leopard's costume which is
A dazzle of spots like a veiled design;
  Or the zebra's marvelous dazzle of line;
  Or the gibbon's gloves or the tufts of hair
Grown in the boots of the polar bear;
  Or the penguin's snowy vest;
  Or the cockatoo's white crest;
Or the morning coat which the wagtails know
Is always *de rigueur*[1] and never *de trop*,
  Or the lamb's white woolly pants,
  Or lumbering elephants'

---

[1] *de rigueur*, indispensable; *de trop*, too much.

Gray overalls that almost might
Be skins they fit so exactly right,
Never too loose or tight,
Never too heavy or light.
But absolutely,
Oh, so minutely,
Adequate, suitable, right.

WALTER DE LA MARE

Walter (John) de la Mare was born in 1873 at Charlton, in Kent, of Huguenot, English, and Scotch ancestry. He attended St. Paul's Cathedral Choir School in London, but his formal education ended at the age of seventeen. For the next eighteen years he was employed in the Anglo-American Oil Company, a branch of the Standard Oil Company. When he was almost thirty years of age he began to break loose from the bondage of his business duties and to write reviews which, appearing in the literary weeklies, soon attracted attention by their rare distinction of style.

From this lesser bondage of journalism he was not long in passing to the writing of poems and stories. His first collection of poems, *Songs of Childhood* (1902), appeared under the pseudonym of Walter Ramal; a revised edition appeared in 1916. These first verses, originally written for his own children, were conceived so completely in the mood of childhood that only those who have kept something of their own childhood intact and unspoiled can appreciate them. In *Poems* (1906) and *The Listeners* (1912) there is the same ability to make visible the lovely imaginings of children and to create, by delicate suggestion, sometimes by the mere play of words, a world of fairy beauty. Other poems than those for children will be found in these volumes, but all are haunted by the play of the author's fancy. In *Peacock Pie* (1913) Mr. De la Mare has brought together the best of his children's verses, with the result that this book is clearly the finest thing of its kind since Stevenson. For here Mr. De la Mare's mastery of that subtlest quality of poetry—magic—produces an illusion of the supernatural without taxing our credulity. His fairies are good, honest English elves, without the more extravagant attributes of the Irish leprechauns; his fairyland is no more than the moonlit meads of his own countryside—and yet so completely is every subject translated in his glamorous and sensitive fancy that his readers willingly become children for an hour. And that is no mean achievement, as Stuart P. Sherman pointed out in a passage of inspired beauty:

"In a world that is old and cold and bright with frost and stars, bliss is a little thing like a spark in the night, and the cozy and quiet folk are few—rabbits in their burrows, birds in their nests, and children in their beds. If one could draw a magic circle around their 'infant joy' and keep it young forever! If a man had three wishes, would not the first bring back the roses to the old mother's cheek, and the second seat him at her knee, a boy again? Who could desire to be very great that had the choice of being very little?"

The later volumes of Mr. De la Mare's poetry, *Motley* (1918), *Flora* (1921), and *The Veil* (1921) show a change of tone. The fascinating music is still there, but the words are of soberer import and addressed more often to the mature and thoughtful. At Mr. De la Mare's request, two of the poems reprinted herewith are taken from these recent books, and "The Sleeper" is from *The Listeners*. *Collected Poems 1901-1918* appeared in 1920, *Selected Poems*, in 1927.

Mr. De la Mare's place is not less secure in prose than in poetry. He has a number of novels to his credit, and especially *Memoirs of a Midget* (1921), a story of peculiar originality, intimate insight, and ingenious symbolism. He has also written many short stories and prose fantasies and has compiled a sumptuous anthology of children's verse, *Come Hither* (1923), garnished with inimitably discursive and informal "notes."

SUPPOSE

WALTER DE LA MARE

Suppose . . . and suppose that a wild little Horse of Magic
    Came cantering out of the sky,
With bridle of silver, and into the saddle I mounted,
    To fly—and to fly;

And we stretched up into the air, fleeting on in the sunshine,
    A speck in the gleam,
On galloping hoofs, his mane in the wind out-flowing,
    In a shadowy stream;

And oh, when, all lone, the gentle star of evening
    Came crinkling into the blue,
A magical castle we saw in the air, like a cloud of moonlight,
    As onward we flew;

And across the green moat on the drawbridge we foamed and
    we snorted,
    And there was a beautiful Queen
Who smiled at me strangely; and spoke to my wild little Horse,
    too—
    A lovely and beautiful Queen;

And she cried with delight—and delight—to her delicate
    maidens,
    "Behold my daughter—my dear!"
And they crowned me with flowers, and then to their harps
    sate playing,
    Solemn and clear;

And magical cakes and goblets were spread on the table;
    And at window the birds came in;
Hopping along with bright eyes, pecking crumbs from the
    platters,
    And sipped of the wine;

And splashing up—up to the roof tossed fountains of crystal;
    And Princes in scarlet and green
Shot with their bows and arrows, and kneeled with their dishes
    Of fruits for the Queen;

And we walked in a magical garden with rivers and bowers,
    And my bed was of ivory and gold;
And the Queen breathed soft in my ear a song of enchantment—
    And I never grew old. . . .

And I never, never came back to the earth, oh, never and never;
    How mother would cry and cry!
There'd be snow on the fields then, and all these sweet flowers
    in the winter
    Would wither, and die. . . .

Suppose . . . and suppose . . .

THE SLEEPER

WALTER DE LA MARE

As Ann came in one summer's day,
    She felt that she must creep;
So silent was the clear cool house,
    It seemed a house of sleep.
And sure, when she pushed open the door,
    Rapt in the stillness there,
Her mother sat, with stooping head,
    Asleep upon a chair;
Fast—fast asleep; her two hands laid
    Loose-folded on her knee,
So that her small unconscious face
    Looked half unreal to be;
So calmly lit with sleep's pale light
    Each feature was; so fair

Her forehead—every trouble was
Smoothed out beneath her hair.
But though her mind in dream now moved,
Still seemed her gaze to rest
From out beneath her fast-sealed lids,
Above her moving breast,
On Ann, as quite, quite still she stood;
Yet slumber lay so deep
Even her hands upon her lap
Seemed saturate with sleep.
And as Ann peeped, a cloudlike dread
Stole over her, and then
On stealthy, mouselike feet she trod,
And tiptoed out again.

GOOD-BYE

Walter de la Mare

The last of last words spoken is, Good-bye—
The last dismantled flower in the wood-grown hedge,
The last thin rumor of a feeble bell far ringing,
The last blind rat to spurn the mildewed rye.

A hardening darkness glasses the haunted eye,
Shines into nothing the watcher's burnt-out candle,
Wreathes into scentless nothing the wasting incense,
Faints in the outer silence the hunting cry.

Love of its muted music breathes no sigh,
Thought in her ivory tower gropes in her spinning,
Toss on in vain the whispering trees of Eden,
Last of all last words spoken is, Good-bye.

H. L. DOAK

Hugo L. Doak was born in 1890 in Dublin, where he still lives. He attended Dublin University. Although he has written poems in the Irish-English dialect, such a piece as "The Bathers" shows his command of the more conventional language of English poetry. It shows his command, also, of the difficult art of compression, which is a large part of the art of the lyric. Mr. Doak's work has been published under the title of *The Three-Rock Road* (1919).

THE BATHERS

H. L. DOAK

Spill hither, girls, the orient gold
    Of your bright hair in disarray,
Ere all the summer hours be told,
    And youth a dream of yesterday.

Come, bathe you fearless in the brook
    That ripples in the lonely sun.
Actaeon[1] lurks not here to look
    On that whereby he was undone.

Only the forest thrills like him
    In token of the old distress,
Trembling in every leafy limb
    Before your naked loveliness.

[1] *Actaeon*, a hunter who, having by chance seen Artemis while she was bathing, was changed into a stag and torn to pieces by his dogs.

CAMILLA DOYLE

Camilla Doyle was born in 1888 in the Cathedral Close of the ancient city of Norwich, Norfolk, and grew up in the same fortunate environment. For five years she studied art at the Slade School of Art, University College, London. She also traveled in North Italy, France, and Belgium, and is especially familiar with English localities noted for their historical associations. Poetry is to her only second to painting. She has not only exhibited oil paintings and drawings, but is known for furniture of her own design and painting. Her poems are marked by a delicate perceptiveness and an unfailing gayety.

She has published two volumes: *Poems* (1923) and *Poems* (1927).

CUCKOOS, LARKS, AND SPARROWS

Camilla Doyle

The cuckoo is a heartless bird,
　　Enraging kindly pairs;
But he sounds gayer, being rid
　　Of home and all his cares.

He has a merry double note,
　　Copied quite verbatim
From the imps that laughed when Adam fell;
　　And decent sparrows hate him.

Though the lark can sing with mouths to fill,
　　Not everyone can be
A genius and a housekeeper
　　Together, as can he.

Housework would make the cuckoo
　　Too tired to cuckoo more;
His head would ring all day with dreams
　　That came the night before,

Hammering against his brows
　　For notes to let them through—
He'd put them off all day and then
　　At night postpone them, too.

The sparrows live in dusty crowds
　　With endless quarreling
For building-straws and crumbs of bread—
　　No wonder they don't sing.

The lark is strong enough for both
　　Singing and home-affairs;
But the cuckoo's gayest, being rid
　　Of home and all his cares.

JOHN DRINKWATER

John Drinkwater was born in 1882 in Birmingham and attended the Oxford High School. Like Mr. De la Mare, he went to poetry from business, having spent some twelve years as an insurance clerk before he was free to devote himself entirely to literature. Although his first book, *Poems* (1903), was published when he was twenty-one, his development was slow, and he was long in gaining recognition. He is not a spontaneous lyricist but instead a quiet thinker who has found, in poetry, an intellectual rather than an emotional outlet. With some justice his poetry has been accused of coldness and austerity, but it has never been found wanting in sincerity. The best of his poems have been collected in *Poems, 1908-1919* (1919), to which must be added the subsequent volumes *Tides* (1917), *Seeds of Time* (1921), and *New Poems* (1925).

It is as a dramatist that Drinkwater has scored his greater success. *Abraham Lincoln—A Play* (1919), appearing at the close of the World War, achieved a sensational popularity on both sides of the Atlantic for the simple nobility of its portraiture. As manager of the Birmingham Repertory Theater Company, Mr. Drinkwater produced several poetic plays during the War, which were published as *Pawns* (1920). Of these "X=O: A Night of the Trojan War" is an unforgetable illustration of the futility of warfare.

ANTHONY CRUNDLE

John Drinkwater

Here lies the body of
ANTHONY CRUNDLE
Farmer, of this parish,
Who died in 1849 at the age of 82.
"He delighted in music."
R. I. P.
And of
SUSAN,
For fifty-three years his wife,
Who died in 1860, aged 86.

Anthony Crundle of Dorrington Wood
    Played on a piccolo. Lord was he,
For seventy years, of sheaves that stood
    Under the perry and cider tree;
    Anthony Crundle, R. I. P.

And because he prospered with sickle and scythe,
    With cattle a-field and laboring ewe,
Anthony was uncommonly blithe,
    And played of a night to himself and Sue;
    Anthony Crundle, eighty-two.

The earth to till, and a tune to play,
    And Susan for fifty years and three,
And Dorrington Wood at the end of day. . . .
    May Providence do no worse by me;
    Anthony Crundle, R. I. P.

RECIPROCITY

John Drinkwater

I do not think that skies and meadows are
Moral, or that the fixture of a star
Comes of a quiet spirit, or that trees
Have wisdom in their windless silences.
Yet these are things invested in my mood
With constancy, and peace, and fortitude,
That in my troubled season I can cry
Upon the wide composure of the sky,
And envy fields, and wish that I might be
As little daunted as a star or tree.

JOHN FERGUSON

John Ferguson was born in Callander, Scotland, in 1891, a collateral descendant of the eighteenth-century Scottish poet, Robert Beattie. His early years were spent in the wild and bleak Hebrides; later he traveled on the Continent and lived for some time in Paris and Vienna. He was educated privately and at Edinburgh University. The major part of Mr. Ferguson's work has been as dramatist and novelist. His plays, which treat Scottish material much as the Irish had already treated the material from their own national life, have been produced by the Scottish Repertory Theater, Glasgow, the Abbey Theater, Dublin, and the Arts League, London. His novels are *Stealthy Terror* (1917), *The Dark Geraldine* (1920), and *The Secret Road* (1925).

The amusing thumb-nail portrait called "The Optimist" is taken from *On Vimy Ridge and Other Poems* (1917). Its originality appears to justify the comment of the *London Times Literary Supplement:* "Mr. Ferguson is a poet who sees his own visions and finds his own inspirations."

THE OPTIMIST

John Ferguson

For miles around the parish steeple
The curate he goes in and out,
And up and down and round about
The houses of the working-people;
He listens to their newest bickers,
Smiles wanly to the merry fire,
And hopes they'll come to hear the Vicar's
Impromptu thoughts on Jeremiah.

JAMES ELROY FLECKER

James Elroy Flecker, a son of the headmaster of Dean Close School, Cheltenham, was born in London in 1884. He attended Uppingham and Trinity Colleges, Oxford, and afterwards went to Cambridge to complete his study of Oriental languages. After travel in France and Italy, he went to the East in the British Consular Service. Between 1910 and 1913 he was stationed at Constantinople, Smyrna, Beirut, and other points in Turkey and Syria. This experience in the East, coupled with his enthusiastic study of Oriental literatures, is reflected in much of his work, especially his play "Hassan" and his well-known poem "The Golden Journey to Samarkand."

In 1913 tuberculosis forced him to give up his diplomatic work and retire to Switzerland, where he died of the disease two years later, at the age of thirty-one. Thus England lost one of her most brilliant younger poets at the very time when she could least spare him.

Flecker's poetry is, for the most part, the poetry of sheer romanticism, thrilling with the gorgeous colors and the magical names of the East. The passion for beauty deliberately evoked by the craft of the poet was sufficient for his earlier period. When illness came upon him, a new preoccupation with the thought of death appeared in his pages, and his verse took a sober tone. "To a Poet a Thousand Years Hence" is one of the tenderest and most wistful lyrics of our time. It is reprinted from *Collected Poems* (1917).

TO A POET A THOUSAND YEARS HENCE

James Elroy Flecker

I who am dead a thousand years,
    And wrote this sweet archaic song,
Send you my words for messengers
    The way I shall not pass along.

I care not if you bridge the seas,
    Or ride secure the cruel sky,
Or build consummate palaces
    Of metal or of masonry.

But have you wine and music still,
    And statues and a bright-eyed love,
And foolish thoughts of good and ill,
    And prayers to them who sit above?

How shall we conquer? Like a wind
    That falls at eve our fancies blow,
And old Maeonides[1] the blind
    Said it three thousand years ago.

O friend unseen, unborn, unknown,
    Student of our sweet English tongue,
Read out my words at night, alone:
    I was a poet, I was young.

Since I can never see your face,
    And never shake you by the hand,
I send my soul through time and space
    To greet you. You will understand.

---

[1] *Maeonides*, Homer.

JOHN FREEMAN

John Freeman was born in London in 1882. His place is, however, among the country poets, for most of his poems are landscape pieces which reflect a close observation of the English countryside. The influence of the World War is seen in his later poems, as in the memorable pathos of "The Visit." Even in such narrative poems, the technique is still basically pictorial.

The best of his poetry written between 1909 and 1920 has been collected in *Poems New and Old* (1920). He has also published *Music: Lyrical and Narrative Poems* (1921) and various volumes of critical studies. In 1920 his poetry was awarded the annual Hawthornden prize of £100.

THE VISIT

John Freeman

I reached the cottage. I knew it from the card
He had given me—the low door heavily barred,
Steep roof, and two yews whispering on guard.

Dusk thickened as I came, but I could smell
First red wallflower and an early hyacinth bell,
And see dim primroses. "Oh, I can tell,"

I thought, "they love the flowers he loved." The rain
Shook from fruit bushes in new showers again
As I brushed past, and gemmed the window pane.

Bare was the window yet, and the lamp bright.
I saw them sitting there, streamed with the light
That overflowed upon the inclosing night.

"Poor things, I wonder why they've lit up so,"
A voice said, passing on the road below.
"Who are they?" asked another. "Don't you know?"

Their voices crept away. I heard no more
As I crossed the garden and knocked at the door.
I waited, then knocked louder than before,

And thrice, and still in vain. So on the grass
I stepped, and tap-tapped on the rainy glass.
Then did a girl without turning toward me pass

From the room. I heard the heavy barred door creak,
And a voice entreating from the doorway speak,
"Will you come this way?"—a voice childlike and quick.

The way was dark. I followed her white frock,
Past the now-chiming, sweet-tongued unseen clock,
Into the room. One figure like a rock

Draped in an unstarred night—his mother—bowed
Unrising and unspeaking. His aunt stood
And took my hand, murmuring, "So good, so good!"

Never such quiet people had I known.
Voices they scarcely needed, they had grown
To talk less by the word than muted tone.

"We'll soon have tea," the girl said. "Please sit here."
She pushed a heavy, low, deep-seated chair
I knew at once was his; and I sat there.

I could not look at them. It seemed I made
Noise in that quietness. I was afraid
To look or speak until the aunt's voice said,

"You were his friend." And that "You were!" awoke
My sense, and nervousness found voice and spoke
Of what he had been, until a bullet broke

A too-brief friendship. The rock-like mother kept
Night still around her. The aunt silently wept,
And the girl into the screen's low shadow stepped.

"You were great friends," said with calm voice the mother.
I answered, "Never friend had such another."
Then the girl's lips, "Nor sister such a brother."

Her words were like a sounding pebble cast
Into a hollow silence; but at last
She moved and, bending to my low chair, passed

Swift, leaf-like fingers o'er my face and said,
"You are not like him." And as she turned her head
Into full light beneath the lamp's green shade

I saw the sunken spaces of her eyes.
Then, her face listening to my dumb surprise,
"Forgive," she said, "a blind girl's liberties.

"You were his friend; I wanted so to see
The friends my brother had. Now let's have tea."
She poured, and passed a cup and cakes to me.

"These are my cakes," she smiled; and as I ate
She talked, and to the others cup and plate
Passed as they in their shadow and silence sat.

"Thanks, we are used to each other," she said when I
Rose in the awkwardness of seeing, shy
Of helping and of watching helplessly.

And from the manner of their hands 'twas clear
They too were blind; but I knew they could hear
My pitiful thoughts as I sat aching there.

. . . I needs must talk, until the girl was gone
Awhile out of the room. The lamp shone on,
But the true light out of the room was gone.

"Rose loved him so!" her mother said, and sighed.
"He was our eyes, he was our joy and pride,
And all that's left is but to say he died."

She ceased as Rose returned. Then as before
We talked and paused until, "Tell me once more,
What was it he said?" And I told her once more.

She listened; in her face was pride and pain
As in her mind's eye near he stood and plain. . . .
Then the thin leaves fell on my cheek again

And on my hands. "He must have loved you well,"
She whispered, as her hands from my hands fell.
Silence flowed back with thoughts unspeakable.

It was a painful thing to leave them there
Within the useless light and stirless air.
"Let me show you the way. Mind, there's a stair

"Here, then another stair ten paces on . . .
Isn't there a moon? Good-bye."
                                And she was gone.
Full moon upon the drenched fruit garden shone.

H. W. GARROD

"Revolt" is reprinted from *Worms and Epitaphs* (1919), a thin volume of verse by Heathcote William Garrod, Professor of Poetry in Oxford University since 1913, and Fellow and Tutor of Merton College. He was born in 1878 and is self-educated.

During the World War he visited the United States as a member of a Labor Mission. He has translated and edited various Latin texts, has published several volumes of essays on poets and poetry, and compiled *The Oxford Book of Latin Verse* (1912).

REVOLT

H. W. Garrod

Cat of my aunt, a word with you.
This is the limit. Oh, it's true,
In days gone by, cats, on the Nile,
Were sacred. Still it stirs my bile,
Staggers my reason, racks my rimes,
That you should sit upon the *Times*,
And I not dare to indicate
A distant interest in the fate
Of empires or the large affairs
Of armies or the price of shares.
West is West, and East is East,
Egypt be damned; I'll be high-priest
To that insufferable purr
And smug amenity of fur
Not an hour longer . . . And that's that:
So, shhhh—, unconscionable cat!

WILFRID WILSON GIBSON

Wilfrid Wilson Gibson was born in 1878 at Hexham, Northumberland. He was educated in private schools. For some years he lived in the eastern slums of London as a sympathetic observer and recorder of the life of the poor. He served as a private in the World War. In 1917 he visited the United States on a reading tour. Since then he has been living quietly and writing in Gloucestershire and, more recently, in Wales.

The sharp difference between his early poetic interests and his later is seen in the titles of such volumes as *The Queen's Vigil* (1902) and *Daily Bread* (1910). In other words, he started out to be another ineffectual imitation of Tennyson by writing medieval romances; but something—partly his slum experience, partly the realism of Masefield's longer poems—turned his attention to the unromantic facts of an industrial civilization. Between 1910 and 1915 he produced an astonishing amount of powerful poetry, dominated by the tragic injustices of society and at its best in narrative or dramatic forms.

The World War furnished him with new material, and in a series of unforgetable brief poems he caught pictures out of the reality of war which might have been seen in the momentary flare of a bursting shell. These intense and ghastly vignettes were published as *Battle* (1915) and remain today one of the bitterest indictments of war by one who saw it at first hand.

The War changed Mr. Gibson as it did many other British poets whose lives it spared. Perhaps his poem "Lament" helps to explain the lassitude which came over British poetry following the War. Recalling those who went, he asks:

> But we, how shall we turn to little things
> And listen to the birds and winds and streams
> Made holy by their dreams,
> Nor feel the heart-break in the heart of things?

Collected Poems, 1905-1925, appeared in 1926, and contains the contents of more than a dozen previous volumes.

FIRES*

Wilfrid Wilson Gibson

Snug in my easy chair
I stirred the fire to flame.
Fantastically fair
The flickering fancies came,
Born of heart's desire;
Amber woodlands streaming;
Topaz islands dreaming,
Sunset-cities gleaming,
Spire on burning spire;
Ruddy-windowed taverns;
Sunshine-spilling wines;
Crystal-lighted caverns
Of Golconda's mines;
Summers, unreturning;
Passion's crater yearning;
Troy, the ever-burning;
Shelley's lustral pyre;[1]
Dragon-eyes, unsleeping;
Witches' caldrons leaping;
Golden galleys sweeping
Out from sea-walled Tyre:
Fancies fugitive and fair,
Flashed with winging through the air;
Till, dazzled by the drowsy glare,
I shut my eyes to heat and light;
And saw, in sudden night,
Crouched in the dripping dark,
With streaming shoulders stark,
The man who hews the coal to feed my fire.

---

*From *Fires* by Wilfrid Wilson Gibson. Copyright 1912 by The Macmillan Company. Reprinted by permission.
[1]*Shelley's lustral pyre*, Shelley's body, washed up on the shores of the Bay of Spezia, was cremated in the ancient Greek manner.

DOUGLAS GOLDRING

Douglas Goldring was born in London in 1887, and attended Oxford without completing his course. He is an all-round man of letters, having been on the staff of *Country Life* and later, under Ford Madox Hueffer, on *The English Review*. Besides poetry he has written criticisms, a play, books of travel, and novels. All of his poetry written prior to 1922 which he cares to preserve was published in that year as *Streets*, the title of an earlier volume published in England. Of this Rebecca West has written, "I insist on saying that his volume *Streets* contains some of the loveliest verse that has ever been written about London."

Owing to the scattering of his interests, Mr. Goldring has not followed up his earlier successes as a poet, and hence remains, as a poet, comparatively unread. There are, however, in his slender production, playful wit and biting satire as well as atmospheric beauty. He is deserving of a larger audience, especially among young readers, for he has said, "My verses are mostly a young man's verses, and it is precisely young men whom I should like to read them."

DINNER-TIME (SLOANE STREET)[1]

Douglas Goldring

The lamp gives a softened light that is like a caress,
And the fire gleams cosy and red in the open grate,
Warming your bosom and neck and your shimmering dress;
And the people begin to arrive, for it's five to eight.

I'm not very near you at dinner—it wouldn't be wise,
And nobody guesses the things that we say, you and I,
When, perhaps, from the frail little tumbler, we lift our eyes
And agree that the wine's a success, and deliciously dry. . . .

Fine wine and fine jewels, white linen and beautiful frocks,
Kind glances and musical laughter and delicate food!
And my tie's well tied, and I'm pleased with my black silk
 socks;
Is it earthy of me to find these good things good?

THE SPANISH SAILOR

Douglas Goldring

Through lines of lights the river glides,
 Bestrewn with many a green-eyed ship,
And swiftly down the slinking tides
 All night the heavy steamers slip.

Bright shone the moon when he slunk down,
 A-sailing to some foreign parts,
Past Greenwich and past Gravesend Town
 And caring nought for broken hearts.

[1] *Sloane Street*, the western boundary of Belgravia, a fashionable residential section of London.

'Twas in July.   He kissed and fled:
    He stole my all and slipped to sea,
And now I wish that I was dead
    —Or that his arms were crushing me.

WEST END LANE[1]

Douglas Goldring

Off through the dripping, moonless night,
Up West End Lane and Frognal Rise,[2]
They trace their footsteps by the light
Of love that fills their weary eyes.

"Nellie, though Town's a tiresome place,
With far less joy in it than tears,
To set my lips to your warm face
Is worth a sight of dismal years!"

"And I'm so happy, Jack, with you,"
She whispers softly. . . . "See, the rain
Has stopped, the clouds are broken through,
And stars shine out, as plain as plain!"

Pausing, they gaze across the Heath[3]
Submerged in fog—a dim hushed lake
Wherein the wretched might seek death,
And lovers drown for dear love's sake.

Then clasping hands, and touching lips,
They dream beneath great somber trees,
Whence large and solemn-falling drips
Are shaken by the restless breeze.

---

[1] *West End Lane*, a street in the London suburb of Hampstead.
[2] *Frognal Rise*, a street in Hampstead.
[3] *the Heath*, Hampstead Heath, a large park in the northern part of London.

"Oh, nothing's half so sweet, my dear,
As kisses in the quiet night:
Lean close, and let me hold you near,
Put out your arms and clasp me tight!

"Why should we wait, so cold and wise?
We're only human, Nell, we two;
And even if love fades and dies—
I shall remember this; won't you?"

GERALD GOULD

Gerald Gould was born at Scarborough, Yorkshire, in 1885. He attended Magdalen College, Oxford, and was a Fellow of Merton College from 1906 to 1916. The influence of this quiet, scholastic background is evident in the cool and even restraint of his verse. "Portrait," reprinted from *Lyrics* (1906), has little of modernity in its smoothly modulated measures. It is of the classical school which belongs to no age and acknowledges only the one ideal of perfection. Mr. Gould's later lyrics are contained in *The Happy Tree* (1919) and *The Journey* (1920).

PORTRAIT

GERALD GOULD

O perfect quiet lips and hands,
   And brows made marvelous no less,
Eyes as of one that understands,
   And face fulfilled of happiness!
—O thou whose gait, whose glance, whose touch
Are quick with comfort, overmuch!—

Because thy thought is kind, thy will
   Compassionate, thy heart not hard;
So by thy grace my life shall still
   Pass in the light of thy regard,
And from thy living beauty draw
Its hope, its discipline, its law.

Thou hast that utter skill to wear
   The morning in thy brows of light,
And catch in gathering up thine hair
   The innumerable stars of night,
And from thy throat let forth the tune
Of winds and waters hushed at noon.

In thy few brief bright yesterdays
   Thou hast not dwelt with grief at all;
Yet through the stillness of thy gaze
   Tears of the grievous ages fall,
And autumn twilights have not brought
A sadder or a stranger thought.

In thee do many visions meet
   Of longing and remembering;
Thou art too young, too keen, too sweet,
   And thy mere beauty has a sting,

Whereby the eyes are wet that see
Earth's joy and sorrow joined in thee.

Thou art so excellently made
    That in thy being stand confessed
All curve and color, light and shade,
    All song and silence, speed and rest,
Blue seas, gray winds, and dawn and rain,
And dreams dreamt once but not again.

ROBERT GRAVES

Heredity and environment conspired to make Robert (Ranke) Graves a man of letters. Born in 1895 in London, the son of Alfred Percival Graves, an Irish poet, he was educated at Charterhouse and at Oxford. He went from the University to the Army, and saw active service in France. He was one of a group of friends, young soldiers and poets, who found in the World War a terrific stimulus to poetic expression. Others of this group were Siegfried Sassoon, Robert Nichols, and Charles Hamilton Sorley. Mr. Graves was the only one of this group who was not stirred to profound questionings of life and death nor moved to bitter and passionate protest against the realities of warfare. Neither did he lend himself to any falsification or glorification of these same realities. Merely he came through the War with a native gift of sanity and sweet mirth intact and undismayed.

The poems reprinted here are typical of Mr. Graves's refreshing gayety. "Free Verse" is an irreverent treatment of a form which he has no apparent need of, for regular rimes and rhythms flow from his pen with uncanny ease.

His first book, *Fairies and Fusiliers* (1917), contains some of his pleasantest writing. In *Country Sentiment* (1919) he turns, as he says, to Arcadia in trying to escape the War neurosis. More sophisticated are *The Pier Glass* (1921), *Whipperginny* (1923), and *Mock Beggar Hall* (1924). His *Collected Poems* were published in 1926.

Since 1926 Mr. Graves has been Professor of English Literature at the Egyptian National University.

In *A Survey of Modernist Poetry* (1927) Mr. Graves, with the collaboration of Laura Riding, has furnished the reader of the newer writers with a helpful and illuminating study of a dark subject. Not content with the usual generalities of criticism, he fearlessly attempts the analysis and explanation of some of the most cryptic of the modernist productions. His attitude toward his subject is, in general, sympathetic.

CAREERS

Robert Graves

Father is quite the greatest poet
That ever lived anywhere.
You say you're going to write great music—
I chose that first; it's unfair.
Besides, now I can't be the greatest painter
and do Christ and angels, or lovely pears
and apples and grapes on a green dish, or
storms at sea, or anything lovely,
Because that's been taken by Claire.

It's stupid to be an engine-driver,
And sailors are horrible men.
I won't be a tailor, I won't be a sailor,
And gardener's taken by Ben.
It's unfair if you say that you'll write great
music, you horrid, you unkind (I simply
loathe you, though you are my sister), you
beast, cad, coward, bully, liar!
Well? Say what's left for me then!

But *we* won't go to your ugly music.
(Listen!) Ben will garden and dig,
And Claire will finish her wondrous pictures
All flaming and splendid and big.
And I'll be a perfectly marvelous
carpenter, and I'll make cupboards
and benches and tables and . . . and
baths, and nice wooden boxes for
studs and money,
And you'll be jealous, you pig!

WEATHERS

THOMAS HARDY

This is the weather the cuckoo likes,
    And so do I;
When showers betumble the chestnut spikes,
    And nestlings fly;
And the little brown nightingale bills his best,
And they sit outside at "The Travelers' Rest,"
And maids come forth sprig-muslin dressed,
And citizens dream of the south and west,
    And so do I.

This is the weather the shepherd shuns,
    And so do I;
When beeches drip in browns and duns,
    And thresh, and ply;
And hill-hid tides throb, throe on throe,
And meadow rivulets overflow,
And drops on gate-bars hang in a row,
And rooks in families homeward go,
    And so do I.

UNDER THE WATERFALL

THOMAS HARDY

"Whenever I plunge my arm, like this,
In a basin of water, I never miss
The sweet, sharp sense of a fugitive day
Fetched back from its thickening shroud of gray.
  Hence the only prime
  And real love-rime
  That I know by heart,
  And that leaves no smart,

Is the purl of a little valley fall
About three spans wide and two spans tall
Over a table of solid rock,
And into a scoop of the selfsame block;
The purl of a runlet that never ceases
In stir of kingdoms, in wars, in peaces;
With a hollow, boiling voice it speaks
And has spoken since hills were turfless peaks."

"And why gives this the only prime
Idea to you of a real love-rime?
And why does plunging your arm in a bowl,
Full of spring water, bring throbs to your soul?"

"Well, under the fall, in a crease of the stone,
Though where precisely none ever has known,
Jammed darkly, nothing to show how prized,
And by now with its smoothness opalized,
    Is a drinking-glass;
    For, down that pass
    My lover and I
    Walked under a sky
Of blue with a leaf-wove awning of green,
In the burn of August, to paint the scene,
And we placed our basket of fruit and wine
By the runlet's rim, where we sat to dine;
And when we had drunk from the glass together,
Arched by the oak-copse from the weather,
I held the vessel to rinse in the fall,
Where it slipped, and sank, and was past recall,
Though we stooped and plumbed the little abyss
With long, bared arms. There the glass still is.
And, as said, if I thrust my arm below
Cold water in basin or bowl, a throe
From the past awakens a sense of that time,

And the glass we used, and the cascade's rime.
The basin seems the pool, and its edge
The hard, smooth face of the brookside ledge,
And the leafy pattern of chinaware
The hanging plants that were bathing there.

"By night, by day, when it shines or lours,
There lies intact that chalice of ours,
And its presence adds to the rime of love
Persistently sung by the fall above.
No lip has touched it since his and mine
In turns therefrom sipped lovers' wine."

IN THE SERVANTS' QUARTERS

THOMAS HARDY

"Man, you, too, aren't you, one of these rough followers of the
    criminal?
All hanging hereabout to gather how he's going to bear
Examination in the hall."   She flung disdainful glances on
The shabby figure standing at the fire with others there,
        Who warmed them by its flare.

"No, indeed, my skipping maiden; I know nothing of the trial
    here,
Or criminal, if so he be.   —I chanced to come this way,
And the fire shone out into the dawn, and morning airs are
    cold now;
I, too, was drawn in part by charms I see before me play,
        That I see not every day."

"Ha, ha!" then laughed the constables who also stood to warm
    themselves,
The while another maiden scrutinized his features hard,
As the blaze threw into contrast every knot and line that
    wrinkled them,

Exclaiming, "Why, last night when he was brought in by the guard,
    You were with him in the yard!"

"Nay, nay, you teasing wench, I say! You know you speak mistakenly,
Cannot a tired pedestrian who has legged it long and far
Here on his way from northern parts, engrossed in humble marketings,
Come in and rest awhile, although judicial doings are
    Afoot by morning star?"

"O, come, come!" laughed the constables. "Why, man, you speak the dialect
He uses in his answers; you can hear him up the stairs.
So own it. We sh'n't hurt ye. There he's speaking now! His syllables
Are those you sound yourself when you are talking unawares,
    As this pretty girl declares."

"And you shudder when his chain clinks!" she rejoined. "Oh, yes, I noticed it.
And you winced, too, when those cuffs they gave him echoed to us here.
They'll soon be coming down, and you may then have to defend yourself
Unless you hold your tongue, or go away and keep you clear
    When he's led to judgment near!"

"No! I'll be damned in hell if I know anything about the man!
No single thing about him more than everybody knows!
Must not I even warm my hands but I am charged with blasphemies?" . . .
—His face convulses as the morning cock that moment crows,
    And he droops, and turns, and goes.

A BROKEN APPOINTMENT

THOMAS HARDY

You did not come,
And marching Time drew on, and wore me
  numb.—
Yet less for loss of your dear presence there
Than that I thus found lacking in your make
That high compassion which can overbear
Reluctance for pure lovingkindness' sake
Grieved I, when, as the hope-hour stroked its
  sum,
    You did not come.

You love not me,
And love alone can lend you loyalty;
—I know and knew it. But, unto the store
Of human deeds divine in all but name,
Was it not worth a little hour or more
To add yet this: Once, you, a woman, came
To sooth a time-torn man; even though it be
    You love not me?

"AH, ARE YOU DIGGING ON MY GRAVE?"

THOMAS HARDY

"Ah, are you digging on my grave,
  My loved one?—planting rue?"
—"No; yesterday he went to wed
One of the brightest wealth has bred.
'It cannot hurt her now,' he said,
  'That I should not be true.' "

"Then who is digging on my grave?
  My nearest, dearest kin?"

—"Ah, no; they sit and think, 'What use!
What good will planting flowers produce?
No tendance of her mound can loose
   Her spirit from Death's gin.' "[1]

"But someone digs upon my grave?
   My enemy?—prodding sly?"
—"Nay; when she heard you had passed the gate
That shuts on all flesh soon or late,
She thought you no more worth her hate,
   And cares not where you lie."

"Then, who is digging on my grave?
   Say—since I have not guessed!"
—"Oh, it is I, my mistress dear,
Your little dog, who still lives near,
And much I hope my movements here
   Have not disturbed your rest?"

"Ah, yes! *You* dig upon my grave . . .
   Why flashed it not upon me
That one true heart was left behind!
What feeling do we ever find
To equal among human kind
   A dog's fidelity!"

"Mistress, I dug upon your grave
   To bury a bone, in case
I should be hungry near this spot
When passing on my daily trot.
I am sorry, but I quite forgot
   It was your resting-place."

---

[1] gin, snare or trap.

RALPH HODGSON

Ralph Hodgson was born in Darlington, Northumberland, in 1871. His first volume, *The Last Blackbird and other Lines* (1907), appeared when he was almost forty. His subsequent production has been small but of distinguished quality, much of it appearing in the broadsides of The Flying Fame Press with Lovat Fraser's jolly "embellishments." A collected edition of his work, *Poems*, was published in 1917. In 1924, following the example of Mr. Blunden, Mr. Vines, and other British poets, he visited Japan as a lecturer in English literature at Sendai University. Besides being a poet, Mr. Hodgson unites such diverse interests as draftsmanship and being an authority on bull terriers. His love of animals appears in many of his poems.

The outstanding quality of Mr. Hodgson's verse is its lucent simplicity and purity. The singing quality of "Time, You Old Gypsy Man" has inspired several composers with lovely musical settings. In his apparently naïve lines may be concealed the wonder of the universe—as in his long poem, "The Song of Honor," in which we hear

> The sons of Light exalt their Sire
> With universal song,

and so, through "the song of every singing bird," the songs of poets, painters, "men divinely wise," of beggars and kings, of sailors and fighters and lovers—"the whole harmonious hymn of being" rolls on and upward to a mighty climax of comprehension and communion with the infinite. And yet he can tell it in words of one syllable:

> I stood upon that silent hill
> And stared into the sky until
> My eyes were blind with stars, and still
> I stared into the sky.

TIME, YOU OLD GYPSY MAN*

RALPH HODGSON

Time, you old gypsy man,
　Will you not stay,
Put up your caravan
　Just for one day?

All things I'll give you
Will you be my guest,
Bells for your jennet[1]
Of silver the best,
Goldsmiths shall beat you
A great golden ring,
Peacocks shall bow to you,
Little boys sing,
Oh, and sweet girls will
Festoon you with may.
Time, you old gypsy,
Why hasten away?

Last week in Babylon,
Last night in Rome,
Morning, and in the crush
Under Paul's dome;
Under Paul's dial
You tighten your rein—
Only a moment,
And off once again;
Off to some city
Now blind in the womb,

---

*From *Poems* by Ralph Hodgson.   Copyright 1917 by The Macmillan Company.   Reprinted
by permission.
[1]*jennet*, a small Spanish horse.

Off to another
Ere that's in the tomb.

Time, you old gypsy man,
    Will you not stay,
Put up your caravan
    Just for one day?

A. E. HOUSMAN

Alfred Edward Housman prepared for college at Bromsgrove School in Worcestershire and was graduated from St. John's College, Oxford, of which he is now an Honorary Fellow. He was for ten years employed in the government service, then became Professor of Latin at University College, London (1892-1911). Since 1911 he has been Professor of Latin at Cambridge and Fellow of Trinity College.

It is doubtful if any other first slender volume of a poet's work held more of pure lyric gold than *A Shropshire Lad* (1896). The uniformly high quality of the poems in this little book was due partly to the fact that they had been written over a long period of years and partly to the severe literary standards which the poet's classical education and profession had caused him to set upon his work. It is impossible to believe that these sixty-three poems were other than the gleanings from a much larger body of work.

Mr. Housman's classicism is apparent in the purity and chaste restraint of the style; yet these poems are too intensely human to be the mere product of a scholar's study. Against the sweetness of the English countryside, with all the bloom of new life in the springtime, he sees the "rose-lipped maidens" and "lightfoot lads" haunted by the hopelessness of destiny and, instead of the reckless fatalism of Fitzgerald, he tinges his philosophy with a bitter and tender pity. With rare understanding of the soul of youth, he voices the eternal revolt against things which must change, grow old, and pass away. All this he does in lines so simple and natural that they sing themselves into the memory. There can hardly be a better sign that they will live.

After a silence of a quarter of a century, another thin volume came from his pen, *Last Poems* (1922). Here are found the same qualities which made *A Shropshire Lad* famous, though the second volume has received less notice, perhaps because the influence of the first, which stood out in an age of empty jingling, had made Mr. Housman's qualities the accepted and expected style in English pastoral poetry.

It is a curious fact that Mr. Housman is said never to have been in the county of Shropshire. However, these poems are far less important as pictures of any particular scene than as expressions of universal human experience.

REVEILLE

A. E. Housman

I

Wake! The silver dusk returning
  Up the beach of darkness brims,
And the ship of sunrise burning
  Strands upon the eastern rims.

Wake! The vaulted shadow shatters,
  Trampled to the floor it spanned,
And the tent of night in tatters
  Straws the sky-pavilioned land.

Up, lad, up! 'Tis late for lying;
  Hear the drums of morning play;
Hark, the empty highways crying,
  "Who'll beyond the hills away?"

II

Towns and countries woo together,
  Forelands beacon, belfries call;
Never lad that trod on leather
  Lived to feast his heart with all.

Up, lad! Thews that lie and cumber
  Sunlit pallets never thrive;
Morns abed and daylight slumber
  Were not meant for man alive.

Clay lies still, but blood's a rover;
  Breath's a ware that will not keep.
Up, lad; when the journey's over
  There'll be time enough to sleep.

LOVELIEST OF TREES

A. E. HOUSMAN

Loveliest of trees, the cherry now
Is hung with bloom along the bough,
And stands about the woodland ride[1]
Wearing white for Eastertide.

Now, of my threescore years and ten,
Twenty will not come again,
And take from seventy springs a score,
It only leaves me fifty more.

And since to look at things in bloom
Fifty springs are little room,
About the woodlands I will go
To see the cherry hung with snow.

WITH RUE MY HEART IS LADEN

A. E. HOUSMAN

With rue my heart is laden
For golden friends I had,
For many a rose-lipped maiden
And many a lightfoot lad.

By brooks too broad for leaping
The lightfoot lads are laid;
The rose-lipped girls are sleeping
In fields where roses fade.

---

[1]*ride*, a bridle path.

BREDON HILL[1]

A. E. Housman

In summertime on Bredon
  The bells they sound so clear;
Round both the shires they ring them
  In steeples far and near,
  A happy noise to hear.

Here of a Sunday morning
  My love and I would lie,
And see the colored counties,
  And hear the larks so high
  About us in the sky.

The bells would ring to call her
  In valleys miles away:
"Come all to church, good people;
  Good people, come and pray."
  But here my love would stay.

And I would turn and answer
  Among the springing thyme,
"Oh, peal upon our wedding,
  And we will hear the chime,
  And come to church in time."

But when the snows at Christmas
  On Bredon top were strown,
My love rose up so early
  And stole out unbeknown
  And went to church alone.

---

[1] *Bredon*, pronounced brē′dŭn.

They tolled the one bell only,
   Groom there was none to see,
The mourners followed after,
   And so to church went she,
   And would not wait for me.

The bells they sound on Bredon,
   And still the steeples hum.
"Come all to church, good people"—
   Oh, noisy bells, be dumb;
   I hear you, I will come.

And each girl squeals to show she feels
It's a treat to be treated so;
Ah! your spirits be up, lad;
But my spirits be low!

I don't think as I used to think,
Nor do as I used to do;
But I still can drink as I used to drink,
A darned sight better than you!
You care a lot for the pewter pot,
But you're only the rag-tag sort;
A pint of stuff for you is enough,
But I'm for the double quart!

DOUGLAS HYDE

Born at Frenchpark, County Roscommon, Ireland, about 1860, the son of a Protestant clergyman, Douglas Hyde was graduated with high honors from Trinity College, Dublin, having distinguished himself in languages, history, and oratory. As a youth he had already deeply interested himself in the folklore of the Connaught countryside surrounding his birthplace. With the enthusiasm of a fanatic he traveled from village to village picking up from aged and unlettered peasants the vanishing remnants of the old Gaelic culture. These tales and poems he was later to publish, both in Gaelic and in English translations which undertook to preserve the spirit and rhythms of the originals.

At first he merely translated into conventional English, but, later, not satisfied with this, he contrived Anglo-Irish versions. The poem reprinted here, "Ringleted Youth of My Love," from *The Love Songs of Connacht* (1894), shows that in conventional English, Dr. Hyde is an artist of rare lyrical ability; this translation into verse should be compared, however, with the Anglo-Irish version in prose which is reprinted in the Introduction, page 45. In the prose version are apparent the origins of the beautiful language which Synge was to bring to perfection in his plays. It is significant that Synge was a constant student of these translations. To Dr. Hyde, therefore, is due first credit for the brilliant achievements of Synge and later members of the Dublin school. He himself did not court such credit, however, for with him the Anglo-Irish translations were but an unavoidable means to an end, and the end is "the de-Anglicizing of Ireland" by the return to the ancient speech of the country. As president of the Gaelic League from its foundation in 1893 until 1915 he fought ardently for the teaching of Gaelic in the public schools.

A further important contribution of this scholar to the interest in Irish literature was *The Literary History of Ireland* (1899), an authoritative work. The body of folklore and folk-poetry which he has collected, edited, and translated is staggering: besides *The Love Songs of Connacht*, he has published *Songs Ascribed to Raftery* (1903) and *Religious Songs of Connacht* (1906). He has received the degrees of LL.D. and Litt. D. from his alma mater, and has been Professor of Modern Irish in the National University of Ireland since 1909.

RINGLETED YOUTH OF MY LOVE
Douglas Hyde

Ringleted youth of my love,
With thy locks bound loosely behind thee,
You passed by the road above,
But you never came in to find me;
Where were the harm for you
If you came for a little to see me;
Your kiss is a wakening dew
Were I ever so ill or so dreamy.

If I had golden store
I would make a nice little boreen,[1]
To lead straight up to his door,
The door of the house of my storeen;[2]
Hoping to God not to miss
The sound of his footfall in it,
I have waited so long for his kiss
That for days I have slept not a minute.

I thought, O my love! you were so—
As the moon is, or sun on a fountain,
And I thought after that you were snow,
The cold snow on top of the mountain;
And I thought after that, you were more
Like God's lamp shining to find me,
Or the bright star of knowledge before,
And the star of knowledge behind me.

You promised me high-heeled shoes,
And satin and silk, my storeen,
And to follow me, never to lose,
Though the ocean were round us roaring;
Like a bush in a gap in a wall
I am now left lonely without thee,
And this house I grow dead of is all
That I see around or about me.

---

[1]boreen, lane.   [2]storeen, darling.

VIOLET JACOB

A native of Forfarshire, Scotland, Violet Jacob (Mrs. Arthur Otway Jacob) is one of the few writers of good Scottish dialect poetry at the present time. "Tam i' the Kirk" is something more than dialect: it is alive with the wistful ardor of a boy's love, calling with the same music that Robert Burns put into his poetry.

Mrs. Jacob's poetry includes *Songs of Angus* (1915), *More Songs of Angus* (1918), *Bonnie Joann* (1921), *Tales of My Own Country* (1923). She has also written two novels, *The Sheep Stealers* (1902) and *The Interloper* (1904).

TAM I' THE KIRK

VIOLET JACOB

O Jean, my Jean, when the bell ca's the congregation
Owre valley an' hill wi' the ding frae its iron mou',
When a'body's thochts is set on his ain salvation,
    Mine's set on you.

There's a reid rose lies on the Buik o' the Word afore ye
That was growin' braw on its bush at the keek[1] o' day,
But the lad that pu'd yon flower i' the mornin's glory,
    He canna pray.

He canna pray; but there's nane i' the kirk will heed him
Whaur he sits sae still his lane[2] at the side o' the wa',
For nane but the reid rose kens what my lassie gie'd him—
    It an' us twa!

He canna sing for the sang that his ain he'rt raises,
He canna see for the mist that's afore his een,[3]
And a voice drouns the hale[4] o' the psalms an' the
    paraphrases,
    Cryin' "Jean, Jean, Jean!"

---

[1]*keek*, peep.
[2]*his lane*, by himself.
[3]*een*, eyes.
[4]*hale*, whole.

FRANCIS LEDWIDGE

Francis Ledwidge was born in 1891 in Slane, County Meath, Ireland. With no opportunity for schooling, he learned life at first hand, working as miner, farmhand, grocer's boy, and road-mender. In 1912 he sent a copybook full of his verses to the Irish dramatist, Lord Dunsany, who, happily, realized their true worth. Under the patronage of Dunsany, *Songs of the Fields* (1914) and *Songs of Peace* (1916) were published, although in the meantime the young poet had enlisted in the Inniskilling Fusiliers and was seeing service far from the River Boyne. He fought at Gallipoli, Salonika, and in Serbia. Returning to the Flanders front, he was killed in action in 1917.

His *Complete Poems* were published in 1919 with a warmly appreciative preface by Lord Dunsany. As they represent the work of a youth, it is impossible to give them the place which Ledwidge might have attained had he not fallen in the War. Despite the signs of immaturity in some of the poems, however, the larger number proclaim a gift of song which is as natural and as inexplicable as the song of the blackbird which he loved to write about.

> And wondrous impudently sweet,
> Half of him passion, half conceit,
> The blackbird calls adown the street . . .

He has, too, the gift of poetic description, having left us many landscapes of intimate and affectionate detail. There is no striking originality in these pictures, for he follows the traditions of the English nature poets. Neither is there any attempt to write in other than conventional poetic English and conventional poetic form. Nevertheless there is such a splendid spontaneity in everything he writes, like that of another peasant-poet, Robert Burns, that nothing else much matters.

DESIRE IN SPRING

Francis Ledwidge

I love the cradle songs the mothers sing
In lonely places when the twilight drops,
The slow endearing melodies that bring
Sleep to the weeping lids; and, when she stops,
I love the roadside birds upon the tops
Of dusty hedges in a world of spring.

And when the sunny rain drips from the edge
Of midday wind, and meadows lean one way,
And a long whisper passes through the sedge,
Beside the broken water let me stay,
While these old airs upon my memory play,
And silent changes color up the hedge.

JUNE

Francis Ledwidge

Broom out the floor now, lay the fender by,
And plant this bee-sucked bough of woodbine there,
And let the window down. The butterfly
Floats in upon the sunbeam, and the fair
Tanned face of June, the nomad gypsy, laughs
Above her widespread wares, the while she tells
The farmers' fortunes in the fields, and quaffs
The water from the spider-peopled wells.

The hedges are all drowned in green grass seas,
And bobbing poppies flare like Elmor's light,[1]

---

[1] *Elmor's light* (St. Elmo's light), a flame-like electrical appearance playing about trees or steeples.

While siren-like the pollen-stainéd bees
Drone in the clover depths.   And up the height
The cuckoo's voice is hoarse and broke with joy.
And on the lowland crops the crows make raid,
Nor fear the clappers of the farmer's boy,
Who sleeps, like drunken Noah, in the shade.

And loop this red rose in that hazel ring
That snares your little ear, for June is short
And we must joy in it, and dance and sing,
And from her bounty draw her rosy worth.
Ay! soon the swallows will be flying south,
The wind wheel north to gather in the snow,
Even the roses spilt on youth's red mouth
Will soon blow down the road all roses go.

THE SHADOW PEOPLE

Francis Ledwidge

Old lame Bridget doesn't hear
Fairy music in the grass
When the gloaming's on the mere
And the shadow people pass;
Never hears their slow gray feet
Coming from the village street
Just beyond the parson's wall,
Where the clover globes are sweet
And the mushroom's parasol
Opens in the moonlit rain.
Every night I hear them call
From their long and merry train.
Old lame Bridget says to me,
"It is just your fancy, child."

She cannot believe I see
Laughing faces in the wild,
Hands that twinkle in the sedge,
Bowing at the water's edge
Where the finny minnows quiver,
Shaping on a blue wave's ledge
Bubble foam to sail the river.
And the sunny hands to me
Beckon ever, beckon ever.
Oh! I would be wild and free
And with the shadow people be.

SHANE LESLIE

Shane Leslie was born at Monaghan, Ireland, in 1886, and was educated at Eton, the University of Paris, and King's College, Cambridge. He was affected by the Celtic literary revival; since 1916 he has edited *The Dublin Review*. His *Verses in Peace and War* (1916) look upon war without illusion. His style is often compact to the point of the epigrammatic. His "Epitaphs for Aviators" prove that the ancient and difficult art of the epitaph is not entirely lost.

EPITAPHS FOR AVIATORS
(Capt. Aidan Liddell, V. C.)

Shane Leslie

Another one of mortal birth
Hath set his spirit free.
Lie very lightly on him, Earth,
Who did not tread on thee.

WINIFRED M. LETTS

Winifred M. Letts was born in Ireland in 1887 and educated at Alexandra College, Dublin. During the World War she served as a masseuse in various army hospitals, and gained experiences which are faithfully reflected in *The Spires of Oxford* (1917). Although these poems, especially the title poem, made her famous, her more characteristic material is the life of simple Irish folk, townspeople as well as peasants. "Says She" and "In Service" are from *Songs From Leinster* (1913), a volume which contains her best pieces in this manner. There is a firm and virile impudence in these *genre* sketches, and such others as "The Retort Courteous" and "The Town," which makes it hard to believe that the author is a woman. She has indeed a broad nub to her pen.

The contents of *Hallowe'en and Poems of the War* (London, 1916), were largely reprinted in *The Spires of Oxford* (New York, 1917). Other volumes of her poetry are *Corporal's Corner* (1919) and *More Songs from Leinster* (1926). Miss Letts has also written three novels and two plays which were produced at the Abbey Theater, Dublin.

THE SPIRES OF OXFORD

Winifred M. Letts

I saw the spires of Oxford
  As I was passing by,
The gray spires of Oxford
  Against the pearl-gray sky.
My heart was with the Oxford men
  Who went abroad to die.

The years go fast in Oxford,
  The golden years and gay;
The hoary Colleges look down
  On careless boys at play.
But when the bugles sounded war
  They put their games away.

They left the peaceful river,
  The cricket-field, the quad,
The shaven lawns of Oxford,
  To seek a bloody sod—
They gave their merry youth away
  For country and for God.

God rest you happy, gentlemen,
  Who laid your good lives down,
Who took the khaki and the gun
  Instead of cap and gown.
God bring you to a fairer place
  Than even Oxford town.

IN SERVICE

Winifred M. Letts

Little Nellie Cassidy has got a place in town;
    She wears a fine white apron,
    She wears a new black gown
An' the quarest little cap at all with straymers hanging down.

I met her one fine evening stravagin'[1] down the street,
    A feathered hat upon her head,
    And boots upon her feet.
"Och, Mick," says she, "may God be praised that you and I
    should meet.

"It's lonesome in the city with such a crowd," says she;
    "I'm lost without the bog-land,
    I'm lost without the sea,
An' the harbor an' the fishing-boats that sail out fine and free.

"I'd give a golden guinea to stand upon the shore,
    To see the big waves lepping,
    To hear them splash and roar,
To smell the tar and the drying nets, I'd not be asking more.

"To see the small white houses, their faces to the sea,
    The childher in the doorway,
    Or round my mother's knee;
For I'm strange and lonesome missing them, God keep them
    all," says she.

Little Nellie Cassidy earns fourteen pounds and more,
    Waiting on the quality,
    And answering the door—
But her heart is some place far away upon the Wexford[2] shore.

[1] *stravagin'*, strolling.
[2] *Wexford*, a county in Leinster, on the east coast of Ireland.

SAYS SHE

WINIFRED M. LETTS

My Granny she often says to me,
Says she, "You're terrible bold,
It's you have a right to mend your ways
Before you'll ever grow old,"
  Says she.
"Before you'll ever grow old.
For it's steadfast now that you ought to be,
An' you going on sixteen," says she.
"What'll you do when you're old like me?
What'll you do?" says she.

"What will I do when I'm old?" says I.
"Och Musha, I'll say my prayers,
I'll wear a net an' a black lace cap
To cover my silver hairs,"
  Says I.
"To cover my silver hairs.
When I am as old as Kate Kearney's cat
I'll sell my dress and featherdy hat,
An' buy an old bedgown the like o' that,
The very like o' that."

My Granny she sighs and says to me,
"The years fly terrible fast,
The girls they laugh an' talk with the boys,
But they all grow old at last,"
  Says she.
"They all grow old at last.
At Epiphany cocks may skip," says she,
"But kilt by Easter they're like to be.
By the Hokey! you'll grow as old as me,
As weak an' old," says she.

"Maybe you tell me no lie," says I,
"But I've time before me yet.
There's time to dance, and there's time to sing;
So why would I need to fret?"
    Says I.
"So why would I need to fret?
Old age may lie at the foot of the hill,
Twixt hoppin' and trottin' we'll get there still.
Why wouldn't we dance while we have the will,
Dance while we have the will?"

JOHN McCRAE

John (D.) McCrae, author of perhaps the most widely-quoted poem of the World War, was born in 1872 at Guelph, Ontario, Canada, of Scotch pioneer parents. With a family tradition of sound education he attended the University of Toronto, first as an arts student, then as a student of medicine. After internships at the Toronto General and Johns Hopkins Hospitals, he went to Montreal in 1900 as Fellow in Pathology at McGill University and pathologist to the Montreal General Hospital. From then until the outbreak of the War, McCrae's life was one of crowding activities, professional, social, literary, and civic. He was everywhere a favorite for his friendliness, his gayety, and his endearing boyishness. In the autumn of 1914 he went overseas as surgeon to the First Brigade Artillery. After fourteen months in the Ypres sector he was transferred to the direction of a military hospital at Boulogne with the rank of Lieutenant Colonel. His health steadily failed, and he died of pneumonia in January, 1918.

In Flanders Fields, and Other Poems was published in 1919 with an appreciative study of McCrae's character by Sir Andrew MacPhail. The title poem is by no means the only good poem in the volume, but it is incomparably the best. In form it is a rondeau. After its first appearance in *Punch*, December, 1915, it became "the poem of the army," circulating largely by word of mouth throughout the British Expeditionary Forces.

IN FLANDERS FIELDS*

John McCrae

In Flanders fields the poppies blow
   Between the crosses, row on row,
  That mark our place; and in the sky
  The larks, still bravely singing, fly
Scarce heard amid the guns below.
We are the Dead. Short days ago
We lived, felt dawn, saw sunset glow,
   Loved and were loved, and now we lie,
     In Flanders fields.

Take up our quarrel with the foe;[1]
To you from failing hands we throw
  The torch; be yours to hold it high.
  If ye break faith with us who die
We shall not sleep, though poppies grow
     In Flanders fields.

[1]*Take up our quarrel with the foe*. The foe against whom the man of ideals fought in the World War was not so much a particular enemy nation as the entire political system that made war possible. It was for many "the war to end war."

PATRICK MacGILL

Patrick MacGill was born in 1889 in Donegal, on the rugged west coast of Ireland. He grew up in a peasant household amid the utmost poverty. Schooling or a trade were alike out of the question; he could capitalize only his sturdy muscles as a common laborer. As farmhand, potato-digger, and harvester he passed his boyhood and youth in Ireland and Scotland. Later he became a railroad section-hand, and it is as the "navvy-poet" that he is best known. By some unaccountable miracle, out of this unpromising background he has emerged as singer and novelist. His writings are vivid indictments of industrial society as he has experienced it. *Songs of the Dead End* (1913) is the voice of the underdog.

Mr. MacGill saw service during the World War and was wounded at Loos. In *Soldier Songs* (1917) he turns back to the country of his childhood:

> A candle stuck on the muddy floor,
> Lights up the dugout wall,
> And I see in its flame the prancing sea
> And the mountains straight and tall;
> For my heart is more than often back
> By the hills of Donegal.

The same theme is carried on in another of his books, *Songs of Donegal* (1921).

From PLAYED OUT

Patrick MacGill

As a bullock falls in the crooked ruts, he fell when the day
  was o'er,
The hunger gripping his stinted guts, his body shaken and sore.
They pulled it out of the ditch in the dark, as a brute is pulled
  from its lair,
The corpse of the navvy[1], stiff and stark, with the clay on its
  face and hair.

In Christian lands, with calloused hands, he labored for others'
  good,
In workshop and mill, ditchway and drill, earnest, eager, and
  rude;
Unhappy and gaunt with worry and want, a food to the whims
  of fate,
Hashing it out and booted about at the will of the goodly and
  great.

. . . .

He tramped through the colorless winter land, or swined in the
  scorching heat,
The dry skin hacked on his sapless hands or blistering on his
  feet;
He wallowed in mire unseen, unknown, where your houses of
  pleasure rise,
And hapless, hungry, and chilled to the bone, he builded the
  edifice.

In cheerless "model"[2] and filthy pub his sinful hours were
  passed,
Or footsore, weary, he begged his grub, in the sough of the hail-
  whipped blast,

---

[1] navvy, a laborer employed in road-building, railroad construction, etc.
[2] model, a lodging-house maintained by philanthropy.

So some might riot in wealth and ease, with food and wine be
    crammed,
He wrought like a mule, in muck to his knees, dirty, dissolute,
    damned.

          .   .   .   .   .   .

They pulled it out of the ditch in the dark,
The chilling frost on its hair,
The mole-skinned[3] navvy stiff and stark
From no particular where.

[3]*mole-skinned*, dressed in corduroy.

JOHN MASEFIELD

John Masefield, a lawyer's son, was born in 1874 at Ledbury, Herefordshire. As a youth he ran away to sea and shipped as a cabin boy. His love of "that sea-beauty man has ceased to build" and his intimate knowledge of sailors' lives are thus the result of years of salt-water wanderings. Eventually he turned up in New York, where, in 1895, he was employed in Luke O'Connor's saloon, a landmark of Greenwich Avenue only recently demolished. He has modestly denied that he served as bartender, explaining that his duty was to clean the spittoons.

Chaucer, whose poetry he discovered in a seventy-five cent book when he was working in a Bronx carpet factory and boarding in Yonkers, New York, first determined him to become a poet. "I read the *Parliament* [*of Fowls*] all through one Sunday afternoon, with the feeling that I had been kept out of my inheritance and had then suddenly entered upon it, and had found it a new world of wonder and delight. I had never realized, until then, what poetry could be." He was then twenty-two years old.

The following year he returned to London, where he found precarious employment at first as a hack-writer. *Salt-Water Ballads* (1902) was his first and is still one of his most popular volumes. In this collection of sea lyrics he writes with the fresh enthusiasm of a youth not too old to have forgotten the romance of buccaneers and "stately Spanish galleons." The influence of Mr. Kipling's *Barrack-Room Ballads* is apparent in the headlong zest of this and the succeeding volume, *Ballads* (1903). Here are not only vigorous rhythms and lusty themes, but more—a sense of the beauty and mystery and passion which is life.

Mr. Masefield first won wide notice, however, by *The Everlasting Mercy* (1911), the first of a series of long narrative poems produced within a few years: *The Widow in the Bye Street* (1912), *Dauber* (1912), and *The Daffodil Fields* (1913). Employing in most of these the Chaucerian rime royal, Mr. Masefield has adapted the traditional limpidity of this form to a stark and powerful simplicity. But the greatest strength of these poems is their realism: Mr. Masefield, like his own "dirty British coaster," discovers cargoes of poetic beauty in "the dirt and the dross, the dust and scum of the earth." Over-nice readers are repelled by the coarseness of his characters and their speech; but the reader of perception sees through the surface crudities to the starved but aspiring souls of these pitiful ones. And his range is wider than his own confession of faith would indicate.

Like Chaucer, Mr. Masefield is a born spinner of yarns. So skillfully are his ingredients mixed that the action moves swiftly and dramatically in spite of many passages of serene description or sublime reflection. The chief criticism heard against him is that the alternation of his moods is sometimes too violent.

The World War robbed the world's literature of four years of Mr. Masefield's production. During this time he served with the Red Cross in Gallipoli. His account of this campaign, *Gallipoli* (1916), has been overpraised. Since the War his style has become less emphatic, more mellow. *Reynard the Fox* (1919) is the most important of the later works. There is no room for detailed mention of his plays (*The Tragedy of Nan*, 1909, is the most famous), or his novels, except the strange and beautiful *Multitude and Solitude* (1909), or his essay on *Shakespeare* (1911) which contains many flashes of insight. A collected edition of his works appeared in 1924 and *Midsummer Night and Other Tales in Verse* in 1928.

Mr. Masefield derives from many antecedents. His kinship to Chaucer has been noted—a kinship as much in spirit as in form. Like Wordsworth he uses the actual language of men, but dares to be more literal than Wordsworth ever dreamed of being. The contemporary with whom he has most in common is another sailor, Joseph Conrad. The writers with whom Mr. Masefield has little in common are, however, more numerous. Contrast his gory realism, for instance, with the exquisite conceits of Tennyson. Mr. Masefield goes beyond many moderns in the completeness of his realism.

Copyright restrictions prevent the reprinting here of any of Mr. Masefield's shorter poems except the universally known "Sea Fever," probably his finest lyric; and the length of his narrative poems makes it impracticable to include anything but one magnificent fragment from "Dauber."

SEA FEVER*

John Masefield

I must go down to the seas again, to the lonely sea and the sky,
And all I ask is a tall ship and a star to steer her by,
And the wheel's kick and the wind's song and the white sail's
    shaking,
And a gray mist on the sea's face and a gray dawn breaking.

I must go down to the seas again, for the call of the running
    tide
Is a wild call and a clear call that may not be denied;
And all I ask is a windy day with the white clouds flying,
And the flung spray and the blown spume, and the sea-gulls
    crying.

I must go down to the seas again, to the vagrant gypsy life,
To the gull's way and the whale's way where the wind's like a
    whetted knife;
And all I ask is a merry yarn from a laughing fellow-rover,
And quiet sleep and a sweet dream when the long trick's over.

From DAUBER†[1]

John Masefield

Then came the cry of "Call all hands on deck!"
The Dauber knew its meaning; it was come:
Cape Horn, that tramples beauty into wreck,
And crumples steel and smites the strong man dumb.

*From *Salt-Water Ballads* by John Masefield. Copyright 1913 by The Macmillan Company.
Reprinted by permission.
    †From *The Story of a Round House and Other Poems* by John Masefield. Copyright 1912 by
The Macmillan Company. Reprinted by permission.
    [1]"Dauber" tells the story of a youth who goes to sea to learn how to paint "ships and the
sea; there's nothing finer made." In spite of his shipmates' mockery he is true to his artistic
ambition. As the vessel approaches Cape Horn, the Dauber quails at the prospect of tempest
and disaster. Nevertheless, from the first onslaught of the storms, he plays his part and proves
himself a man.

Down clattered flying kites and staysails; some
Sang out in quick, high calls; the fairleads[2] skirled,
And from the southwest came the end of the world. . . .

Darkness came down—half darkness—in a whirl;
The sky went out, the waters disappeared.
He felt a shocking pressure of blowing hurl
The ship upon her side.   The darkness speared
At her with wind; she staggered, she careered,
Then down she lay.   The Dauber felt her go;
He saw his yard tilt downwards.   Then the snow

Whirled all about—dense, multitudinous, cold—
Mixed with the wind's one devilish thrust and shriek,
Which whiffled out men's tears, deafened, took hold,
Flattening the flying drift against the cheek.
The yards buckled and bent, man could not speak.
The ship lay on her broadside; the wind's sound
Had devilish malice at having got her downed.

     *   *   *   *   *   *   *

How long the gale had blown he could not tell,
Only the world had changed, his life had died.
A moment now was everlasting hell.
Nature an onslaught from the weather side,
A withering rush of death, a frost that cried,
Shrieked, till he withered at the heart; a hail
Plastered his oilskins with an icy mail.

"Cut!" yelled his mate.   He looked—the sail was gone,
Blown into rags in the first furious squall;
The tatters drummed the devil's tattoo.   On
The buckling yard a block thumped like a mall.

[2]*fairleads*, rings of wood or iron by means of which running rigging is led in any direction.
(Author's note).

The ship lay—the sea smote her, the wind's bawl
Came, "loo, loo, loo!"   The devil cried his hounds
On to the poor spent stag strayed in his bounds.

"Cut!   Ease her!" yelled his mate; the Dauber heard.
His mate wormed up the tilted yard and slashed,
A rag of canvas skimmed like a darting bird.
The snow whirled, the ship bowed to it, the gear lashed,
The sea-tops were cut off and flung down smashed;
Tatters of shouts were flung, the rags of yells—
And clang, clang, clang, below beat the two bells. . . .

"Up!" yelled the Bosun; "up and clear the wreck!"
The Dauber followed where he led; below
He caught one giddy glimpsing of the deck
Filled with white water, as though heaped with snow.
He saw the streamers of the rigging blow
Straight out like pennons from the splintered mast,
Then, all sense dimmed, all was an icy blast

Roaring from nether hell and filled with ice,
Roaring and crashing on the jerking stage,
An utter bridle given to utter vice,
Limitless power mad with endless rage
Withering the soul; a minute seemed an age.
He clutched and hacked at ropes, at rags of sail,
Thinking that comfort was a fairy tale

Told long ago—long, long ago—long since
Heard of in other lives—imagined—dreamed—
There where the basest beggar was a prince
To him in torment where the tempest screamed,
Comfort and warmth and ease no longer seemed
Things that a man could know: soul, body, brain,
Knew nothing but the wind, the cold, the pain.

CHARLOTTE MEW

Charlotte Mew followed the example of A. E. Housman and other meticulous poets by publishing only the rigorously selected few of her best verses. In her single volume, *The Farmer's Bride* (1916), are but seventeen poems. The American edition, under the title *Saturday Market* (1921), adds eleven others to this meager offering. But if her poems are small in number they are rich in beauty. It is hard to be temperate in speaking of them, so flawless is their art, so profound their emotion. In a sense, Miss Mew was always the impersonal observer, but this is simply a matter of method. Actually she so identified herself with the intense emotions of her subjects that her poems are one and all subjective in effect. She died in 1928.

ARRACOMBE WOOD*

Charlotte Mew

Some said, because he wud'n spaik
   Any words to women but Yes and No,
Nor put out his hand for Parson to shake
   He mun be bird-witted.   But I do go
   By the lie of the barley that he did sow,
And I wish no better thing than to hold a rake
   Like Dave, in his time, or to see him mow.

   Put up in churchyard a month ago,
"A bitter old soul," they said, but it wadn't so.
His heart were in Arracombe Wood where he'd used to go
To sit and talk wi' his shadder till sun went low,
Though what it was all about us'll never know.
   And there baint no mem'ry in the place
   Of th' old man's footmark, nor his face;
   Arracombe Wood do think more of a crow—
'Will be violets there in the spring; in summertime the
      spider's lace;
   And come the fall, the whizzle and race
Of the dry, dead leaves when the wind gies chase;
   And on the Eve of Christmas, fallin' snow.

THE FARMER'S BRIDE*

Charlotte Mew

Three Summers since I chose a maid,
   Too young maybe—but more's to do
At harvest-time than bide and woo.
   When us was wed she turned afraid
   Of love and me and all things human;

*From *Saturday Market* by Charlotte Mew. Copyright 1921 by The Macmillan Company.
Reprinted by permission.

Like the shut of a winter's day.
Her smile went out, and 'twasn't a woman—
   More like a little frightened fay.
      One night, in the fall, she runned away.

"Out 'mong the sheep, her be," they said,
'Should properly have been abed;
But sure enough she wasn't there
Lying awake with her wide brown stare.
So over seven-acre field and up-along across the down
   We chased her, flying like a hare
   Before our lanterns.   To Church-Town
     All in a shiver and a scare
   We caught her, fetched her home at last
    And turned the key upon her, fast.

She does the work about the house
As well as most, but like a mouse:
   Happy enough to chat and play
    With birds and rabbits and such as they,
    So long as men-folk keep away.
"Not near, not near!" her eyes beseech
When one of us comes within reach.
   The women say that beasts in stall
   Look round like children at her call.

Shy as a leveret,[1] swift as he,
Straight and slight as a young larch tree,
Sweet as the first wild violets, she,
To her wild self.   But what to me?
The short days shorten, and the oaks are brown,
   The blue smoke rises to the low gray sky,
One leaf in the still air falls slowly down,
   A magpie's spotted feathers lie
On the black earth spread white with rime,

---

[1] *leveret*, a young hare.

The berries redden up to Christmas-time.
What's Christmas-time without there be
Some other in the house than we!

She sleeps up in the attic there
Alone, poor maid.   'Tis but a stair
Betwixt us.   Oh! my God! the down,
The soft young down of her, the brown,
The brown of her—her eyes, her hair, her hair!

ALICE MEYNELL

Alice (Christina) Meynell (née Thompson) was born in 1850 in London; she was privately educated by her father, a Cambridge graduate, and lived during her youth in Italy. The family was a distinguished one, her sister being a notable painter. She married Wilfrid Meynell, critic and journalist, who later edited the works of Francis Thompson. A son, Francis Meynell, has become a writer, and a daughter, Viola Meynell, is a novelist and poet.

The home life of the Meynells was particularly rich in friends. Francis Thompson, the unfortunate poetic genius, was discovered and helped by them, and when he became famous remained their intimate companion. Among the names of those who knew and admired Alice Meynell are Ruskin, Stevenson, Rossetti, Coventry Patmore, W. E. Henley, George Meredith, and "Fiona Macleod"— a list which testifies to the length of years spanned by her career. Indeed her earliest volume, *Preludes*, appeared in 1876, and the record was not complete until *The Poems of Alice Meynell* were published in 1923, the year after her death. A selected edition of her essays appeared in 1914.

Her poetry is primarily the poetry of religious feeling—inward, intimate lyrics in which she explores the significance of spiritual experience. For her poetry was obviously a mode of escape from the world too much with us into the larger world of mystical being. Yet in all that she wrote, whether poems or essays, she never allows her mysticism to become misty. With a sure and firm command of the finest shades of language she joins a "heavenly tenderness" to "invulnerable, self-disciplined control." So severe becomes the passion for perfection that some of her later poetry lacks the spontaneity of her earlier work and becomes overwrought. So hard a critic of her own writing was she that when an edition entitled *Collected Poems* was brought out in 1913, she included in it only seventy-six pieces.

"The Shepherdess" is one of the best known poems of our time. It is also familiar in MacMurrough's charming musical setting.

THE SHEPHERDESS

ALICE MEYNELL

She walks—the lady of my delight—
　　A shepherdess of sheep.
Her flocks are thoughts.　She keeps them white;
　　She guards them from the steep;
She feeds them on the fragrant height,
　　And folds them in for sleep.

She roams maternal hills and bright,
　　Dark valleys safe and deep.
Into that tender breast at night
　　The chastest stars may peep.
She walks—the lady of my delight—
　　A shepherdess of sheep.

She holds her little thoughts in sight,
　　Though gay they run and leap.
She is so circumspect and right;
　　She has her soul to keep.
She walks—the lady of my delight—
　　A shepherdess of sheep.

RENOUNCEMENT

ALICE MEYNELL

I must not think of thee; and, tired yet strong,
　　I shun the love that lurks in all delight—
　　The love of thee—and in the blue heaven's height,
And in the dearest passage of a song.
Oh, just beyond the sweetest thoughts that throng
　　This breast, the thought of thee waits hidden yet bright;
　　But it must never, never come in sight;

I must stop short of thee the whole day long.
   But when night comes to close each difficult day,
When night gives pause to the long watch I keep,
And all my bonds I needs must loose apart,
Must doff my will as raiment laid away—
   With the first dream that comes with the first sleep
I run, I run, I am gathered to thy heart.

HAROLD MONRO

Harold Monro was born in Brussels in 1879, and educated at Radley School and Caius College, Cambridge. In 1912 he founded the Poetry Bookshop in London, for the sale of poetry and drama only. As compiler and publisher of the important anthologies of *Georgian Poetry*, and editor of the quarterly *Poetry and Drama*, which, suspended during the War, was revived in 1919 as *The Chapbook*, and as a public reader of poetry, he has been inevitably a leader of the modern poetic revival in England, and his shop has become a meeting-place for the younger poets and other writers.

Himself a poet, he has created a curiously original art, many of his poems concerning the souls of inanimate things, a sort of pan-psychism. "A psychological realist," Conrad Aiken has called him. Such he is in his whimsical "Week End Sonnets," as he describes his arrival at the familiar country-house:

> Your homely floor is creaking for our tread;
>   The smiling teapot with contented spout
> Thinks of the boiling water, and the bread
>   Longs for the butter. All their hands are out
>   To greet us, and the gentle blankets seem
>   Purring and crooning: "Lie in us and dream."

Pathetic fallacy, Ruskin might have called this—but it is not meant to be taken so seriously.

Mr. Monro's poems are contained in *Children of Love* (1914), *Strange Meetings* (1917), *Real Property* (1922).

MILK FOR THE CAT

Harold Monro

When the tea is brought at five o'clock,
And all the neat curtains are drawn with care,
The little black cat with bright green eyes
Is suddenly purring there.

At first she pretends, having nothing to do,
She has come in merely to blink by the grate,
But, though tea may be late, or the milk may be sour,
She is never late.

And presently her agate eyes
Take a soft, large, milky haze,
And her independent casual glance
Becomes a stiff, hard gaze.

Then she stamps her claws or lifts her ears,
Or twists her tail and begins to stir,
Till suddenly all her lithe body becomes
One breathing, trembling purr.

The children eat and wriggle and laugh;
The two old ladies stroke their silk;
But the cat is grown small and thin with desire,
Transformed to a creeping lust for milk.

The white saucer like some full moon descends
At last from the clouds of the table above;
She sighs and dreams and thrills and glows,
Transfigured with love.

She nestles over the shining rim,
Buries her chin in the creamy sea;
Her tail hangs loose; each drowsy paw
Is doubled under each bending knee.

A long dim ecstasy holds her life;
Her world is an infinite shapeless white,
Till her tongue has curled the last holy drop,
Then she sinks back into the night,

Draws and dips her body to heap
Her sleepy nerves in the great armchair,
Lies defeated and buried deep
Three or four hours unconscious there.

OVERHEARD ON A SALT-MARSH

Harold Monro

"Nymph, nymph, what are your beads?"
"Green glass, goblin.   Why do you stare at them?"
"Give them me."
        "No."
"Give them me.   Give them me."
                "No."
"Then I will howl all night in the reeds,
Lie in the mud and howl for them."
"Goblin, why do you love them so?"
"They are better than stars or water,
Better than voices of winds that sing,
Better than any man's fair daughter,
Your green glass beads on a silver ring."
"Hush, I stole them out of the moon."
"Give me your beads, I want them."
                "No."
"I will lie and howl in a deep lagoon
For your green glass beads, I love them so.
Give them me.   Give them."
                "No."

HENRY NEWBOLT

Sir Henry (John) Newbolt, barrister and man of letters, was born at Bilston in 1862; he attended Clifton College and Corpus Christi College, Oxford. He practiced law at Lincoln's Inn from 1887 until his retirement in 1899. Newbolt is the voice of the English naval tradition, and his many books, both in prose and in verse, glorify British rule of the seas. Following the World War he was Official Naval Historian. His long life records a wide range of activities. Of recent years he has turned himself more to literature, editing important anthologies of standard authors and writing critical essays (see especially *A New Study of English Poetry*, 1917).

His poems are chiefly ballads, many of the sea, some—like that reprinted here—of Britain's colonies. All are marked by a robust style, a swinging meter, and frequently a narrative interest which has commended them to a wide popularity. *Admirals All* (1897), *The Island Race* (1898), and *Poems New and Old* (1912) contain Sir Henry's best verse.

"HE FELL AMONG THIEVES"

Henry Newbolt

"Ye have robbed," said he, "ye have slaughtered and made an
    end,
  Take your ill-got plunder and bury the dead;
What will ye more of your guest and sometime friend?"
  "Blood for our blood," they said.

He laughed: "If one may settle the score for five,
  I am ready; but let the reckoning stand till day;
I have loved the sunlight as dearly as any alive."
  "You shall die at dawn," said they.

He flung his empty revolver down the slope,
  He climbed alone to the eastward edge of the trees;
All night long in a dream untroubled of hope
  He brooded, clasping his knees.

He did not hear the monotonous roar that fills
  The ravine where the Yassim River[1] sullenly flows;
He did not see the starlight on the Laspur hills
  Or the far Afghan snows.

He saw the April noon on his books aglow,
  The wistaria trailing in at the window wide;
He heard his father's voice from the terrace below,
  Calling him down to ride.

He saw the gray little church across the park,
  The mounds that hide the loved and honored dead,
The Norman arch, the chancel softly dark,
  The brasses black and red.

---

[1] *Yassim River, Laspur hills*, in northern Kashmir, India.

He saw the School Close, sunny and green,
　　The runner beside him, the stand by the parapet wall,
The distant tape, and the crowd roaring between
　　His own name over all.

He saw the dark wainscot and timbered roof,
　　The long tables, and the faces merry and keen;
The College Eight, and their trainer, dining aloof,
　　The Dons on the dais serene.

He watched the liner's stem plowing the foam,
　　He felt her trembling speed and the thrash of her screw;
He heard her passengers' voices talking of home,
　　He saw the flag she flew.

And now it was dawn. He rose strong on his feet,
　　And strode to his ruined camp below the wood;
He drank the breath of the morning cool and sweet;
　　His murderers round him stood.

Light on the Laspur hills was broadening fast,
　　The blood-red snow-peaks chilled to a dazzling white:
He turned and saw the golden circle at last,
　　Cut by the Eastern height.

"O glorious Life, Who dwellest in earth and sun,
　　I have lived, I praise and adore Thee."
　　　　A sword swept.
Over the pass the voices one by one
　　Faded, and the hill slept.

ROBERT NICHOLS

Robert (Malise Bowyer) Nichols, son of J. B. Nichols, also a poet, was born in the Isle of Wight in 1893. He attended Winchester, and was an undergraduate at Trinity College, Oxford, when the World War began. From October, 1914, to August, 1916, he served as a Second Lieutenant in the Royal Field Artillery, seeing active service on the Western Front. Disabled by shell shock, he was sent to the United States in 1918 on a propaganda tour for the Ministry of Information. Since 1921 he has held the chair of Professor of English Literature in the Imperial College, Tokyo, a post first filled by Lafcadio Hearn. Some hint of his interesting personality may be gathered from what he names as his recreations: "conversation (especially with scientists), sauntering (particularly through crowds), music, reading, aeronautics, art galleries, dreaming in a boat."

Although Mr. Nichols leaped into fame by his war poems in *Ardours and Endurances* (1917), he had already given high promise in the field of pure poetry, where the search for beauty is the sole end. His first book is not all war poems: "The Faun's Holiday," which fills almost seventy pages, is rich in sensuous perceptions. Even the War poems are not all such agonized documents of battle experience as "The Assault"—that ghastly and veracious moving picture. Often, as in "Last Words" or "Farewell to Place of Comfort," visions of beauty are discovered in the midst of pain.

In his later volumes of verse, *The Budded Branch* (1918) and *Aurelia* (1920), he reverts to his earlier moods. Laurence Binyon credits him with "an ardent temperament, extreme impressibility of the senses, and the power of rendering sensation with subtlety and exactness."

LAST WORDS

ROBERT NICHOLS

Oh, let it be
Just such an eve as this when I must die!
To see the green bough soaking, still against a sky
Washed clean after the rain.
To watch the rapturous rainbow flame and fly
Into the gloom where drops fall goldenly,
And in my heart to feel the end of pain.
The end of pain: the late, the long expected!—
To see the skies clear in a sudden minute,
The gray disparting on the blue within it,
And on the low, far sea the clouds collected.

In that deep quiet, die to all has been,
To be renewed, to bud, to flower again:
My second spring!—whose hope was nigh rejected
Before I go hence and am no more seen.

To hear the blackbird ring out, gay and bold,
The low renewal of the ringdove's moan
From among high, sheltered boughs, and ceaseless fall
Pitter, pitter, patter,
A dribble of gold
From leaves nodding each on the other one,
The hush, calm piping, and the slow sweet mood!
To drink the ripe warm scent of soaking matter,
Wet grass, wet leaves, wet wood,
Wet mold,
The saddest and the grandest scent of all.

So when my dying eyes have loved the trees
Till with huge tears turned blind,
When the vague ears for the last time have hearkened

To the cool stir of the long evening breeze,
The blackbird's tireless call,
Having drunk deep of earth-scent strong and kind,
Come then, O Death, and let my day be darkened.

I shall have had my all.

ALFRED NOYES

Alfred Noyes was born in Staffordshire in 1880. He is a graduate of Exeter College, Oxford, and holds the honorary degree of Litt. D. from Yale. From 1914 to 1923 he filled the chair of Modern English Literature at Princeton University. He has made several successful lecture tours in the United States, in the course of which he has given admirable renderings of his own poetry.

That Mr. Noyes has been one of the most prolific poets of our time is attested by nine volumes of verse, consolidated into three large volumes as *Collected Poems* (Volumes I and II, 1913; Volume III, 1920). That he is also one of our most popular poets is proved by the fact that he has been able to make poetry pay. The secret of his popularity is largely his facility in rime and rhythm—a natural ability to sing. To this must be added his ability to tell a good story. In an age when introspection and impressionism largely dominate poetry, Mr. Noyes's simple objectiveness, his lilting lyricism, and his narrative skill satisfy the demands of readers who cannot thrill to the eccentricities of modernism. All the best of Mr. Noyes is shown in "The Highwayman," a rarely successful re-creation of the forthright old ballad style.

THE HIGHWAYMAN*

Alfred Noyes

PART ONE

I

The wind was a torrent of darkness among the gusty trees,
The moon was a ghostly galleon tossed upon cloudy seas,
The road was a ribbon of moonlight over the purple moor,
And the highwayman came riding—
    Riding—riding—
The highwayman came riding, up to the old inn-door.

II

He'd a French cocked-hat on his forehead, a bunch of lace at
    his chin,
A coat of the claret velvet, and breeches of brown doeskin;
They fitted with never a wrinkle; his boots were up to the
    thigh!
And he rode with a jeweled twinkle,
    His pistol butts a-twinkle,
His rapier hilt a-twinkle, under the jeweled sky.

III

Over the cobbles he clattered and clashed in the dark inn-
    yard,
And he tapped with his whip on the shutters, but all was locked
    and barred;
He whistled a tune to the window, and who should be waiting
    there
But the landlord's black-eyed daughter,
    Bess, the landlord's daughter,
Plaiting a dark red love-knot into her long black hair.

*Reprinted by permission from *Collected Poems*, Volume I, by Alfred Noyes. Copyright,
1906, by Frederick A. Stokes Company.

IV

And dark in the dark old inn-yard a stable-wicket creaked
Where Tim the hostler listened; his face was white and peaked;
His eyes were hollows of madness, his hair like moldy hay,
But he loved the landlord's daughter,
   The landlord's red-lipped daughter,
Dumb as a dog he listened, and he heard the robber say—

V

"One kiss, my bonny sweetheart, I'm after a prize tonight,
But I shall be back with the yellow gold before the morning light;
Yet, if they press me sharply, and harry me through the day,
Then look for me by moonlight;
   Watch for me by moonlight;
I'll come to thee by moonlight, though hell should bar the way."

VI

He rose upright in the stirrups; he scarce could reach her hand,
But she loosened her hair i' the casement! His face burned like
    a brand
As the black cascade of perfume came tumbling over his breast;
And he kissed its waves in the moonlight,
   (Oh, sweet black waves in the moonlight!)
Then he tugged at his rein in the moonlight, and galloped away
    to the West.

PART TWO

I

He did not come in the dawning; he did not come at noon;
And out o' the tawny sunset, before the rise o' the moon,
When the road was a gypsy's ribbon, looping the purple moor,
A redcoat troop came marching—
   Marching—marching—
King George's men came marching, up to the old inn-door.

II

They said no word to the landlord; they drank his ale instead;
But they gagged his daughter and bound her to the foot of her
    narrow bed;
Two of them knelt at her casement, with muskets at their side!
There was death at every window;
    And hell at one dark window;
For Bess could see, through her casement, the road that *he*
    would ride.

III

They had tied her up to attention, with many a sniggering jest;
They had bound a musket beside her, with the barrel beneath
    her breast!
"Now keep good watch!" and they kissed her.
    She heard the dead man say—
Look for me by moonlight;
    Watch for me by moonlight;
I'll come to thee by moonlight, though hell should bar the way!

IV

She twisted her hands behind her; but all the knots held good!
She writhed her hands till her fingers were wet with sweat or
    blood!
They stretched and strained in the darkness, and the hours
    crawled by like years,
Till, now, on the stroke of midnight,
    Cold on the stroke of midnight,
The tip of one finger touched it! The trigger at least was hers!

V

The tip of one finger touched it; she strove no more for the rest!
Up, she stood up to attention, with the barrel beneath her
    breast,
She would not risk their hearing; she would not strive again;

For the road lay bare in the moonlight;
   Blank and bare in the moonlight,
And the blood of her veins in the moonlight throbbed to her
      love's refrain.

VI

Tlot-tlot; tlot-tlot! Had they heard it? The horse-hoofs ringing
      clear;
Tlot-tlot, tlot-tlot, in the distance? Were they deaf that they did
      not hear?
Down the ribbon of moonlight, over the brow of the hill,
The highwayman came riding,
   Riding, riding!
The redcoats looked to their priming! She stood up, straight
      and still!

VII

Tlot-tlot, in the frosty silence! *Tlot-tlot,* in the echoing night!
Nearer he came and nearer! Her face was like a light!
Her eyes grew wide for a moment; she drew one last deep breath,
Then her finger moved in the moonlight,
   Her musket shattered the moonlight,
Shattered her breast in the moonlight and warned him—with
      her death.

VIII

He turned; he spurred to the westward; he did not know who
      stood
Bowed, with her head o'er the musket, drenched with her own
      red blood!
Not till the dawn he heard it, and slowly blanched to hear
How Bess, the landlord's daughter,
   The landlord's black-eyed daughter,
Had watched for her love in the moonlight, and died in the
      darkness there.

IX

Back, he spurred like a madman, shrieking a curse to the sky,
With the white road smoking behind him and his rapier brand-
  ished high!
Blood-red were his spurs i' the golden noon; wine-red was his
  velvet coat;
When they shot him down on the highway,
  Down like a dog on the highway,
And he lay in his blood on the highway, with the bunch of lace
  at his throat.

*   *   *   *   *   *   *

X

*And still of a winter's night, they say, when the wind is in the
  trees,*
When the moon is a ghostly galleon tossed upon cloudy seas,
When the road is a ribbon of moonlight over the purple moor,
A highwayman comes riding—
  Riding—riding—
A highwayman comes riding, up to the old inn-door.

XI

Over the cobbles he clatters and clangs in the dark inn-yard;
*And he taps with his whip on the shutters, but all is locked and
  barred;*
He whistles a tune to the window, and who should be waiting there
But the landlord's black-eyed daughter,
  Bess, the landlord's daughter,
Plaiting a dark red love-knot into her long black hair.

SEUMAS O'SULLIVAN

(James Starkey)

James Starkey, better known by his pseudonym of Seumas (pro-nounced Shā'mas) O'Sullivan, is one of the most brilliant of the "song-birds" sponsored by A. E.'s *New Songs* (1904). In fact his and Padraic Colum's are the two most important names in this collection of the younger poets. He was born in Dublin in 1878.

His earlier verse is tenuous to the point of frailty, but never quite breaks down and becomes mere beautiful words. He has described it best in his own lines:

> It is a whisper among the hazel bushes;
> It is a long, low, whispering voice that fills
> With a sad music the bending and swaying rushes;
> It is a heartbeat deep in the quiet hills.

The rhythms and the music of his technique are in perfect keeping with the exquisite, twilight beauty in which his fancy lives. There is, too, entire harmony between these delicate imaginings and the poet's love of beautiful things; in other words, his art is based on sincerity of emotion.

Although this is the mood which pervades *The Twilight People* (1905), his later volumes, *The Earth Lover* (1909), *Poems* (1912), and *An Epilogue* (1914), show a steady extension of his powers and his interests. Particularly interesting are his pictures of Dublin street scenes wherein the fairy-like fragility of his earlier shadow poetry is replaced by a semi-realism. "In Mercer Street: a Piper" has been set to music and is often sung.

Mr. O'Sullivan's keen eye and ear for beauty and his admirable skill in metrics make him one of the most important of the followers of Mr. Yeats.

HAVE THOU NO FEAR

SEUMAS O'SULLIVAN

Have thou no fear though round this heart
The winds of passion are.
The image of your love is set
Within, serene and far;
As in some lonely mountain lake
The reflex of a star.

But deeper than the deepest lake,
And stiller than its deep,
Is your immortal image set,
And round it steep on steep
Like guardians, peace-enturreted,
The winds of passion sleep.

IN MERCER STREET[1]: A PIPER

SEUMAS O'SULLIVAN

A piper in the streets today
Set up, and tuned, and started to play,
And away, away, away on the tide
Of his music we started; on every side
Doors and windows were opened wide,
And men left down their work and came,
And women with petticoats colored like flame
And little bare feet that were blue with cold
Went dancing back to the age of gold,
And all the world went gay, went gay,
For half an hour in the street today.

---

[1]*Mercer Street*, a short business street in the heart of Dublin.

THE ROSSES[1]

Seumas O'Sullivan

My sorrow that I am not by the little dun[2]
By the lake of the starlings at Rosses under the hill,
And the larks there, singing over the fields of dew,
Or evenings there, and the sedges still.
For plain I see now the length of the yellow sand,
And Lissadell[3] far off and its leafy ways,
And the holy mountain whose mighty heart
Gathers into it all the colored days.
My sorrow that I am not by the little dun
By the lake of the starlings at evening when all is still,
And still in whispering sedges the herons stand,
'Tis there I would nestle at rest till the quivering moon
Uprose in the golden quiet over the hill.

[1] *Rosses*, a point on Sligo Bay, northwestern coast of Ireland.
[2] *dun*, a mound or earthworks.
[3] *Lissadell*, a resort across the bay from Rosses Point.

WILFRED OWEN

"Killed in action, November 4, 1918"—Wilfred Owen's place in English poetry was left forever undetermined by the battle of the Sambre, seven days before the Armistice. He was born at Oswestry, Shropshire in 1893, and educated at Birkenhead Institute and London University. He was a private tutor for two years and then, in spite of ill health, enlisted in the Artists' Rifles. He served in France, was invalided home for a year, and went back, winning the Military Cross just a month before he joined "the unreturning army that was youth."

Here was a man whom no one could accuse of softness. Such a picture of warfare as "The Chances" must therefore be taken as faithful to the truth. It was at first supposed that the only writing to survive his death was "Strange Meeting," an extraordinary unfinished poem in which "the pity war distilled" rose above the reality of battle. Then Siegfried Sassoon discovered the other pieces which, published as *Poems* (1920), gave him, in the words of J. C. Squire, "a place among the unchallengeable poets."

THE CHANCES*

WILFRED OWEN

I mind as 'ow the night afore that show
Us five got talking—we was in the know,
"Over the top tomorrer; boys, we're for it,
First wave we are, first ruddy wave; that's tore it."[1]
"Ah, well," says Jimmy—an' 'e's seen some scrappin'—
"There ain't more nor five things as can 'appen;
Ye get knocked out[2]; else wounded—bad or cushy;
Scuppered; or nowt except yer feeling mushy."

One of us got the knock-out, blown to chops.
T'other was hurt-like, losin' both 'is props.
An' one, to use the word of 'ypocrites,
'Ad the misfortoon to be took by Fritz.
Now me, I wasn't scratched, praise God Almighty
(Though next time, please, I'll thank 'im for a blighty),[3]
But poor young Jim, 'e's livin' an' 'e's not;
'E reckoned 'e'd five chances, an' 'e's 'ad;
'E's wounded, killed, and pris'ner, all the lot—
The ruddy lot all rolled in one.   Jim's mad.

*From *Poems*, by Wilfred Owen; B. W. Huebsch, 1920. New York: The Viking Press, Inc.
By permission of the publishers.
[1]*that's tore it*, that means we're in for it.
[2]*knocked out*, killed; *cushy*, soft, easy; *scuppered*, taken prisoner; *mushy*, unnerved.
[3]*blighty*, a wound serious enough to invalid a soldier home to England.

ALEXANDER ROBERTSON

Alexander Robertson, a corporal in the Twelfth York and Lancaster Regiment, is one of the surprisingly many British soldiers who turned to writing poetry under the stress of the World War. Much of this poetry which was preserved in printed form might charitably have been allowed to die. Occasionally, however, the lines are strong and beautiful, and the song, however obscure its author, deserves not to be forgotten. Such are these stinging reflections on a thought from Thomas Campbell, war poet of an earlier and different tradition. The poem appeared in a pamphlet, *Soldier Poets*, published by Erskine MacDonald, London.

"WE SHALL DRINK TO THEM THAT SLEEP"[1]

Alexander Robertson

Yes, you will do it, silently of course;
For after many a toast and much applause,
One is in love with silence, being hoarse,
—Such more than sorrow is your quiet's cause.

Yes, I can see you at it, in a room
Well-lit and warm, high-roofed and soft to tread,
Satiate and briefly mindful of the tomb
With its poor victim of Teutonic lead.

Some unknown notability will rise,
Ridiculously solemn, glass a-brim,
And say, "To our dear brethren in the skies"—
Dim are all eyes, all glasses still more dim.

Your pledge of sorrow but a cup to cheer,
Your sole remark some witless platitude,
Such as, "Although it does not yet appear,
To suffer is the sole beatitude.

Life has, of course, good moments such as this
(A glass of sherry we should never spurn),
But where our brethren are, 'tis perfect bliss;
Still, we are glad *our* lot was—to return."

Yes, I can see you and can see the dead,
Keen-eyed at last for truth, with gentle mirth
Intent.   And having heard, smiling, they said:
"Strange are our little comrades of the earth."

[1] The title is a line from a poem by Thomas Campbell (1777-1843). (Author's note.)

MARGARET SACKVILLE

Lady Margaret Sackville comes from literary stock on both sides, inheriting her taste especially from her father, the seventh Earl de la Warr. She was born in 1881, and much of her early life was spent in the Sussex country, which she loves as do all who have come under its spell. She has written verse ever since she was six years old. A grave but not cold classicism rules her style. A special aptitude for compact and polished expression has found outlet in the writing of epitaphs, a volume of which has appeared under the title *Epitaphs* (1921). Other volumes are *Lyrics* (1912), *Selected Poems* (1919), and *Poems* (1923). She has also written fairy tales and short stories.

She makes her home near Edinburgh.

VALE

Margaret Sackville

Go forth; the snow
    So fast upon thy track
Shall fall, no man may know
Whether thou goest on
    Or turnest back.

The cold winds over thee
    Snowing shall hide
Thy pathway; not the sea
Shall so efface all footprints from the sand
    With the incoming tide.

But when at last
    Glad early morning like an anthem thrills
The skies, how wilt thou lie? In sleep locked fast
In a warm bed, or where the snow drifts deep
    Out there among the hills?

V. SACKVILLE-WEST

Virginia (Mary) Sackville-West (the Hon. Mrs. Harold George Nicolson) is the daughter of the third Baron Sackville and wife of a First Secretary of the Diplomatic Service. Her childhood was spent in the romantic surroundings of the family seat, Knole, at Sevenoaks, Kent, the greatest private house in England, which was granted by Queen Elizabeth to a Sackville in 1586. This background of noble traditions is graphically and delightfully described in her *Knole and the Sackvilles* (1923). As a small girl she lived in the vast old house with an aged and unsociable grandfather, occupying herself by writing endless stories in an old ledger.

She is equally well known as novelist and as poet. Of her novels, *Challenge* (1923) affords an interesting comparison with Joseph Conrad's masterpiece, *Nostromo*. Her poetry has a substantial quality which is not common in the work of women poets. It is clear, plain, not richly musical, definite. "Sailing Ships" reflects the poet's travels with her diplomat husband; it is instinct with love of country, pride of empire, and the ancient British comradeship with the sea. The poetry of Mrs. Sackville-West has been published in *Poems of East and West* (1917), *Orchard and Vineyard* (1921), and *The Land* (1926). The last-named received the Hawthornden Prize for 1926.

SAILING SHIPS

V. SACKVILLE-WEST

Lying on Downs[1] above the wrinkling bay
I with the kestrels shared the cleanly day,
The candid day; wind-shaven, brindled turf;
Tall cliffs; and long sea-line of marbled surf
From Cornish Lizard[2] to the Kentish Nore[3]
Lipping the bulwarks of the English shore,
While many a lovely ship below sailed by
On unknown errand, kempt and leisurely;
And after each, oh, after each, my heart
Fled forth, as, watching from the Downs apart,
I shared with ships good joys and fortunes wide
That might befall their beauty and their pride;

Shared first with them the blessed void repose
Of oily days at sea, when only rose
The porpoise's slow wheel to break the sheen
Of satin water indolently green,
When for'ard the crew, caps tilted over eyes,
Lay heaped on deck; slept; mumbled; smoked;
    threw dice;
The sleepy summer days; the summer nights
(The coast pricked out with rings of harbor-lights),
The motionless nights, the vaulted nights of June
When high in the cordage drifts the entangled moon,
And blocks go knocking, and the sheets go slapping,
And lazy swells against the sides come lapping;
And summer mornings off red Devon rocks,
Faint inland bells at dawn and crowing cocks;

[1]*Downs*, Sussex hills bordering the English Channel and becoming cliffs at Beachy Head.
[2]*Lizard*, the southernmost point of Great Britain.
[3]*Nore*, a sandbank at the mouth of the River Thames.

Shared swifter days, when headlands into ken
Trod grandly; threatened; and were lost again,
Old fangs along the battlemented coast;
And followed still my ship, when winds were most
Night-purified, and, lying steeply over,
She fled the wind as flees a girl her lover,
Quickened by that pursuit for which she fretted,
Her temper by the contest proved and whetted.
Wild stars swept overhead; her lofty spars
Reared to a ragged heaven sown with stars
As leaping out from narrow English ease
She faced the roll of long Atlantic seas.

Her captain then was I, I was her crew,
The mind that laid her course, the wake she drew,
The waves that rose against her bows, the gales—
Nay, I was more: I was her very sails
Rounded before the wind, her eager keel,
Her straining mastheads, her responsive wheel,
Her pennon stiffened like a swallow's wing;
Yes, I was all her slope and speed and swing,
Whether by yellow lemons and blue sea
She dawdled through the isles off Thessaly,[4]
Or saw the palms like sheaves of scimitars
On desert's verge below the sunset bars,
Or passed the girdle of the planet where
The Southern Cross looks over to the Bear,
And strayed, cool Northerner beneath strange skies,
Flouting the lure of tropic estuaries,
Down that long coast, and saw Magellan's Clouds[5]
   arise.

---

[4]*Thessaly*, a province in Greece.
[5]*Magellan's Clouds*, star-clusters resembling the Milky Way, seen in the southern heavens.

And some that beat up Channel homeward-bound
I watched, and wondered what they might have found,
What alien ports enriched their teeming hold
With crates of fruit or bars of unwrought gold?
And thought how London clerks with paper-clips
Had filed the bills of lading of those ships,
Clerks that had never seen the embattled sea,
But wrote down jettison and barratry,[6]
Perils, Adventures, and the Act of God,
Having no vision of such wrath flung broad;
Wrote down with weary and accustomed pen
The classic dangers of seafaring men;
And wrote "Restraint of Princes," and "the Acts
Of the King's Enemies," as vacant facts,
Blind to the ambushed seas, the encircling roar
Of angry nations foaming into war.

_____

[6] *jettison and barratry*, etc.—legal terms employed in making out a ship's manifest and other papers.

SIEGFRIED SASSOON

Siegfried (Loraine) Sassoon, born in Kent in 1886, of Jewish ancestry, was scarcely known before the World War except as a pleasant
young gentleman of quiet tastes, graduate of Clare College, Cambridge,
a master of fox-hounds, fond of books, tennis, and hunting, and mildly
addicted to the writing of melodious, dreamy verse for his own pleasure
and that of his friends, for whom his books were privately printed.
In 1913, we are told by his fellow poet, Robert Nichols, he fell under
the spell of Mr. Masefield's blunt realism and, starting to parody the
new manner, ended by adopting it in earnest. Hence he was in some
measure prepared to express the mounting horror which swept over
him when the War broke out and he found himself in France as a
captain in the Royal Welsh Fusiliers.

At first he was inarticulate before the truth of his war experience,
but by 1916 he had begun to find words for his burning indignation
at the sacrifice of youth. In *The Old Huntsman* (1917) and *Counter-
Attack* (1918) all pretense of poetizing war in the old way was cast
aside, and a torrent of bitter, passionate protest surged from his pen.
In all the literature of war—and it has always attracted poets—there
was never before such deadly revelation as this. Many readers there
were who, anxious to keep their traditional concepts of pomp and
glory, condemned Mr. Sassoon as raw, barbarous, unfeeling. An
American anthology, published as recently as 1921, even said, "The
imperishable poetry of the War betrays no murmur of revolt, no accents
of despair; it rejoices in the holiness, honor, nobleness, that duty has
recovered for mankind, in the victory that the ages shall attain." So
far as Mr. Sassoon is concerned, or Wilfred Owen or Robert Nichols
or Robert Graves or Wilfrid Wilson Gibson or any other of the men
who saw actual fighting, this is entirely false. One and all they
joined in a terrific denunciation of all that they had seen and felt.
And this not because they were insensitive: rather were they impelled
by intense pity for the tragedy of those who "gave their merry youth
away." Rupert Brooke is an exception to the general rule, but he
died before he saw actual service and his idealism was still safe from
disillusion.

Mr. Sassoon exceeds all other war poets in his savage unrestraint.
There is nothing suave or indirect in his attack. His sarcasm is like the

maddened jab of a bayonet. If his vehemence seems to outrun all bounds it is only, he would say, because his subject can be treated in no other way. If his art is barbaric, so, he would say, is war. Behind his poetry is the burning desire to make later generations see the fact of modern warfare as it appeared to one who took his part in it—no craven or peacemonger, for his bravery won him the Military Cross, but one whose soul was seared by the horror he passed through. "Let no one ever from henceforth say one word in any way countenancing war," he is quoted as saying in Mr. Nichols's preface to *Counter-Attack*. "It is dangerous even to speak of how here and there the individual may gain some hardship of soul by it. For war is hell, and those who institute it are criminals."

Mr. Sassoon's later books are *The War Poems of Siegfried Sassoon* (1919), *Picture Show* (1920), and *Satirical Poems* (1926).

THE KISS

Siegfried Sassoon

To these I turn, in these I trust;
Brother Lead and Sister Steel.
To his blind power I make appeal;
I guard her beauty clean from rust.

He spins and burns and loves the air,
And splits a skull to win my praise;
But up the nobly marching days
She glitters naked, cold, and fair.

Sweet Sister, grant your soldier this:
That in good fury he may feel
The body where he sets his heel
Quail from your downward darting kiss.

AFTERMATH

Siegfried Sassoon

Have you forgotten yet? . . .
For the world's events have rumbled on since those gagged days,
Like traffic checked awhile at the crossing of city ways:
And the haunted gap in your mind has filled with thoughts
that flow
Like clouds in the lit heavens of life; and you're a man reprieved
to go,
Taking your peaceful share of Time, with joy to spare.
But the past is just the same—and war's a bloody game . . .
Have you forgotten yet? . . .
*Look down, and swear by the slain of the War that you'll never
forget.*

Do you remember the dark months you held the sector at
    Mametz—
The nights you watched and wired and dug and piled sandbags
    on parapets?
Do you remember the rats; and the stench
Of corpses rotting in front of the front-line trench—
And dawn coming, dirty-white, and chill with a hopeless rain?
Do you ever stop and ask, "Is it all going to happen again?"

Do you remember that hour of din before the attack—
And the anger, the blind compassion that seized and shook
    you then
As you peered at the doomed and haggard faces of your men?
Do you remember the stretcher-cases lurching back
With dying eyes and lolling heads, those ashen-gray
Masks of the lads who once were keen and kind and gay?

Have you forgotten yet? . . .
Look up, and swear by the green of the spring that you'll never
    forget.

EDITH SITWELL

Edith Sitwell, born in Scarborough, Yorkshire, in 1887, is the daughter of Sir George and Lady Ida Sitwell and sister of Osbert and Sacheverell Sitwell, her brothers being, like herself, prominent members of the modernist or "intellectual" school of British poets. She was privately educated.

From 1916 to 1921 as editor of *Wheels*, an annual anthology of extremely modern poetry, she disturbed the complacency of British letters with her aggressive originality. Nothing just like Miss Sitwell's poetry had been seen before, and there were plenty of critics ready to declare that it was not poetry. Yet she has not failed of a following who admire her poetry for its brilliant oddity and admire the Sitwells for their militant counterblasts against their critics.

A curious perversity of Miss Sitwell's style is the transposition of sense impressions: the stars "howl wolfishly," the morning light "creaks," the fire "caws." Especially startling are the similes: "Whinnying whines like grass the air," "a clang darker than an orang-outang." And yet, for all its strangeness, this poetry now and again throws over reality flashes of illumination which, if fitful, are none the less revealing of new and unsuspected aspects of things.

Behind the glitter and play of her style Miss Sitwell offers plenty of substance, whether the romantic invention of her nursery rimes, the merciless wit of her satire, or the half-weary, half-pitying attitude of her philosophy. For a further description of modernist tendencies, see the Introduction, pages 50 and 51.

Miss Sitwell measurably explains herself in the following passage from that standing refutation of British humorlessness, *Who's Who:* "in early youth she took an intense dislike to simplicity, morris-dancing, a sense of humor, and every kind of sport except reviewer-baiting, and has continued these distastes ever since."

Her books are: *The Mother and Other Poems* (1915), *Clown's Houses* (1918), *The Wooden Pegasus* (1920), *Façade* (1922), *Bucolic Comedies* (1923), *The Sleeping Beauty* (1924), *Troy Park* (1926). Her best and most characteristic work is in the three last-named volumes.

AUBADE[1]

Edith Sitwell

Jane, Jane,
Tall as a crane,
The morning light creaks down again.

Comb your cockscomb-ragged hair;
Jane, Jane, come down the stair.

Each dull blunt wooden stalactite
Of rain creaks, hardened by the light,

Sounding like an overtone
From some lonely world unknown.

But the creaking empty light
Will never harden into sight,

Will never penetrate your brain
With overtones like the blunt rain.

The light would show (if it could harden)
Eternities of kitchen garden,

Cockscomb flowers that none will pluck,
And wooden flowers that 'gin to cluck.

In the kitchen you must light
Flames as staring, red and white

As carrots or as turnips, shining
Where the cold dawn light lies whining.

---

[1] *aubade*, a morning song.

Cockscomb hair on the cold wind
Hangs limp, turns the milk's weak mind . . .

Jane, Jane,
Tall as a crane,
The morning light creaks down again!

THE DRUM[1]

EDITH SITWELL

In January when the blue
Feathered winds like cocks crew,
Then blew old winter's tales down chimneys,
Said the Justice Mompesson,
"What is that harsh beating drum
That we hear rolling like the sea?"
"It is a beggar with a pass
Signed by you." "I signed not one."
They took the ragged drum that we
Once heard rolling like the sea;
In the house of the Justice it must lie
And usher in Eternity.

.   .   .   .

Is it black night?
Black as Hecate[2] howls a star
Wolfishly, and whined
The wind from very far.

---

[1] *The Drum:* The narrative of the Demon of Tedworth and of the disturbances at Mr. Mompesson's house caused by witchcraft, 1661. The Drummer was a beggar who appeared with a false pass and demanded money from the authorities of the places he passed through. His drum was confiscated and placed in Mr. Mompesson's country house. In the dead of night, it played alone, with no hand touching it. The Drummer was tried for witchcraft at Salisbury Assizes and was transported; but he raised a storm at sea and escaped. This narrative is taken from *Saducismus Triumphatus* (1682) by Joseph Glanvill, late Chaplain to His Majesty King Charles the Second.—Author's note.
See also *A blow at modern sadducism in some philosophical considerations about witchcraft. To which is added, the relation of the fam'd disturbance by the drummer, in the house of Mr. John Mompesson: with some reflections on drollery, and atheisme.* (1668).
[2] *Hecate*, goddess of the underworld.

In the pomp of the Mompesson house is one
Candle that lolls like the midnight sun
Or the coral comb of a cock; . . . it rocks . . .
Only the goatish snow's locks
Watch the candles lit by fright
One by one through the black night.

Through the kitchen there runs a hare—
Whinnying whines like grass the air;
It passes; now is standing there
A lovely lady . . . see her eyes—
Black angels in a heavenly place,
Her shady locks and her dangerous grace.

"I thought I heard the wicked old witch in
The richest gallipot[3] in the kitchen!"—
A lolloping galloping candle confesses.
"Outside in the passage are wildernesses
Of darkness rustling like witches' dresses."

Out go the candles one by one
Hearing the rolling of a drum!

What is the march we hear groan
As the hoofèd sound of a drum marched on
With a pang like darkness, with a clang
Darker than an orang-outang?
"Heliogabalus[4] is alone—
Only his bones to play upon!"

The mocking money in the pockets
Then turned black . . . now caws
The fire . . . outside, one scratched the door
As with iron claws—
Scratching under the children's bed

---

[3]*gallipot*, a small earthen jar.
[4]*Heliogabalus* (204-222), a Roman emperor, shamelessly profligate, killed by his soldiers.

And up the trembling stairs. . . . "Long dead,"
Moaned the water black as crape.

Over the snow the wintry moon
Green as henbane or herb paris
Spotted the bare trees; and soon

Whinnying, neighed the maned blue wind
Turning the burning milk to snow,
Whining it shied down the corridor—
Over the floor I heard it go.

.   .   .   .

Let those affecting drollery
And foppish incredulity,
With unbelief in apparitions,
Witchcraft, Satan's black religion—
Go at last into perdition.

Let those who want to loose from prison
Witches, scoffing foolishly
At government and our religion
With a fool's buffoonery,

Let them fear, lest in the house
The sound they took but for a mouse
Be witchery . . . let them beware
The idle phantoms of the air!

OSBERT SITWELL

Osbert Sitwell, the elder son of Sir George Sitwell and brother of the poets Edith and Sacheverell Sitwell, was born in London in 1892. His childhood centered in Renishaw Hall, Derbyshire. The seaside town of Scarborough, his father's castle in Florence, and the places of his wanderings in Spain and Italy also contributed to his fortunate background. He attended Eton, where he attained a reputation as a prodigious reader. At nineteen he entered a yeomanry regiment, later transferring to the Grenadier Guards, with whom he went to France in 1914. He was invalided home after two years' service.

Already his poetry had appeared in his sister's annual of modernist verse, *Wheels*. His first book of poetry, *Argonaut and Juggernaut* (1919), was embittered by memories of the World War; he is unsparing in his denunciation of an institution which he sees only as the exploitation of the masses for the benefit of "profiteers." *Out of the Flame* (1923) contains some of his best satire. Here he lashes at a wide range of victims—the parvenu, the Philistine, the snob, the hypocrite —whatever, in short, is stupid or false or small-souled. The clarity and vehemence of his indignation carry him beyond the finicky passion for words which, in the case of some modernists, obstructs a free communication of ideas. He goes further than other modernists also in the vitality of his criticism: instead of regarding the world with weary and sophisticated pessimism, he boldly attacks the objects of his aversion.

England Reclaimed; a Book of Eclogues (1928) is a closely woven series of pastoral portraits recollected from childhood, in which Mr. Sitwell, in his own words, "aims at recording a broad panorama, essentially English . . . which seems now, by force of circumstance, to be slipping away from us into the past." This book is the first of a trilogy, the second of which is to treat of life in country towns, the third of life in the cities.

Of Mr. Sitwell's style it should be noted that, while he is not without the eccentricities of his school, he seldom forgets that poetry should be intelligible.

For a sympathetic study of the Sitwells and their work, see *The Three Sitwells, a Biographical and Critical Study*, by R. L. Mégroz.

ULTIMATE JUDGMENT

Osbert Sitwell

Within the sunny greenness of the close,
Secure, a heavy breathing fell, then rose—
Here undulating chins sway to and fro,
As heavy blossoms do; the cheek's faint glow
Points to post-prandial port.   The willow weeps;
Hushed are the birds—in fact—the Bishop sleeps.

Then, suddenly, the wide sky blazes red;
Up from their graves arise the solemn dead,
The world is shaken; buildings fall in twain,
Exulting hills shout loud, then shout again,
While, with the thunder of deep rolling drums
The angels sing—At last Salvation comes.
The weak, the humble, the disdained, the poor,
Are judged the first, and climb to heaven's door.

.   .   .   .

The Bishop wakes to see his palace crash
Down on the rocking ground—but in a flash
It dawns upon him—with impressive frown,
He sees his second-housemaid in a crown,
In rainbow robes that glisten like a prism
"I warned them . . . " said the Bishop—
   "Bolshevism!"

J. C. SQUIRE

John Collings Squire was born at Plymouth, Devonshire, in 1884. He was educated at Blundell's School and at St. John's College, Cambridge. He first made his name, while literary editor of *The New Statesman*, by exceedingly amusing and clever parodies: *Imaginary Speeches* (1912), *Tricks of the Trade* (1917), *Collected Parodies* (1921). In the meantime, under the pseudonym of "Solomon Eagle," he was writing a weekly grist of literary criticism, to be collected as *Books in General: First Series* (1918), *Second Series* (1920), *Third Series* (1921). In 1919 he founded *The London Mercury* and became its literary and managing editor. In *Essays at Large* (1922) he proved himself a graceful writer of light personal essays.

Being an all-round man of letters, he has produced several volumes of verse, the most important being *Poems: First Series* (1918) and *Second Series* (1922). An uneasy intellectualism sometimes gets the better of his poetic values, as in the introspective "The Mind of Man." Robert Lynd was thinking of this when he wrote of Mr. Squire: "To read him is again and again to be reminded of Donne. Like Donne he is largely self-occupied, examining the horrors of his own soul, overburdened at times with thought, an intellect at odds with the spirit. Like Donne, he will have none of the merely poetic, either in music or in imagery." Yet in such pieces as "The Ship" or "Winter Nightfall," he wields authentic magic; in his parody of Mr. Masefield he combines an acute critical sense with an equally acute sense of humor.

THE SHIP

J. C. SQUIRE

There was no song nor shout of joy
  Nor beam of moon or sun,
When she came back from the voyage
  Long ago begun;
But twilight on the waters
  Was quiet and gray,
And she glided steady, steady and pensive,
  Over the open bay.

Her sails were brown and ragged,
  And her crew hollow-eyed,
But their silent lips spoke content
  And their shoulders pride;
Though she had no captives on her deck,
  And in her hold
There were no heaps of corn or timber
  Or silks or gold.

WINTER NIGHTFALL[1]

J. C. SQUIRE

The old yellow stucco
  Of the time of the Regent[2]
  Is flaking and peeling;
The rows of square windows
  In the straight yellow building
  Are empty and still;

[1]Compare with Dr. Bridges's poem by the same title, page 355.
[2]the Regent, George IV, regent from 1811 to 1820; stucco was much used at this time under the influence of the architect John Nash.

And the dusky dark evergreens
Guarding the wicket
Are draped with wet cobwebs,
And above this poor wilderness
Toneless and somber
   Is the flat of the hill.

They said that a colonel
Who long ago died here
Was the last one to live here:
An old retired colonel,
Some Fraser or Murray,
   I don't know his name;
Death came here and summoned him,
And the shells of him vanished
Beyond all speculation;
And silence resumed here,
Silence and emptiness,
   And nobody came.

Was it wet when he lived here,
Were the skies dun and hurrying,
Was the rain so irresolute?
Did he watch the night coming,
Did he shiver at nightfall
   Before he was dead?
Did the wind go so creepily,
Chilly and puffing,
With drops of cold rain in it?
Was the hill's lifted shoulder
So lowering and menacing,
   So dark, and so dread?

Did he turn through his doorway
And go to his study,
And light many candles?

And fold in the shutters,
And heap up the fireplace
    To fight off the damps?
And muse on his boyhood,
And wonder if India
Ever was real?
And shut out the loneliness
With pig-sticking memoirs
    And collections of stamps?

Perhaps.   But he's gone now,
He and his furniture
Dispersed now forever;
And the last of his trophies,
Antlers and photographs,
    Heaven knows where.
And there's grass in his gateway,
Grass on his footpath,
Grass on his doorstep;
The garden's grown over,
The well-chain is broken,
    The windows are bare.

And I leave him behind me,
For the straggling, discolored
Rags of the daylight,
And hills and stone walls
And a rick long forgotten
    Of blackening hay:
The road pale and sticky,
And cart-ruts and nail-marks,
And wind-ruffled puddles,
And the slop of my footsteps
In this desolate country's
    Cadaverous clay.

IF MR. MASEFIELD HAD WRITTEN "CASABIANCA"[1]

J. C. Squire

"You dirty hog," "You snouty snipe,"
"You lump of muck," "You bag of tripe,"
Such, as their latest breaths they drew,
The objurgations of the crew.
—— —— —— they roared
As they went tumbling overboard,
Or frizzled like so many suppers
All along the halyard scuppers.
"You ——" . . the last was gone,
And Cassy yelled there all alone.
(He thought the old man was on the ship.)
"Father! this gives me the fair pip!"

"My God, you old vagabond," he cried,
"If only I . . . " No voice replied;
Only the tall flames higher sprang,
Amid the spars, and soared and sang,
Only along the rigging came
God's great unfolding flower of flame,
And Love's divine dim planet shed
Her radiance on the many dead;
And past the battling fleets the sea
Stretched to the world's edge tranquilly,
Breathing with slow, contented breath
As though it were in love with Death,
As it has breathed since first began
Man's inhumanity to man,
As it will do when like a scroll
All the heavens together roll.

---

[1] *Casabianca*, a poem by Felicia Hemans (1793-1835). Louis de Casabianca, a Corsican naval captain at the battle of the Nile, blew up his ship rather than surrender. His ten-year-old son refused to leave the ship and died with his father.

There's that purple passage done,
And I have one less lap to run.

Dogs barked, owls hooted, cockerels crew—
As in my works they often do
When, flagging with my main design,
I pad with a descriptive line.—
Young Cassy cried again: "Oh, damn!
What an unhappy pup I am!
Will nobody go out and search
For dad, who's left me in the lurch?
For dad, who's left me on the poop,
For dad, who's left me in the soup,
For dad, who's left me on the deck.
Perhaps it's what I should expeck
Considerin' 'ow he treated me
Before I came away to sea.

"Often at home he used to beat
My head for talking in the street,
Often for things I didden do,
He brushed my breeches with a shoe.
Oh! but I wish that I was home now,
Treading the soft old Breton loam now
In that old Breton country, where
Mellows the golden autumn air,
And all the tender champaign fills
With hyacinths and daffodils,
And on God's azure uplands now
They plow the plowed fields with a plow,
And earthworms feel averse from laughter,
With hungry white birds following after.
And maids at evening walk with men
Through the meadows and up the glen
To hear the old sweet tale again."

The deck was getting hot and hotter,
"Father!" he screamed, "you ——— rotter!"
The deck was getting red and redder,
And now he thought he'd take a header,
Now he advanced and now he funked it . . .
It had been better had he bunked it,
For as he wavered thus, and swore,
There came a slow tremendous roar.
Lord Nelson suddenly woke up.
"Where is Old Cassy and his pup?
'Don't know,' you say? Why, strike me blind,
I s'pose I'd better ask the wind."
He asked the wind; the brooding sky
At once gave back the wind's reply:
"Wotto, Nelson!"
                    "Wotto, sonny?"
"Do you think you're being funny?
Can't you look around, confound you,
At all these fragments that surround you,
Thick as thieves upon the sea,
Instead of coming bothering me?"

Or, alternatively, if you prefer his other method,
      it would run like this:
And the flames rose, and leaping flames of fire
   Leapt round the masts and made the spars a crown,
A golden crown, as ravenous as desire.
"Father!" he cried, "my feet are getting brown."
"Father!" he cried. The quiet stars looked down,
The flames rose up like flowers overhead.
He was alone, and all the crew were dead.

JAMES STEPHENS

James Stephens was born in Dublin in 1882. After a boyhood of wandering and extreme poverty—he is said to have come near starving in Belfast—he married on twenty-six shillings a week, which he received as typist for a Dublin lawyer. In this plight he was discovered and befriended by the discerning A. E., and helped in publishing his first volume of verse, *Insurrections* (1909). Although this made no stir, it was soon followed by his greatest success, the fantastic, mystic, philosophical novel, *The Crock of Gold* (1912). After that, whatever Mr. Stephens wrote was eagerly received. Another prose novel, *The Demi-Gods* (1914), took its place among his chief works; volumes of poetry were *The Hill of Vision* (1912), *Songs from the Clay* (1914), *The Rocky Road to Dublin; The Adventures of Seumas Beg* (1915), *Green Branches* (1916), *Reincarnations* (1918). Following his American tour in 1925 a volume of the most popular of his readings was published as *A Poetry Recital* (1925). His verse has recently been published in a complete edition, *Collected Poems* (1926). A book of tales, *Etched in Moonlight*, appeared in 1928.

Mr. Stephens's leprechaun-like personality communicates itself to everything that he writes, prose or poetry. And indeed the line between his prose and his poetry is indistinct, for he is always at heart a poet. His favorite trick is to combine the casual with the sublime in a reckless irreverence—and from these odd juxtapositions to strike out new and startling effects of exuberant wit and penetrating wisdom. But beneath all the crackling brilliance of his art lies the human tenderness which has made him beloved.

There is yet another side to Mr. Stephens—the poet of sheer fun. Many of his poems have no other purpose than to amuse, and they do that as few other contemporary poems can do. Such poems are "The Devil's Bag," from *Seumas Beg*, which may well be autobiography for Seumas Beg means "little James"; or "The Fur Coat," or "Righteous Anger."

"The Coolun," after Raftery, is one of the *Reincarnations*. It shows alike Mr. Stephens's skill at re-creating the old poetry of Ireland, and his uncanny mastery of verbal music. To get the latter quality of the poem it must absolutely be read aloud—preferably by Mr. Stephens himself.

THE COOLUN*[1]

James Stephens

Come with me, under my coat,
And we will drink our fill
    Of the milk of the white goat,
Or wine if it be thy will;

    And we will talk until
Talk is a trouble, too,
    Out on the side of the hill;
And nothing is left to do,

    But an eye to look into an eye,
And a hand in a hand to slip,
    And a sigh to answer a sigh,
And a lip to find out a lip.

What if the night be black
Or the air on the mountain chill,
    Where the goat lies down in her track
And all but the fern is still!

    Stay with me, under my coat,
And we will drink our fill
    Of the milk of the white goat,
Out on the side of the hill.

---

*From *Reincarnations* by James Stephens. Copyright 1918 by The Macmillan Company. Reprinted by permission.
[1]*coolun*, darling.

THE DEVIL'S BAG*

James Stephens

I saw the Devil walking down the lane
   Behind our house.—There was a heavy bag
Strapped tightly on his shoulders, and the rain
   Sizzled when it hit him.   He picked a rag
Up from the ground and put it in his sack,
   And grinned and rubbed his hands.   There was a thing
Moving inside the bag upon his back—
   It must have been a soul!   I saw it fling
And twist about inside, and not a hole
   Or cranny for escape!   Oh, it was sad!
I cried, and shouted out, *"Let out that soul!"*
   But he turned round, and, sure, his face went mad,
And twisted up and down, and he said *"Hell!"*
And ran away . . . Oh, mammy!   I'm not well.

L. A. G. STRONG

Leonard A. G. Strong was born in Plympton, Devonshire, in 1896, of Irish and English stock. His background was as mixed as his inheritance, for his childhood was spent partly in Dartmoor, the country of *Lorna Doone*, and partly in the hills of Wicklow, near Dublin. His education was English: a school at Plymouth, Brighton College, and Wadham College, Oxford. He is a teacher at Summer Fields, a preparatory school near Oxford.

In his first small volume of poems, *Dublin Days* (1921), Mr. Strong presents a portrait gallery of Irish types, with a pungent wit which does not prevent sympathetic analysis of these people of the Dublin streets. *The Lowery Road* (1923) exchanges the irresistible impudence of the first book for the stolid bluntness of the Devon peasantry. His annual anthologies are discriminating selections of the best magazine verse published in England and America.

THE BREWER'S MAN

L. A. G. Strong

Have I a wife?   Bedam I have!
    But we was badly mated.
I hit her a great clout one night,
    And now we're separated.

And mornin's going to me work
    I meets her on the quay:
"Good mornin' to ye, ma'am!" says I:
    "To hell with ye!" says she.

THE MADWOMAN OF PUNNET'S TOWN

L. A. G. Strong

A swell within her billowed skirts
    Like a great ship with sails unfurled,
The madwoman goes gallantly
    Upon the ridges of her world.

With eagle nose and wisps of gray
    She strides upon the westward hills,
Swings her umbrella joyously
    And waves it to the waving mills.

Talking and chuckling as she goes
    Indifferent both to sun and rain,
With all that merry company,
    The singing children of her brain.

MICKY-THE-MOON

L. A. G. STRONG

Oho, me little silver moon!
    They run me for a fool,
But I've a wisdom in me head
    Will put them all to school.

I'll stick a bucket in the yard
    The time there's no one round,
And when she's swimmin' grand and gay
    I'll crawl without a sound

And pop a sack tight over her,
    Then drain the water dry,
And catch the little leppin' moon
    And stow her safely by.

I'll rub her brilliant face across
    Each copper coin that's mine,
And every penny of them all
    Will get a florin shine.

Then up to Doyle's for floods o' drink
    To give them gullet's joy:
"Come on," they'll say; "it's Micky's treat:
    Bedam, but Mick's the boy!"

EDWARD THOMAS

(Philip) Edward Thomas, born in England in 1878, attended St.
Paul's School, London, and Lincoln College, Oxford. Early faced
with the responsibility of supporting an increasing family, he turned
himself to whatever writing presented itself. At first he won considerable note for his work as a reviewer, but as the years passed he
lost his zest for this kind of work. The necessity of writing to order
largely destroyed his artistic enthusiasm, but never prevented him from
turning out workmanlike prose. His collected sketches, *Rest and Unrest*
(1910) and *Light and Twilight* (1911) are popular with British readers.

In 1912 he met Robert Frost. The friendship with the American
poet gave Thomas the impulse to write poetry with no other purpose
than the joy of artistic self-expression. Inexplicably, out of the years
of dreary hack-work, the ability to sing suddenly flowered forth. In
the congenial friendship of a small group of poets—Mr. Frost, Mr.
De la Mare, and Mr. Lascelles Abercrombie—he was stimulated to produce the intimate, simple lyrics which began to appear in the magazines under the pseudonym of "Edward Eastaway." He was no
poet to voice the song too high for earth, the surge and thunder of
majestic thoughts—but he could write with a grave charm of a pile
of turnips in an English farmyard, white and gold and purple under
spring sunshine, of the dust-covered nettles in the corner, of hill
roads wet with rain. Without resort to artifice but with an almost
passionate sincerity he described the English countryside in little,
vivid, affectionate lyrics. "Adlestrop" sums up his best qualities.
Of this poem Edward Shanks, a fellow poet, has written: "It captures
not the reflection but the moment of seeing, the very moment itself."

When the War came, Thomas had no hesitation as to his future
course of action. In spite of his age (he was thirty-six), in spite of
the urgings of his friends that his first duty was to his family, he
could see only his duty to the country which was so much a part of
him that he gladly offered it his service. Many of his poems were written
while waiting to enlist, in the training camp, or at the front. Sent to
France with the Artists' Rifles, he was killed in action at Vimy Ridge
in 1917. His first book, *Poems* (1917), is dedicated to Robert Frost.
A further collection, *Last Poems*, appeared in 1918, and *Collected
Poems*, with introduction by Mr. De la Mare, in 1920.

ADLESTROP

Edward Thomas

Yes, I remember Adlestrop—
The name—because one afternoon
Of heat the express-train drew up there
Unwontedly. It was late June.

The steam hissed. Someone cleared his throat.
No one left and no one came
On the bare platform. What I saw
Was Adlestrop—only the name—

And willows, willow-herb, and grass,
And meadowsweet, and haycocks dry;
No whit less still and lonely fair
Than the high cloudlets in the sky.

And for that minute a blackbird sang
Close by, and round him, mistier,
Farther and farther, all the birds
Of Oxfordshire and Gloucestershire.

THE NEW HOUSE

Edward Thomas

Now first, as I shut the door,
    I was alone
In the new house; and the wind
    Began to moan.

Old at once was the house,
    And I was old;
My ears were teased with the dread
    Of what was foretold,

Nights of storm, days of mist, without end;
    Sad days when the sun
Shone in vain; old griefs and griefs
    Not yet begun.

All was foretold me; naught
    Could I foresee;
But I learned how the wind would sound
    After these things should be.

SHERARD VINES

Sherard Vines was born in 1890 at Oxford of clerical and professorial heritage. He grew up in what he terms "the prim atmosphere of Oxford society, charged with both Darwinism and Conservative Anglicanism." He was graduated from New College, Oxford, with honors in English literature, afterwards studying post-impressionist art in Munich and Paris. During the War he saw active service in Flanders, with the same resultant attitude against war as that of the other young British poets.

His travels and studies in Europe and his subsequent life as a teacher of English at Keiogijuku University, Tokyo, have furnished a curious complex of influences on his poetry which he lists as follows: "Bergsonism and the reaction against it, Aristophanes, Apuleius, Aristotle's *Poetics*, Petronius, anthropology, comparative religion, modern French literature, the aesthetic attitude, the tropics, Salomon Reinach, Boileau, Dryden, etching, engraving, mezzotint, aquatint, Japanese art, especially the Ukiyoye school, Coleridge's criticism." Against this must be placed an even more astonishing list of antipathies: "Russian and Irish literature, Ibsen, Hauptmann, nineteenth-century literature—especially Walter Pater, Lafcadio Hearn (a shallow sentimentalist), Botticelli, the Middle Ages (except the Scholastics), Negro art, Marinetti, expressionism."

Out of all this he has wrought a poetic style which becomes increasingly involved in esoteric aesthetics. Starting with the comparative simplicity of such a warm and unaffected poem as "A Song for Grocers," in *The Two Worlds* (1916), he begins to desert the pure poetic impulse in *The Kaleidoscope* (1920); and in *The Pyramid* (1926) he is quite frankly aiming at "ornate poetry on a philosophic basis, the ornament consisting of symbols, conceits, images, etc., which relate to and extend the underlying idea." His critical theories find expression in *Movements in Modern English Poetry and Prose* (1928).

A SONG FOR GROCERS

SHERARD VINES

Heaven bless grocers' shops, wherein
Raisins are with tawny skin,
Murrey[1] wine, and green liqueurs,
Curious spice in canisters,
Honest ham, and mother tea,
Isinglass[2] and caraway,
Rennet,[3] vinegar, and salt
That honor has, and clear cobalt;[4]
Coffee, that swart Mussulman,
Caviar the Caspian,
Suave oil, angry condiments,
Anchovies, and sweet essence
Of clove and almond, honeycomb,
Jam our English orchards from,
Portly cheeses full of mold,
Sugars and treacles brown or gold;
Soap, to keep us pure, and white
Candles, the slim sons of light,
Butter like the flow'r of gorse,
Wheat meal fine and oatmeal coarse,
Soda for our maid's service,
Sago, tapioca, rice—
An economic trinity—
Bacon, friend ham's affinity.
Bananas, which the People please,
Proletarian oranges,
While of fruits in sirup a
Frequent cornucopia.

[1] *murrey*, dark reddish-brown.
[2] *isinglass*, gelatine.
[3] *rennet*, a substance used in making cheese or junket.
[4] *cobalt*, bluing.

Eggs fresh within and white without,
Cocoa of origin devout,
Nuts and string and brooms and mops,
Saveloys[5], and lollipops—
God, be good to grocers' shops!

[5]*saveloys*, dried sausages.

ARTHUR WALEY

Arthur Waley, born at Tunbridge Wells in 1889, was educated at Rugby and at King's College, Cambridge. He is an assistant curator in the Department of Prints and Drawings at the British Museum. As an accomplished Orientalist he has made a large number of translations from Chinese and Japanese sources, as well as having contributed to the study of Chinese painting. His translations faithfully reproduce the quiet simplicity both of words and of emotions for which Oriental poetry is remarkable. Because of the preoccupation of Oriental poets with the thoughts and happenings of everyday life —because, as Mr. Waley says, "Their thoughts set out on no strange quests and adventures, just as their ships discovered no new continents"—the poems of a thousand years ago often strike notes that are startlingly contemporaneous; for life in its essentials—friendship, family life, love of children, solitude, grief of parting, joy of meeting, birth, death, love—is the same today as it was when Po Chü-i and Li Po wrote about it.

There are no heights of ecstasy in Chinese poetry, but in its defense, Mr. Waley writes: "We must recognize that for thousands of years the Chinese maintained a level of rationality and tolerance that the West might well envy. . . . In the poems of Po Chü-i no close reasoning or philosophic subtlety will be discovered; but a power of candid reflection and self-analysis which has not been rivaled in the West."

The renascence of interest in Chinese literature has been largely owing to Mr. Waley's translations: *170 Chinese Poems* (1918), *More Translations* (1919), *Japanese Poetry* (1919), *The Nō Plays of Japan* (1921), *The Temple* (1923), and *The Tale of Genji* (3 volumes, 1925, 1926, 1927).

HOT CAKES[1]

ARTHUR WALEY

Winter has come; fierce is the cold;
In the sharp morning air new-risen we meet.
Rheum freezes in the nose;
Frost hangs about the chin.
For hollow bellies, for chattering teeth and knees shivering
What better than a hot cake?
Soft as the down of spring,
Whiter than autumn wool!
Dense and swift the steam
Rises, swells, and spreads.
Fragrance flies through the air,
Is scattered far and wide,
Steals down along the wind, and wets
The covetous mouth of passer-by.
Servants and grooms
Throw sidelong glances, munch the empty air;
They lick their lips who serve;
While lines of envious lackeys by the wall
Stand dryly swallowing.

---

[1]Translated from Shu Hsi, a Chinese poet of the third century after Christ.

WILLOUGHBY WEAVING

Willoughby Weaving was born at Oxford in 1885. He attended Pembroke College, Oxford, from which he was graduated with the degree of M.A. His interests, as indicated by his poetry, are largely influenced by a classical background. He saw service in the British Army during the early years of the War. Since then he has been headmaster of a preparatory school at Killylea, County Armagh, in the North of Ireland.

His poetic output consists of a half-dozen small volumes: *Poems* (1913), *The Star Fields* (1916), *The Bubble* (1917), *Heard Melodies* (1918), *Daedal Wings* (1920), and *Algazel* (1920), a tragedy. His lyrics are mostly brief and unconcerned with deep emotions. Their best quality is their simple melodiousness.

AUGUST

WILLOUGHBY WEAVING

Now lithe young August like an Indian basks
  His tanned and naked body in the sun,
And who beholds his comeliness but asks,
  "For sure, is this the shy, white-withered one
Who fled in April down the woodland ways,
Hiding his face and weeping half his days?"

SONG

WILLOUGHBY WEAVING

The field is filled with fragrance,
  With song the tree,
The skies with cloudless beauty,
  My heart with thee.

Sweet are the fields that waver,
  The boughs that meet,
Sweet the blue skies between them,
  My heart more sweet.

T. P. CAMÉRON WILSON

Theodore Percival Cameron Wilson was born in South Devon in 1888 and educated at Exeter and Oxford. Before the War he was a schoolmaster at Mt. Arlington School, Surrey, and well known under the pseudonym "Tipuca" as a contributor of articles to *The Westminster Gazette* and other periodicals. When the War began he enlisted in the Grenadier Guards, and was later made a captain in the Sherwood Foresters. He was killed in action in 1918. His poems were collected and edited by Harold Monro under the title *Magpies in Picardy* (1919). He also wrote a novel, *The Friendly Enemy*.

His poetry is written with the lightness of a happy personality and a fresh fancy. Only occasionally does he touch a more serious tone, as in "Dulce et Decorum":

> O young and brave, it is not sweet to die,
>   To fall and leave no record of the race,
> A little dust trod by the passers-by,
>   Swift feet that press your lonely resting-place;
> Your dreams unfinished, and your song unheard—
> Who wronged your youth by such a careless word?

THE MATHEMATICAL MASTER TO
HIS DULLEST PUPIL

T. P. Cameron Wilson

I came to you and caught your eagle wings
And gloomed your soul with Algebra and things,
And cast a net of pale Geometry
Wherein your laughter struggled to be free.

They say that mental discipline is grand
For teaching little striplings how to stand.
They say I cannot fit your soul for life
Without continual pruning with a knife.

And they are clever men, who come from schools
Where they were made successful by these rules,
And where they gained that weight of flesh and bone
Which I would give my oldest pipe to own.

And so they must be right and I be wrong,
Yet when I see sweet thoughts around you throng
Like honeybees above the tousled gorse
In smoke-blue valleys under Devon tors,[1]

And when, O little son! within your eyes
The light that lives on wings of dragon-flies
(More delicate than laughter of dead jests)
Is drowned beneath your pedagogue's requests,

I go and swear and smoke and drink
And dream of vested interests, and think
Of all the poets' fire we might have won
Had you and I been pals, O little son!

[1]*tors*, rocky peaks, especially on Dartmoor in Devonshire.

HUMBERT WOLFE

Humbert Wolfe was born of Jewish parentage in Milan, Italy, in 1885, but spent his childhood in Bradford, Yorkshire. He attended Wadham College, Oxford, and then was appointed to the British Civil Service. He is now attached to the Ministry of Labor, in London; he also represents Great Britain at Geneva in the International Labor Office, an agency associated with the League of Nations. Although he had dabbled in literature, he published nothing until he was thirty-five. Then came, in rapid succession, *London Sonnets* (1920), *Shylock Reasons with Mr. Chesterton* (1921), *Circular Saws* (1923), *Kensington Gardens* (1924), *The Unknown Goddess* and *Lampoons* (1925), *Humoresque* and *News of the Devil* (1926), *Requiem* and *Cursory Rhymes* (1927), *Others Abide* (translations from the Greek Anthology), and *This Blind Rose* (1928).

The most characteristic of his earlier poetry will be found in *Kensington Gardens* and *The Unknown Goddess*. His verse is marked by a most alluring deftness of technique. A single dip into his readable poetry will almost inevitably mean finishing the volume. There is a definiteness of outline, a lucidity of phrasing, which is in refreshing contrast to the fuzzy obscurities of some of Mr. Wolfe's contemporaries. To this is added, in *Humoresque* and *Requiem*, the deepening thought of an artist who has come into philosophic maturity. "Saint Joan" is typical of the newer mood.

PRELUDE TO THE AFTERNOON OF A FAUN

HUMBERT WOLFE

In a cool clearing,
  with no one to crib it,
greatly daring
  a baby rabbit

solemnly dances
  with skips and turns
between the green lances
  of two tall ferns.

Tripping and swaying,
  and straight down the middle,
as though they were playing
  the viol or fiddle,

a little brown faun
  on furry white pads
with the ferns on the lawn
  for his Oreads[1].

Dance, little rabbit,
  whatever the tune!
You will lose the habit
  only too soon!

Only too soon
  on the selfsame lawn
'twill be afternoon
  for another faun.

---

[1]*Oreads*, mountain nymphs.

Only too soon, you,
 like me, will be hearing
the same low tune you
 heard in the clearing.

And you will not shake then,
 and skip, and bow,
but slip through the bracken
 as I do now.

ILIAD

Humbert Wolfe

False dreams, all false,
mad heart, were yours.
The word, and nought else,
in time endures.
Not you long after,
perished and mute,
will last, but the defter
viol and lute.
Sweetly they'll trouble
the listeners
with the cold dropped pebble
of painless verse.
Not you will be offered,
but the poet's false pain.
Mad heart, you have suffered,
and loved in vain.
What joy doth Helen
or Paris have
where these lie still in
a nameless grave?

Her beauty's a wraith,
and the boy Paris
muffles in death
his mouth's cold cherries.
Aye! these are less,
that were love's summer,
than one gold phrase
of old blind Homer?
Not Helen's wonder
nor Paris stirs,
but the bright untender
hexameters.
And thus, all passion
is nothing made,
but a star to flash in
an Iliad.
Mad heart, you were wrong!
No love of yours,
but only what is sung,
when love's over, endures.

THE SAINT

HUMBERT WOLFE

Do you remember, Joan (Oh, vain to wonder
  if you remember how the evening star,
  a thousand times you drove the herd home under,
  admitted you to vision's calendar,
    like any child
  by that tall friendship, and the quiet moon beguiled)?

Do you remember the Domremy you knew,
  the plain and the small mountain-range of ricks,

the poplars at their goose-step, two by two,
the brown hen-church that folded her stone-chicks,
 your father's farm
so dear, so small it almost fitted in your arm?

Do you remember (even through the flame)
 after the long day's labor in the field
 how with the Angelus you heard your name
 mixed with the bells, and hid your face and kneeled
  when sweet and high
 a peasant heard "Ecce ancilla Domini"?

"Behold the servant of the Lord—and France,"
 and in your hands, that never held a sword,
 the country staff was lifted like a lance
 in the hushed aisles of evening, to the Lord,
  and you were gone
 forever, Joan, to put immortal iron on.

What was your sainthood, Joan? You did not guess
 when you restored his lilies to your king
 that you had found beyond the fleur-de-lys
 the lilies in an everlasting spring
  whose wind is blown
 across the centuries, and is fragrant, Joan.

You were not a proud saint. You went alone
 among the soldiers, and you understood
 how men are only frightened angels, Joan,
 and evil only unprotected good;
  you knew these things,
 and knew how pardonable are the hearts of kings.

And, being a woman, you lifted mankind up
 against the devil in their own despite,
 and when they feared, you drank the bitter cup

for all your cowards as by woman's right,
    and, even when
you burned, you did not blame them, knowing they
    were men.

Saint Joan, it may be all things human must
    be dull with earth, and with the darkness faint,
but if it be so, then your mortal dust
    was purged with flame till you were all a saint,
      and when you prayed
fire spoke to fire, and mixed in heaven, Maid.

WILLIAM BUTLER YEATS

William Butler Yeats was born in Dublin in 1865, the son of an artist. A childhood spent in the wilds of Sligo, on the west coast of Ireland, gave him a love for the peasant lore which he was later to transmute into the language of the lyric. He was educated at the Godolphin School, Hammersmith, near London; and at the Erasmus Smith School, Dublin. Originally committed to an art career, he forsook the study of art when he was twenty-one in order to devote himself to literature.

Circumstance and inclination early made him a leader in the revival of Irish letters. Although his first book was published in 1886, it was not until *The Land of Heart's Desire* appeared in 1894 and *Poems* in 1895 that he began to attract a following. From then down to the present he has produced a constant succession of poetical and dramatic works, all but the latest being included in the six-volume *Collected Works* (1924).

For the best of Mr. Yeats's poetry the reader must turn back to the earlier work, especially *The Wind among the Reeds* (1899). By that time he had rid himself of the English influence of Spenser, Shelley, and others, had uncovered the peculiar and tenuous magic which is his version of Irishry, but had not yet succumbed to the French Symbolists and other influences which have made his later poetry a "dream tapestry." At no time has he so deeply identified himself with the soil and toil of Ireland as have Colum, Campbell, Synge, Lady Gregory, Stephens, and some lesser writers. His supreme distinction as a poet is his gift of sheer song, melodies which sing themselves into the memory forever. Such are

> I will arise and go now, and go to Innisfree . . .

and the refrain from *The Land of Heart's Desire:*

> "When the wind has laughed and murmured and sung,
> The lonely of heart is withered away."

In the face of such music, the reader does not seek too closely for meanings; but the feeling remains that in some of Mr. Yeats's later work the bewildering mysticism is not sufficiently compensated for. Indeed, according to Ernest Boyd, it is not true mysticism in so far as mysticism is intellectual. "His appeal is primarily sensuous . . . So long as the mind surrenders to the heart, thought to emotion, Mr. Yeats carries the reader with him . . . Mysticism to Mr. Yeats is not an intellectual belief, but an emotional or artistic refuge. His visions do not convince us, because they are obviously 'literary' rather than spiritual. The concepts which are realities to Blake, or to Mr. Yeats's contemporary, A.E., are to him symbols, nor do they strike the reader as being anything more. Of symbolism—even mystic symbolism—there is plenty, but of mysticism hardly a trace."

But however critics may differ as to Mr. Yeats's poetry, there can be only one opinion as to his influence. That influence, not only on younger Irish poets but on British and American poets as well, has been incalculable. To him perhaps more than to any other one person modern poetry is indebted for its emancipation from the insincerities of former poetic convention. Mr. Yeats showed English-speaking poets how to extract lyric beauty from simple, unadorned language. He proved that the richest music is hidden in the plainest words, that "rhetoric is the thing heard, poetry is the thing overheard."

"The Wild Swans at Coole," from the book by that title, published in 1917, is a notable example of the suggestive power of quite ordinary words. In this poem, Mr. Yeats said, he was trying to rid his poetry of the reds and yellows that Shelley brought back from Italy and get into it the bleak grays of Galway.

THE WILD SWANS AT COOLE[*][1]

WILLIAM BUTLER YEATS

The trees are in their autumn beauty,
The woodland paths are dry,
Under the October twilight the water
Mirrors a still sky;
Upon the brimming water among the stones
Are nine and fifty swans.

The nineteenth autumn has come upon me
Since I first made my count;
I saw, before I had well finished,
All suddenly mount
And scatter wheeling in great broken rings
Upon their clamorous wings.

I have looked upon those brilliant creatures,
And now my heart is sore.
All's changed since I, hearing at twilight,
The first time on this shore,
The bell-beat of their wings above my head,
Trod with a lighter tread.

Unwearied still, lover by lover,
They paddle in the cold,
Companionable streams or climb the air;
Their hearts have not grown old;
Passion or conquest, wander where they will,
Attend upon them still.

*From *Later Poems* by William Butler Yeats. Copyright 1924 by The Macmillan Company. Reprinted by permission.
[1]*Coole*, a small lake in Galway, Ireland.

But now they drift on the still water
Mysterious, beautiful;
Among what rushes will they build,
By what lake's edge or pool
Delight men's eyes, when I awake some day
To find they have flown away?

FRANCIS BRETT YOUNG

Francis (E.) Brett Young, born in Worcestershire in 1884, is equally
well known as novelist and as poet. His novels show a succession of
influences and no final certainty of individual method. In poetry he
is surer of his aim, for he adheres to a classic purity of style which
suggests Robert Bridges. A criticism of his poetry, in *The London
Mercury*, says: "He is not interested in Life for Life's sake, his interest
is far more concentrated. His heart is ranged inalienably beside the
Absolute Beauty . . . in what he conceives is the last battle of her
long losing campaign with the world." The subjects of his poetry
cover a considerable range, for Dr. Young was educated as a physician,
served in the Army Medical Corps in German East Africa during
the War, and is an accomplished musician. He lives at Anacapri,
Italy.

His poetry will be found in *Five Degrees South* (1917) and *Poems
1916-18* (1919). His most notable novel is *Love Is Enough* (1927).

CRISTO MORTO[1]

Francis Brett Young

Forth from the narrow alleys, under the saracen vaultings
That bound the dusty piazza, gathers and clusters
An idle concourse, black-coated, moving and halting,
White faces agonized under the hanging lusters
Of street lamps.   Overhead,
The air vibrates with bells that swing for the dead:
Not mournfully, but with a savage clangor
Of horror and of anger,
Shattering cross-echoes thrown
From blatant cornet and somber-mouthed trombone
Beating the measure of a mocking, ponderous,
Slow-footed *Valse Macabre*.[2]

It is the festival of *Cristo Morto* . . .

They come, the shuffling files of children bearing
Bent candles that flare yellow in the still air
And spatter the stones with tears of molten tallow.
Then, shy and sallow,
With black mantilla and blue ribbon, follow
The vestal Daughters of Mary, idly staring:
Locked hands, slow feet, and faces stony cold.
They come . . . the symbols of passion, thorn and scourge;
The tinseled banners surge
Onward, as driven forth by the mocking band
Beneath the clangor of bells; and now men stand
Bareheaded, and women hunch their shoulders in dread
For the coming of Christ Dead,
Whose bloody shroud bears on before the loud
Blaring of brass, whose advent sways the crowd,

---

[1] *Cristo Morto*, the dead Christ.
[2] *Valse Macabre*, waltz of death.

As a dark cornfield, swept by winds of night,
Quails and recovers.   The pompous dance is still,
While, strained and shrill
Over the shuffle of feet, like a blown candle-flame,
Quavers the dirge of high-pitched voices wailing
Their patter of unintelligible Latin;
And stooping men, haggard, and pressed for breath,
Beneath their staggering burden, carry on high
An image of Christ, who died, with lolling head
And bleeding flanks; his lank limbs overspread
By the green pallor of death.

A woman cries and falls to her knees; old men,
With listless, humble hands, are bowed.   They come . . .
The Masters of Mysteries:
Dark priests, black-robed, proud-eyed,
With cheeks unshaven, gross lips numbed by words,
In an aura of dusty vestment and stale incense,
Preening and peering above the prostrate throng
Like shabby vultures that sniff the odor of death
Blown from the image of the broken God
Whose suffering is the measure of their strength,
Whose sorrow is the symbol of their pride.
Onward the slow procession trails its length
Of tossing lights and tasseled banners: on
Coils, like a shining snake, black-skinned, obscene,
Beneath the cavernous arches . . . and is gone,
Where now the muffled drum
Throbs like a heart in pain,
As the mocking *Valse Macabre* begins again.

And my soul was shaken, as though, in a dark dream,
Its eyes had plumbed the very pit of death:
Death, black beyond redemption or recall:
Death absolute, triumphant, beyond hope,

Savage, unhallowed, terrible, and old . . .
So old . . .
Older than Attis,[3] older than that Adonis
Whose flowery death dyes the pale meadows of Lebanon
With vernal crimson, older than Osiris:[4]
Old as the primal passion of despair
That burned into the dark brain of the first
Man, when he gazed upon mortality!

Thus, when the flowered graft
Of a rose tree dies, from the stock of briar, deep-rooted,
Do thorny shoots arise
That draw their sap from the cruel
Heart of the earth; and the bough,
Sweet-perfumed and gracious, now
Hangs rotten and forgotten . . .

Shaken, I moved apart
And shuddered through the throng with bursting heart,
Until, alone, alone,
I faced the silence of the middle sea,
Thinking of that calm spirit of Galilee
Whose ways were bitter and whose words were sweet
As the cool fragrance of hidden flowers in spring
Or wells of mountain-water; and, as I stood,
I was abased before the humility
Of Him whose life made death a little thing.

---

[3] *Attis, Adonis.* The myths of Attis and Adonis are somewhat similar. Attis, a Phrygian shepherd beloved by the goddess Cybele, killed himself; from his blood sprang violets. Adonis, a youth beloved by Aphrodite, was killed by a boar while hunting; the goddess made the anemone spring from his blood. Both Attis and Adonis were the objects of worship at annual rites of wildest mourning.

[4] *Osiris,* an Egyptian god, judge of the dead.

GEOFFREY WINTHROP YOUNG

Geoffrey Winthrop Young was born in London in 1876, the son of Sir George Young, Bart., one of those English gentlemen who can combine scholarship and poetry with an active life as a civil administrator, and Dame Alice Eacy Young, a Dublin wit and leader in English intellectual society. He is a grandnephew of Winthrop Mackworth Praed, the poet. One brother is an author and poet with a distinguished diplomatic career; another combines literature with politics and finance. Geoffrey Young carries on the family tradition. In his own words, "The motive of my life, if any, has been to attempt to recover something of the Greek balance between the activity of the body and of the mind; to pursue adventurous living, open-air discipline, natural human intercourse; and to attempt to express the rhythms achieved in movement or perceived in nature by means of the rhythm of words, poetry or prose."

Brought up in a family life pervaded by English and Irish liberalism, educated at Marlborough, Trinity College, Cambridge, Jena, and Geneva, given generous opportunities for travel in Europe and the Near East, Mr. Young had every advantage to make for a cultured life; and as a teacher at Eton College, an inspector of secondary schools, a war correspondent, and commandant of various ambulance units, he has followed his ideas of an active life. He was severely wounded at the Italian front, and a dozen war medals have been awarded him.

But the chief passion of his life, since the age of fifteen, has been mountains and mountaineering. In this pursuit he has found both "adventurous living" and the rhythms of his verse and prose. How much mountains have influenced his art is suggested by the titles of some of his books: *Wind and Hill* (1909), *Freedom* (1914), *April and Rain* (1923)—all poetry; *Mountain Craft* (1920) and *On High Hills* (1927)—prose. The keen athleticism of "Mountain Speed" will bear comparison with Browning's famous passage in "Saul":

> "Oh, our manhood's prime vigor! No spirit feels waste,
> Not a muscle is stopped in its playing nor sinew unbraced . . ."

MOUNTAIN SPEED

Geoffrey Winthrop Young

Oh, the winter joy of the flying of feet over snow-clad hill,
the rush and the snow-leap vying with the flight of our will;
the hiss of our ski, and the sighing of speed that frost cannot
  still!

The race of the strong thrust urging the froth of the turn,
the pace of the snow-blast purging with clean heart-burn,
the face of the valley up-surging to meet our sweep of return!

Oh, the sunshine glory of lying a-dream on the steep,
above restless forests defying their burden of sleep,
with the whisper of white worlds dying, lulling our hearts from
  the deep!

As the swoop of the swift keen-shrilling in twilight of May,
as the stoop of the hawk to the killing from visionless gray,
as the plunge of the rainbow filling the haggard spaces of day—

Like the pouring of glacier on ocean, in fiords of the sea,
like the flood of a people's devotion, in arms to be free,
is our soaring of passionate motion o'er mountains, the swirl
  of our ski!

Though the way be uphill and long winding, with irksome sleet,
and a slabbery snow-broth binding our lift and beat,
there'll be day o'er the pass, and the blinding of wind, and all
  heaven in our feet!

Spurn the crest fierce-driven from falling fountain of snow;
Earn the rest that is given to all whom the mountains know;
Learn the best of all living from height, and the glory of speed,
  and the glow!

MOUNTAIN SPEED

(Douglas Wherton Young)

Oh the winter, joy of the thing of far over snow-clad hill,
The rush and the zoom leap away with the flight of our will,
The lilt of the ski and the singing of speed that frost can not
chill!

The roar of the group thrust urging the flight of the drift,
the pace of the snow blast parting with clean heart burn,
the race of the valley up surging to meet our sweep of return!

Oh, the sparkling glory of dawn radiant on the steep,
here reflect forms dark with our burden of sleep,
with the wonder of white worlds dying, lulling our hearts from
the deep!

As the swoop of the swift keen shilling in twilight of May,
as the stoop of the hawk to the killing from viewless grey,
as the plunge of the rainbow filling the haggard spaces of day!

Like the pouring of plaster on plaster, on bursts of the sea,
like the flood of a people's disaster, in arms to be free,
as man sharing of passion, ambition over mountains, the field
of our ski!

Though the way be uphill and long winding, with the song aloft,
and a slackery snow breath limiting our life and heart,
there'll be day o'er the peak and the pink, and the blinding of
wind, and all heaven in our feet!

Upon the crest here driven from falling fountain of snow,
learn the rest that's given to all where the mountains know,
Learn the best of all living from height, and the glory of speed,
and the glow!